ROAD TO
RIVERDALE
VOLUME TWO

P9-BYK-350

15-
Y4

MARLBOROUGH PUBLIC LIBRARY
35 West Main St.
Marlborough, MA 01752

COVER ART BY
FRANCESCO FRANCAVILLA

FEATURING STORIES BY
MARK WAID, CHIP ZDARSKY,
ADAM HUGHES, MARGUERITE BENNETT,
CAMERON DeORDIO, TOM DeFALCO & WILL EWING

WITH ART BY
FIONA STAPLES, ERICA HENDERSON,
ADAM HUGHES, AUDREY MOK, SANDY JARRELL,
ALITHA MARTINEZ, ANDRE SZYMANOWICZ,
JOSÉ VILLARRUBIA, JEN VAUGHN, KELLY FITZPATRICK,
THOMAS CHU, BOB SMITH, JANICE CHIANG
& JACK MORELLI

EDITOR
MIKE PELLERITO

EDITOR-IN-CHIEF
VICTOR GORELICK

CO-EDITOR (*JOSIE*)
ALEX SEGURA

ASSOCIATE EDITOR
STEPHEN OSWALD

GRAPHIC DESIGN BY
KARI McLACHLAN

ASSISTANT EDITOR
JAMIE LEE ROTANTE

PUBLISHER
JON GOLDWATER

ROAD TO RIVERDALE
INTRODUCTION

When Archie Comics relaunched *Archie* with a brand new #1 in 2015, it was only the beginning of what would be a renaissance for the company. After the relaunch, news quickly spread that not only would the company be producing more all-new comics, but there would also be a TV show set to air on the CW network, based on the classic characters.

Now it's 2017, and not only do we have brand new issues of *Archie, Jughead, Betty & Veronica, Josie and the Pussycats* and *Reggie and Me* coming out every month, but we also have a full season of the highly-acclaimed (and recently renewed!) *Riverdale* TV series under our belt. *Riverdale* is written by Archie Comics Chief Creative Officer Roberto Aguirre-Sacasa and produced by Warner Brothers Studios and Berlanti Productions.

The live-action TV series offers a bold, compelling take on Archie Andrews (played by KJ Apa), Betty Cooper (played by Lili Reinhart), Veronica Lodge (played by Camila Mendes), Jughead Jones (played by Cole Sprouse) and their friends and families, exploring small-town life and the darkness and weirdness bubbling beneath Riverdale's wholesome facade.

While the series gives a subversive look at the characters and the town they inhabit, it also focuses on some universal truths that Archie Comics has upheld for the past 75+ years: the eternal love triangle of Archie, girl-next-door Betty, and rich socialite Veronica, Jughead and Archie's undying friendship, Archie and his long-time rivalry with Reggie Mantle and much, much more. Not only was the TV series a hit, but it also spawned a special *RIVERDALE* one-shot comic by Roberto Aguirre-Sacasa and The CW writers room followed by an ongoing series, which features ALL-NEW stories set between the episodes of the TV series. You can find these comics on sale now at your local comic shop.

For fans of the *Riverdale* TV show who are new to the comics: we want to wish you a warm welcome. If you're wondering where these great characters and twists come from, then the answer is in your hands. This second volume continues the stories that launched with the best-selling ROAD TO RIVERDALE collection. Whether it's a primer for the TV show or a handy guide to the new Archie Comics landscape, we're proud to offer this graphic novel as the perfect introduction to Archie, his friends and his world.

Marlborough Public Library
35 West Main Street
Marlborough, MA 01752

ROAD TO RIVERDALE

CONTENTS

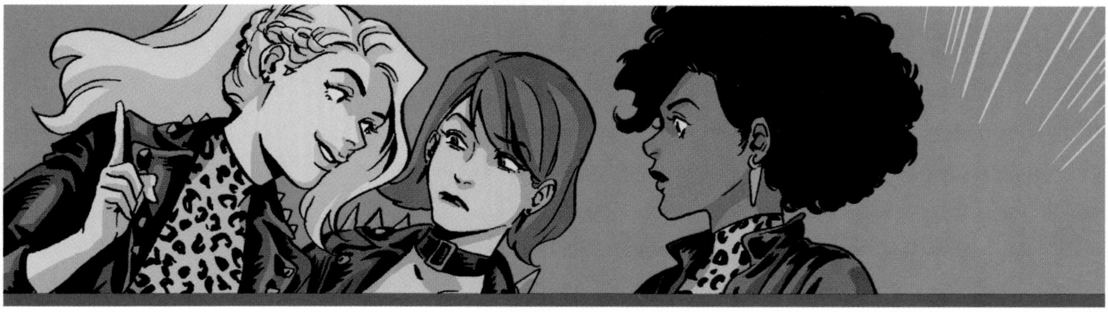

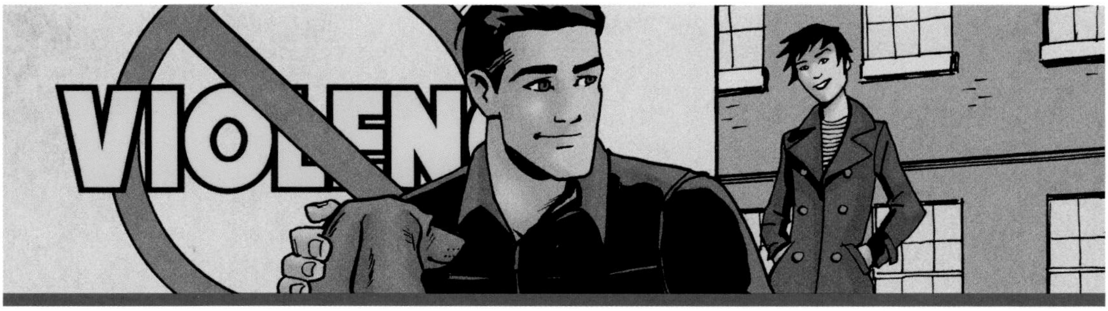

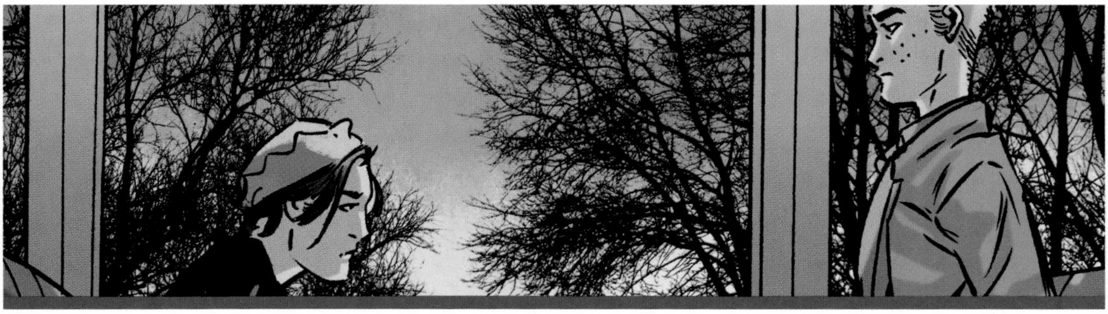

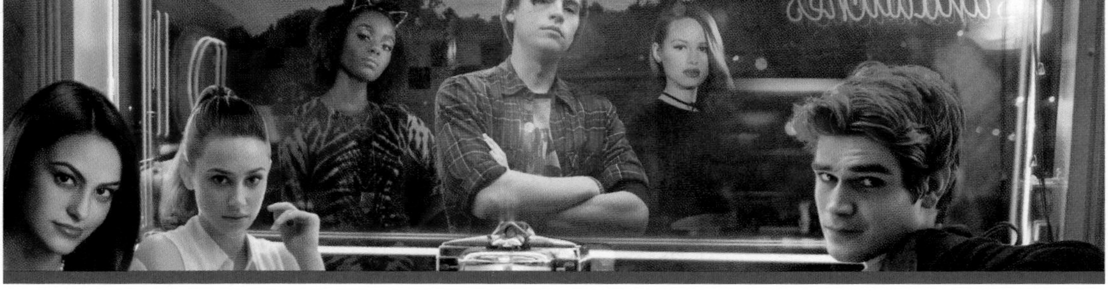

PREVIOUSLY IN THE TOWN OF RIVERDALE...

Riverdale's ideal couple, Archie & Betty... *SPLIT??*

Say it isn't so!

After the infamous "Lipstick Incident" (don't ask), their breakup was all anyone at Riverdale High seemed to talk about! Following a failed attempt to bring them back together (thanks, Jughead!), it now looks like everyone is *FINALLY* ready to accept some change in their small town...

STORY BY
MARK WAID

ART BY
FIONA STAPLES

COLORING BY
ANDRE SZYMANOWICZ
WITH JEN VAUGHN

LETTERING BY
JACK MORELLI

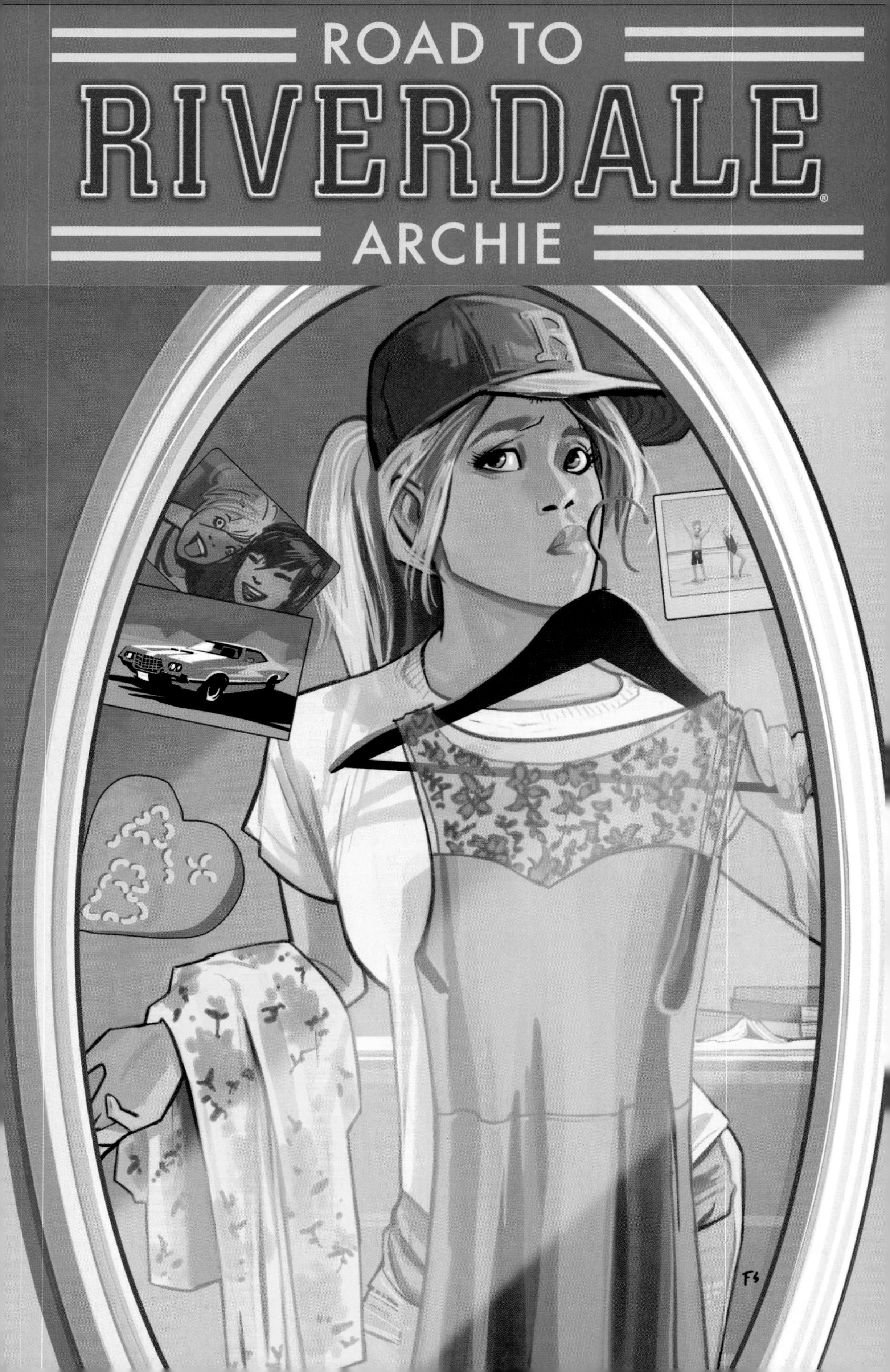
ROAD TO
RIVERDALE®
ARCHIE

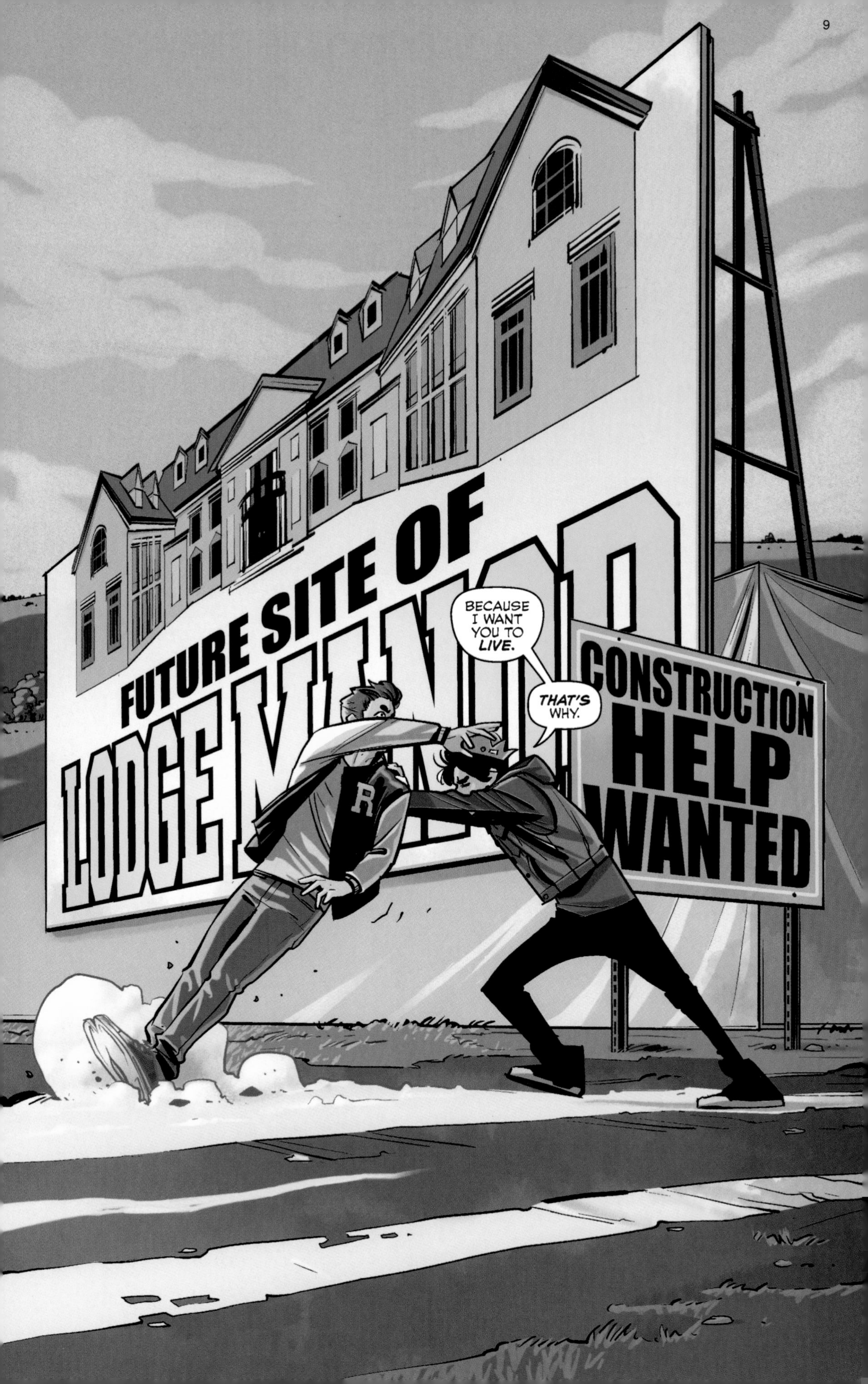
FUTURE SITE OF
LODGE MANOR
BECAUSE I WANT YOU TO *LIVE*.
THAT'S WHY.
CONSTRUCTION HELP WANTED

CHAPTER ONE: IT'S BETTER THAN "FORSYTHE"

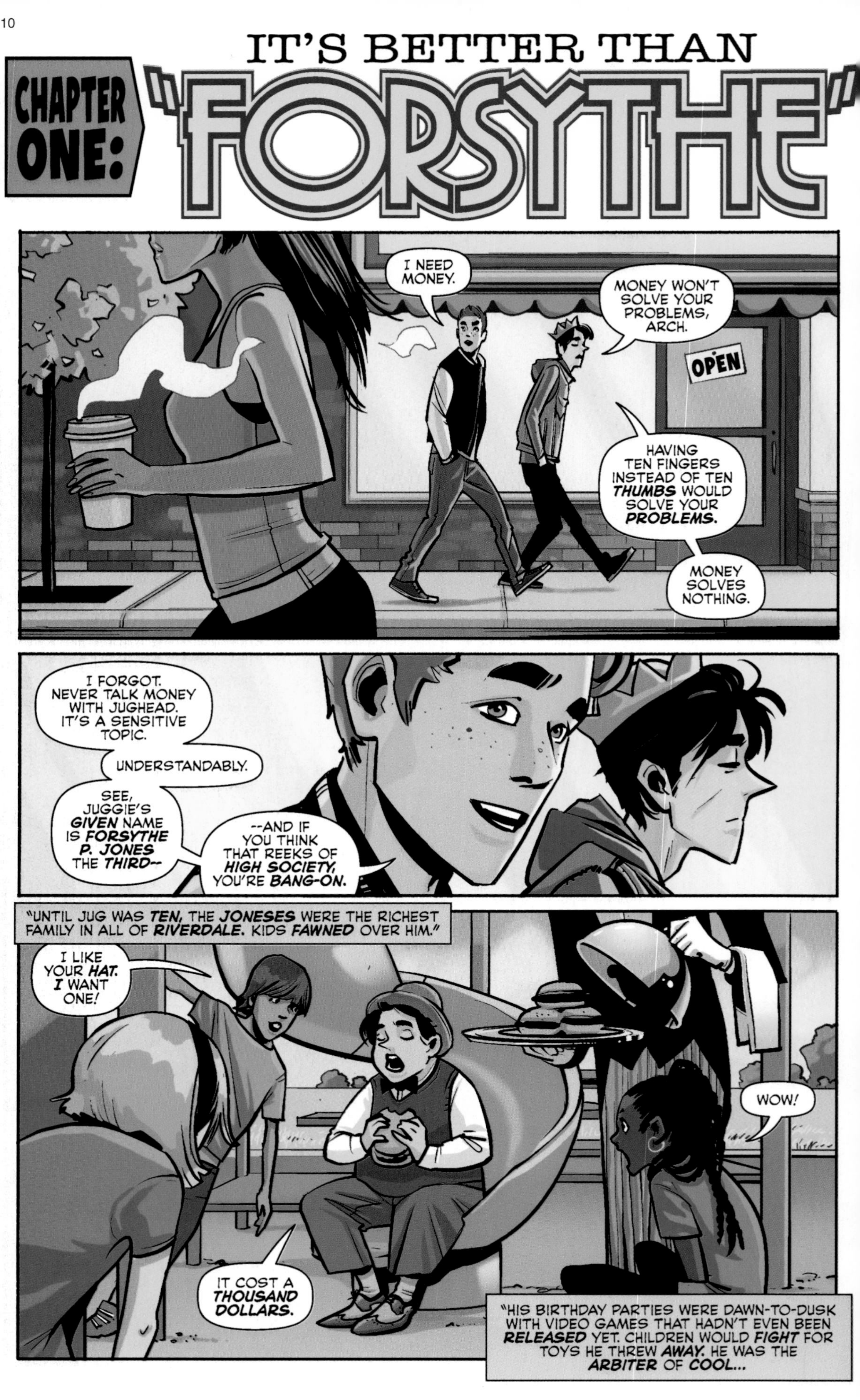
I NEED MONEY.
MONEY WON'T SOLVE YOUR PROBLEMS, ARCH.
HAVING TEN FINGERS INSTEAD OF TEN THUMBS WOULD SOLVE YOUR PROBLEMS.
MONEY SOLVES NOTHING.
OPEN
I FORGOT. NEVER TALK MONEY WITH JUGHEAD. IT'S A SENSITIVE TOPIC.
UNDERSTANDABLY.
SEE, JUGGIE'S GIVEN NAME IS FORSYTHE P. JONES THE THIRD--
--AND IF YOU THINK THAT REEKS OF HIGH SOCIETY, YOU'RE BANG-ON.
"UNTIL JUG WAS TEN, THE JONESES WERE THE RICHEST FAMILY IN ALL OF RIVERDALE. KIDS FAWNED OVER HIM."
I LIKE YOUR HAT. I WANT ONE!
WOW!
IT COST A THOUSAND DOLLARS.
"HIS BIRTHDAY PARTIES WERE DAWN-TO-DUSK WITH VIDEO GAMES THAT HADN'T EVEN BEEN RELEASED YET. CHILDREN WOULD FIGHT FOR TOYS HE THREW AWAY. HE WAS THE ARBITER OF COOL...

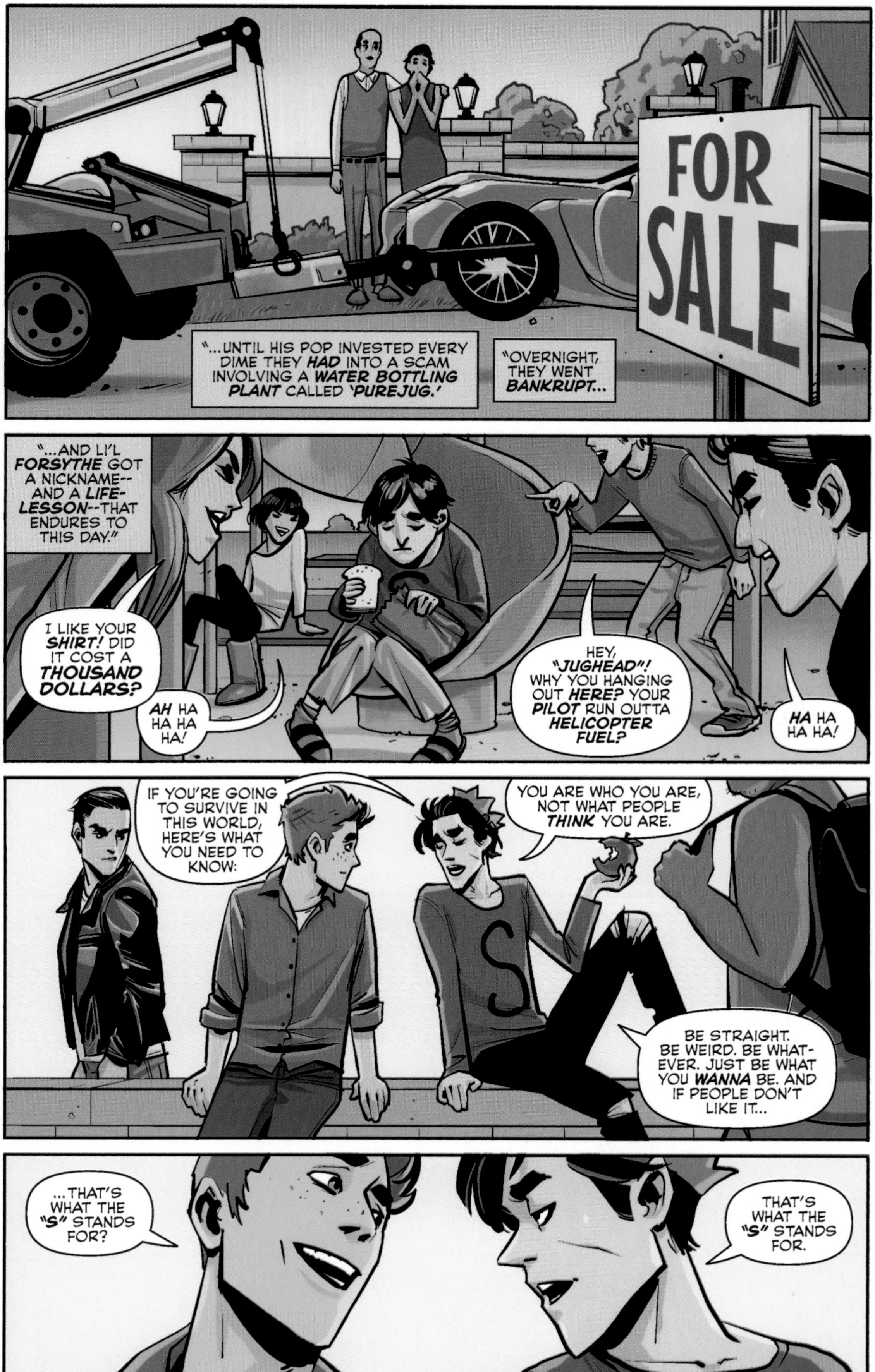
"...UNTIL HIS POP INVESTED EVERY DIME THEY HAD INTO A SCAM INVOLVING A WATER BOTTLING PLANT CALLED 'PUREJUG.'
"OVERNIGHT, THEY WENT BANKRUPT...
FOR SALE
"...AND LI'L FORSYTHE GOT A NICKNAME--AND A LIFE-LESSON--THAT ENDURES TO THIS DAY."
I LIKE YOUR SHIRT! DID IT COST A THOUSAND DOLLARS?
AH HA HA HA HA!
HEY, "JUGHEAD"! WHY YOU HANGING OUT HERE? YOUR PILOT RUN OUTTA HELICOPTER FUEL?
HA HA HA HA!
IF YOU'RE GOING TO SURVIVE IN THIS WORLD, HERE'S WHAT YOU NEED TO KNOW:
YOU ARE WHO YOU ARE, NOT WHAT PEOPLE THINK YOU ARE.
BE STRAIGHT. BE WEIRD. BE WHAT-EVER. JUST BE WHAT YOU WANNA BE. AND IF PEOPLE DON'T LIKE IT...
...THAT'S WHAT THE "S" STANDS FOR?
THAT'S WHAT THE "S" STANDS FOR.

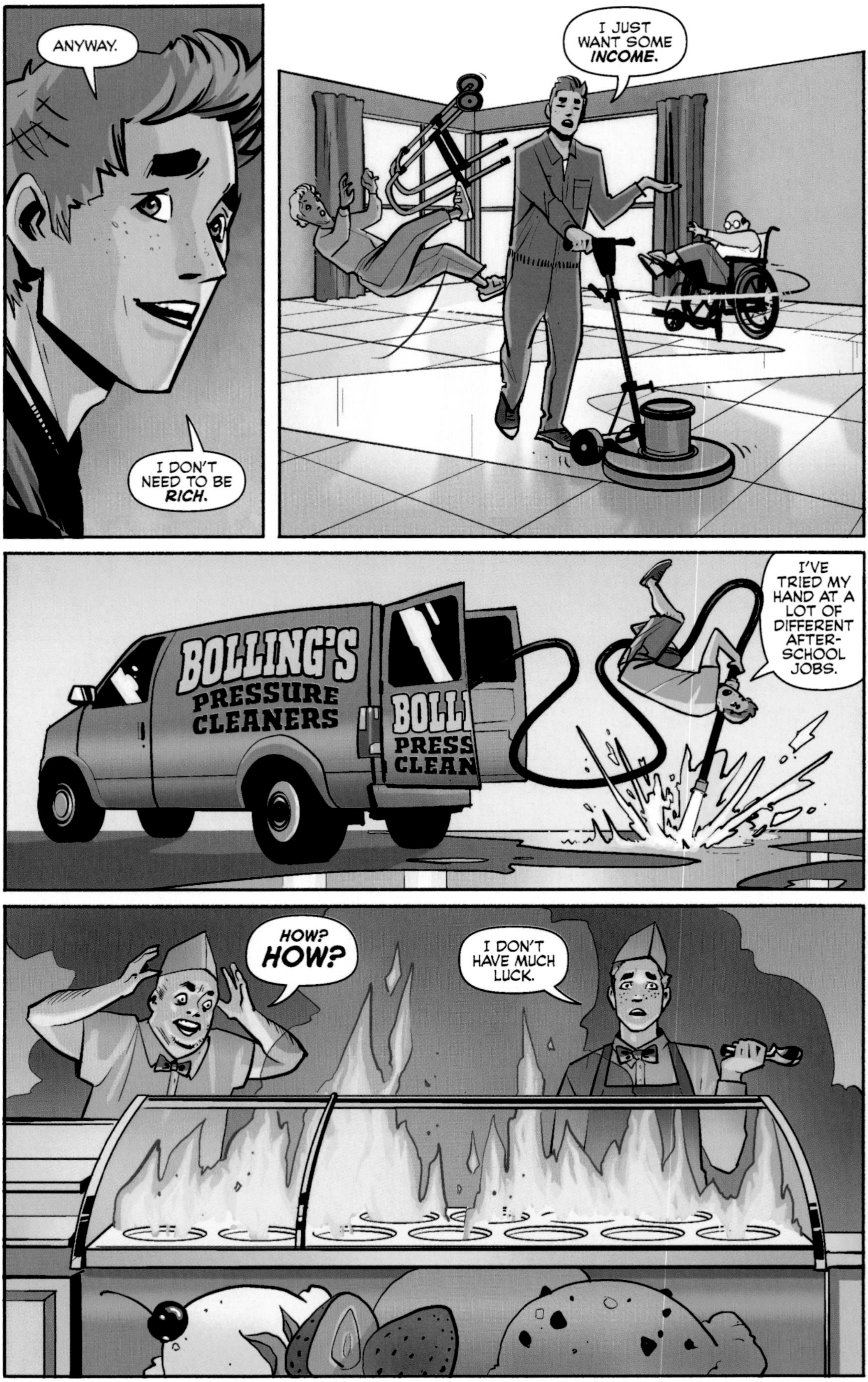
ANYWAY.
I DON'T NEED TO BE RICH.
I JUST WANT SOME INCOME.
BOLLING'S PRESSURE CLEANERS
I'VE TRIED MY HAND AT A LOT OF DIFFERENT AFTER-SCHOOL JOBS.
HOW? HOW?
I DON'T HAVE MUCH LUCK.

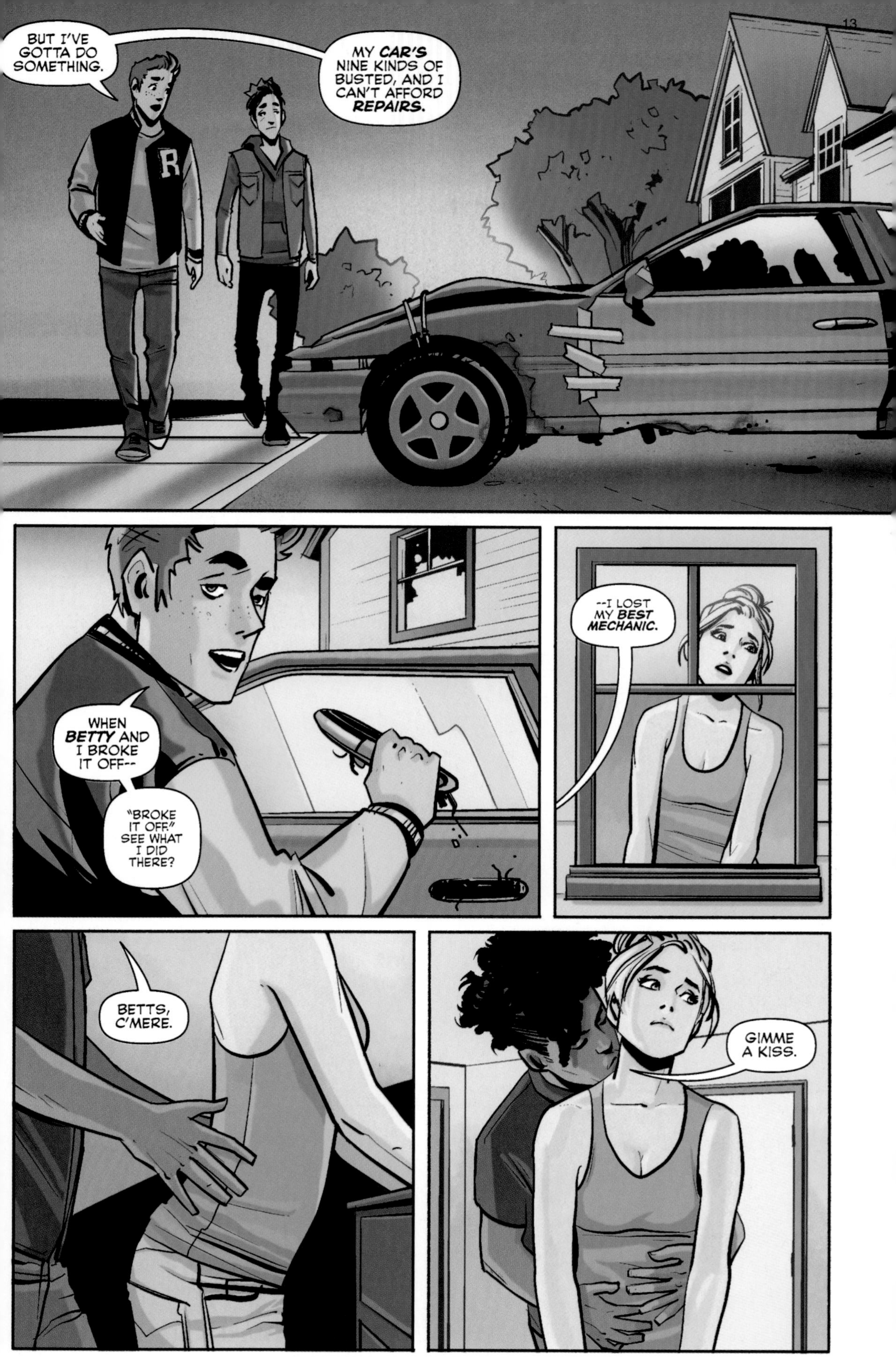
BUT I'VE GOTTA DO SOMETHING.
MY CAR'S NINE KINDS OF BUSTED, AND I CAN'T AFFORD REPAIRS.
WHEN BETTY AND I BROKE IT OFF--
"BROKE IT OFF." SEE WHAT I DID THERE?
--I LOST MY BEST MECHANIC.
BETTS, C'MERE.
GIMME A KISS.

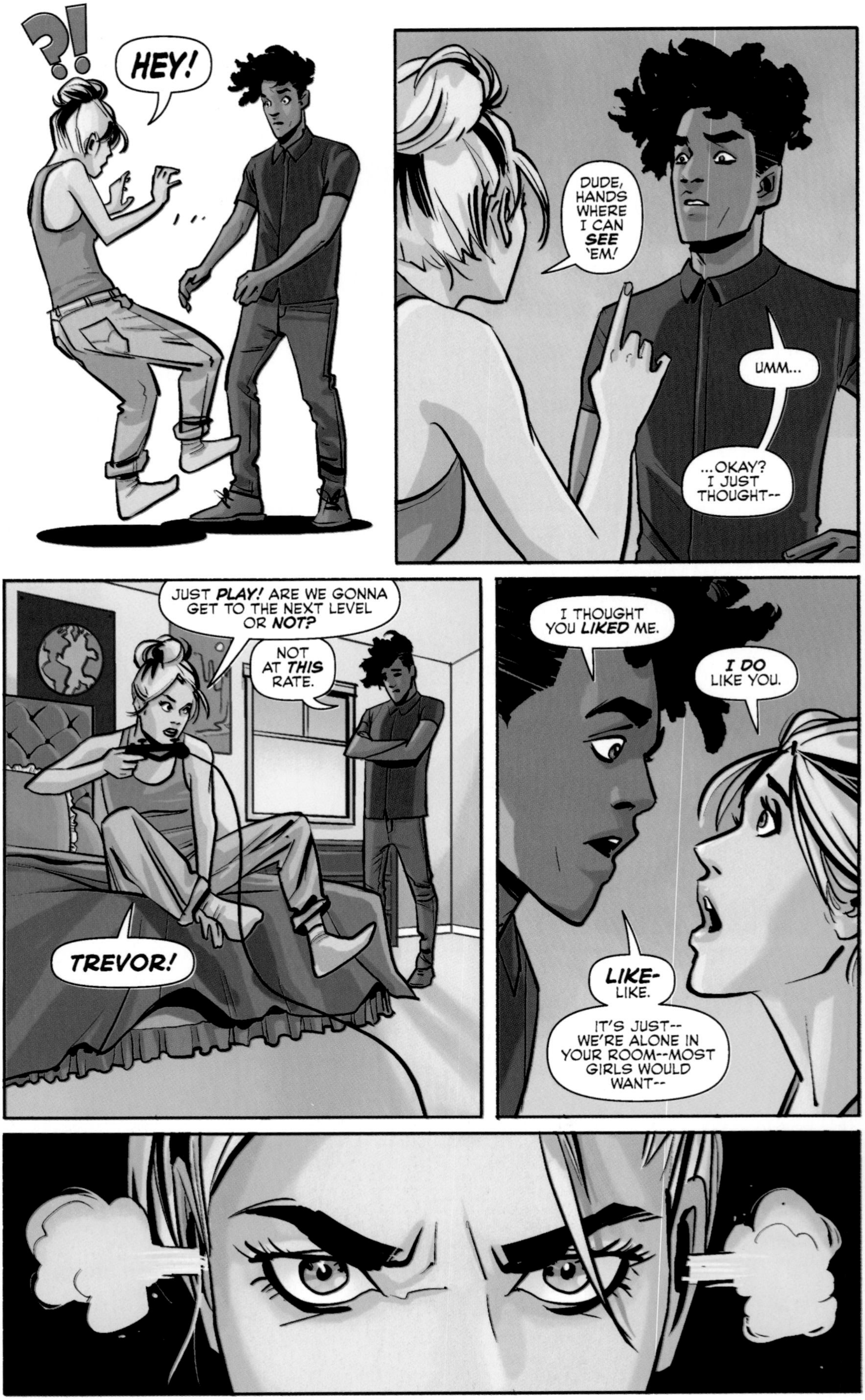
?!
HEY!
DUDE, HANDS WHERE I CAN SEE 'EM!
UMM...
...OKAY? I JUST THOUGHT--
JUST PLAY! ARE WE GONNA GET TO THE NEXT LEVEL OR NOT?
NOT AT THIS RATE.
TREVOR!
I THOUGHT YOU LIKED ME.
I DO LIKE YOU.
LIKE-LIKE.
IT'S JUST-- WE'RE ALONE IN YOUR ROOM--MOST GIRLS WOULD WANT--

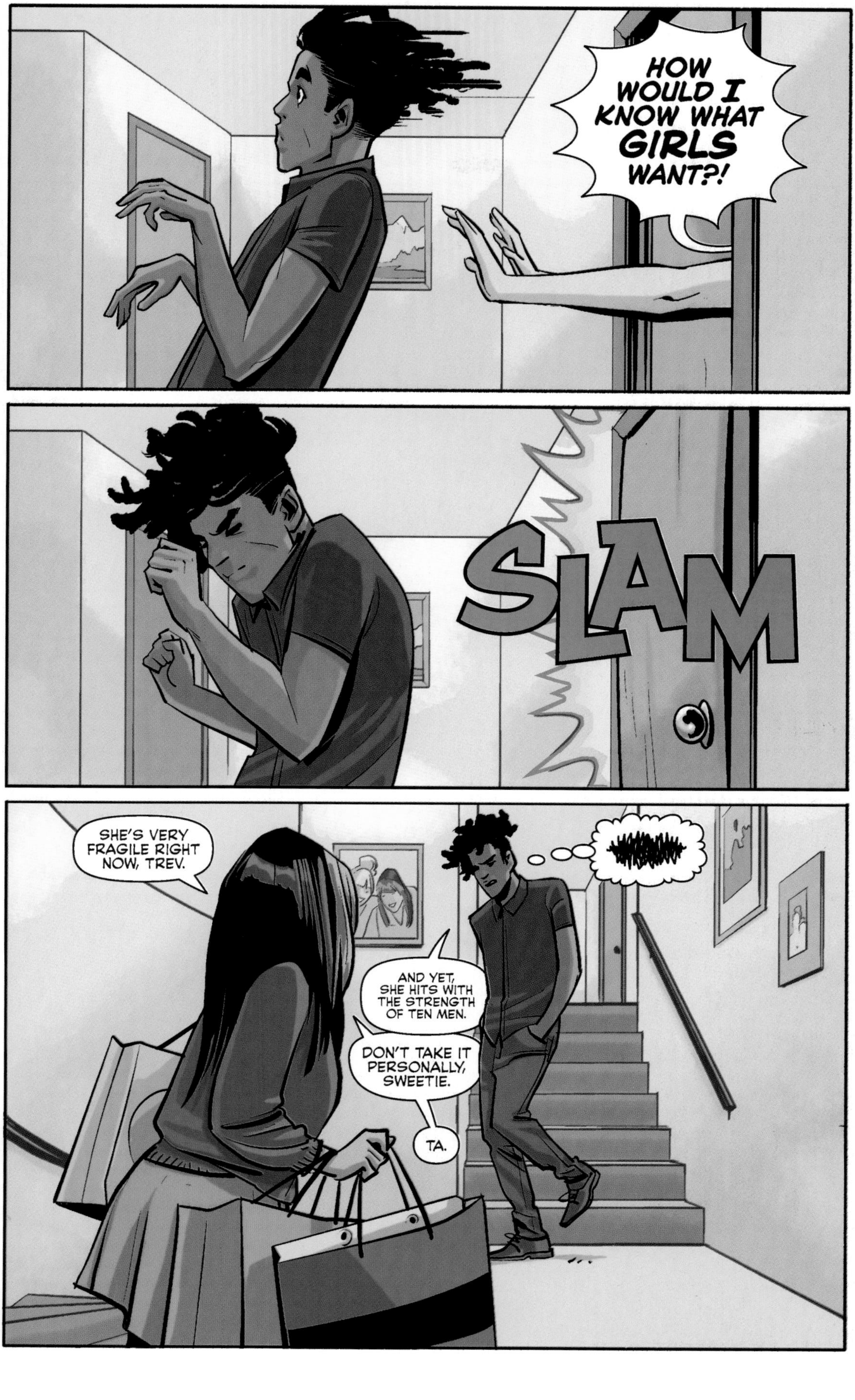
HOW WOULD I KNOW WHAT GIRLS WANT?!
SLAM
SHE'S VERY FRAGILE RIGHT NOW, TREV.
AND YET, SHE HITS WITH THE STRENGTH OF TEN MEN.
DON'T TAKE IT PERSONALLY, SWEETIE.
TA.

CHAPTER TWO: ONE OF THE GUYS

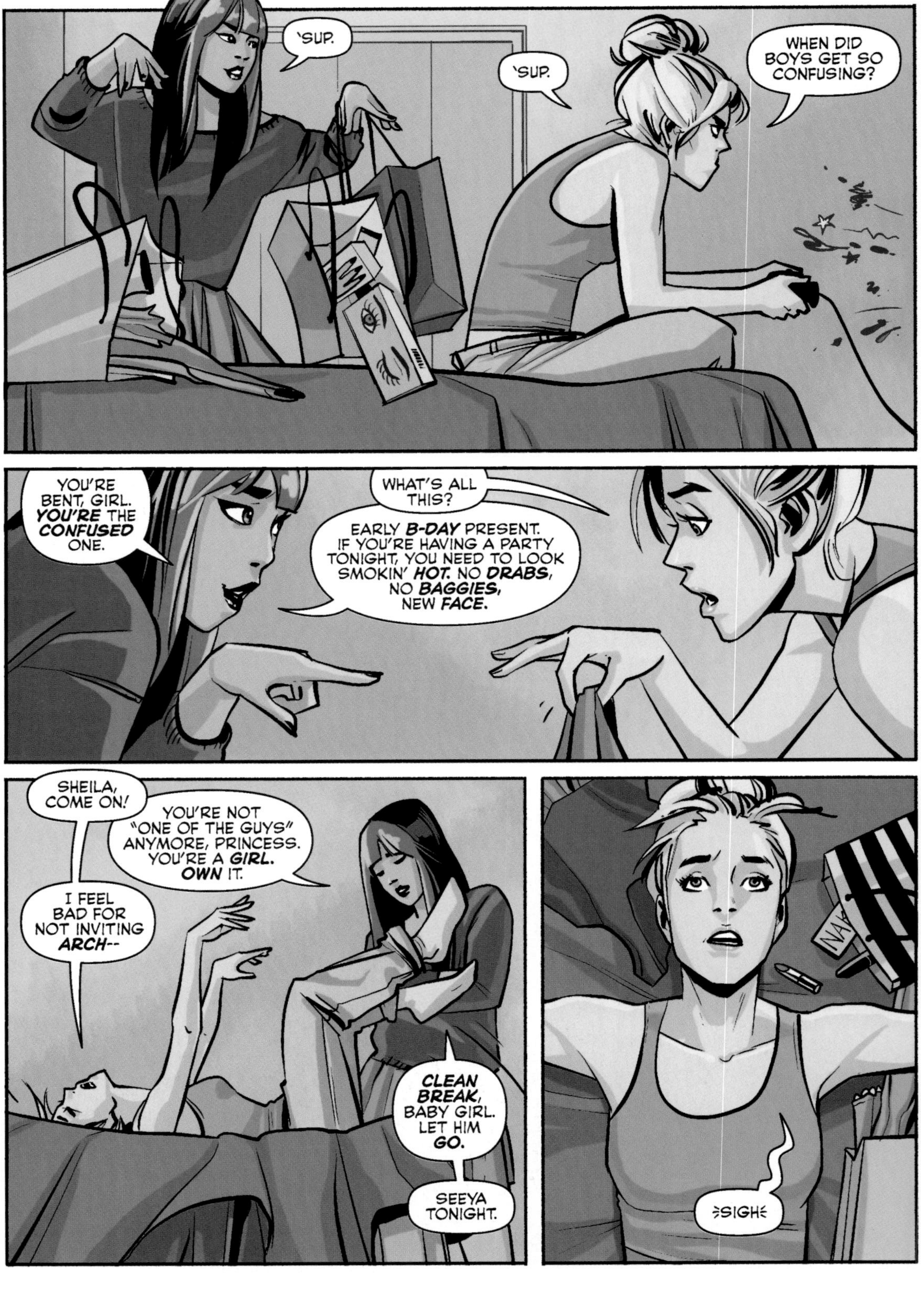

'SUP.
'SUP.
WHEN DID BOYS GET SO CONFUSING?
YOU'RE BENT, GIRL. ***YOU'RE*** THE ***CONFUSED*** ONE.
WHAT'S ALL THIS?
EARLY ***B-DAY*** PRESENT. IF YOU'RE HAVING A PARTY TONIGHT, YOU NEED TO LOOK SMOKIN' ***HOT.*** NO ***DRABS,*** NO ***BAGGIES,*** NEW ***FACE.***
SHEILA, COME ON!
YOU'RE NOT "ONE OF THE GUYS" ANYMORE, PRINCESS. YOU'RE A ***GIRL. OWN*** IT.
I FEEL BAD FOR NOT INVITING ***ARCH--***
CLEAN BREAK, BABY GIRL. LET HIM ***GO.***
SEEYA TONIGHT.
NAK
SIGH

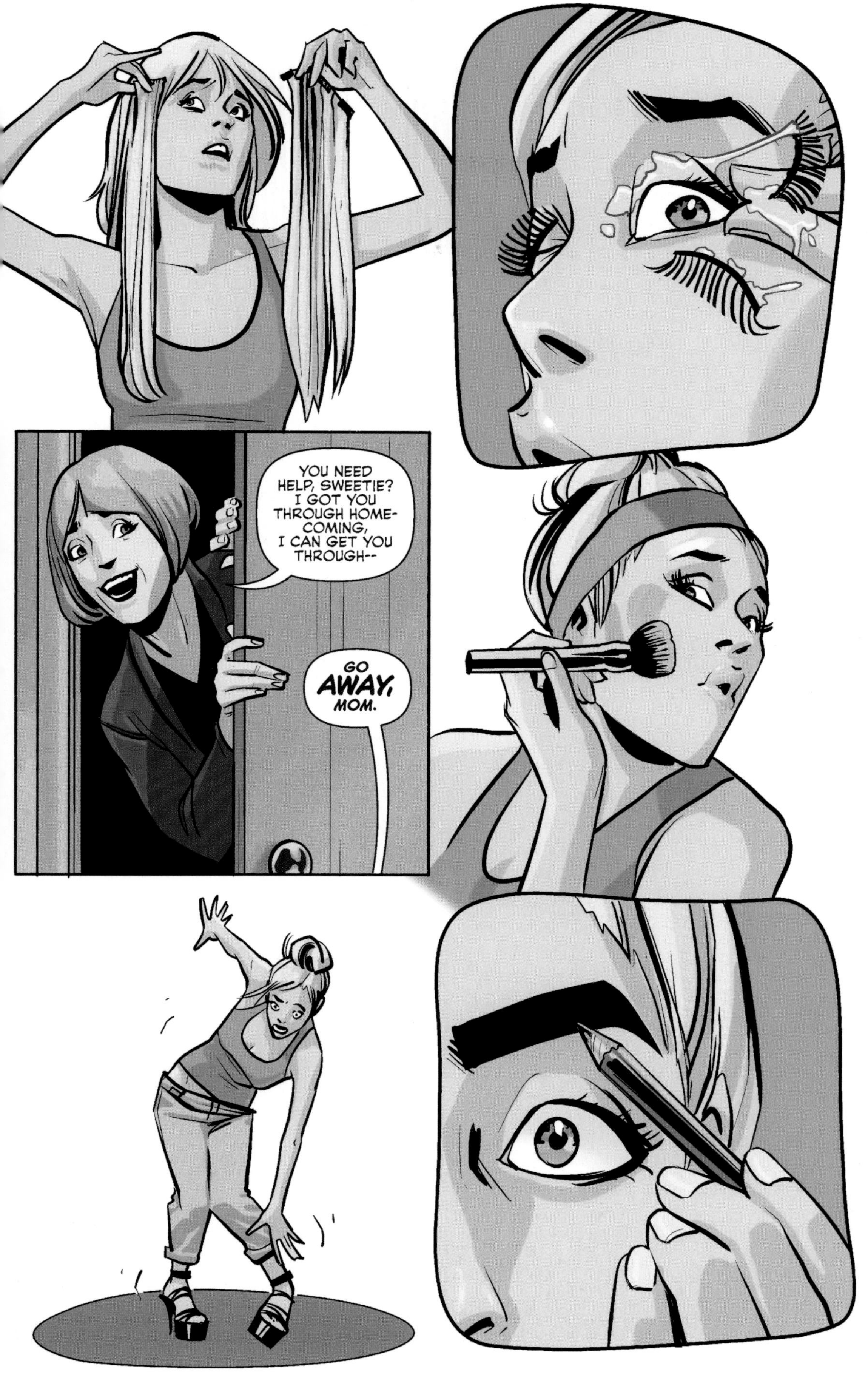
YOU NEED HELP, SWEETIE? I GOT YOU THROUGH HOME-COMING, I CAN GET YOU THROUGH--
GO AWAY, MOM.

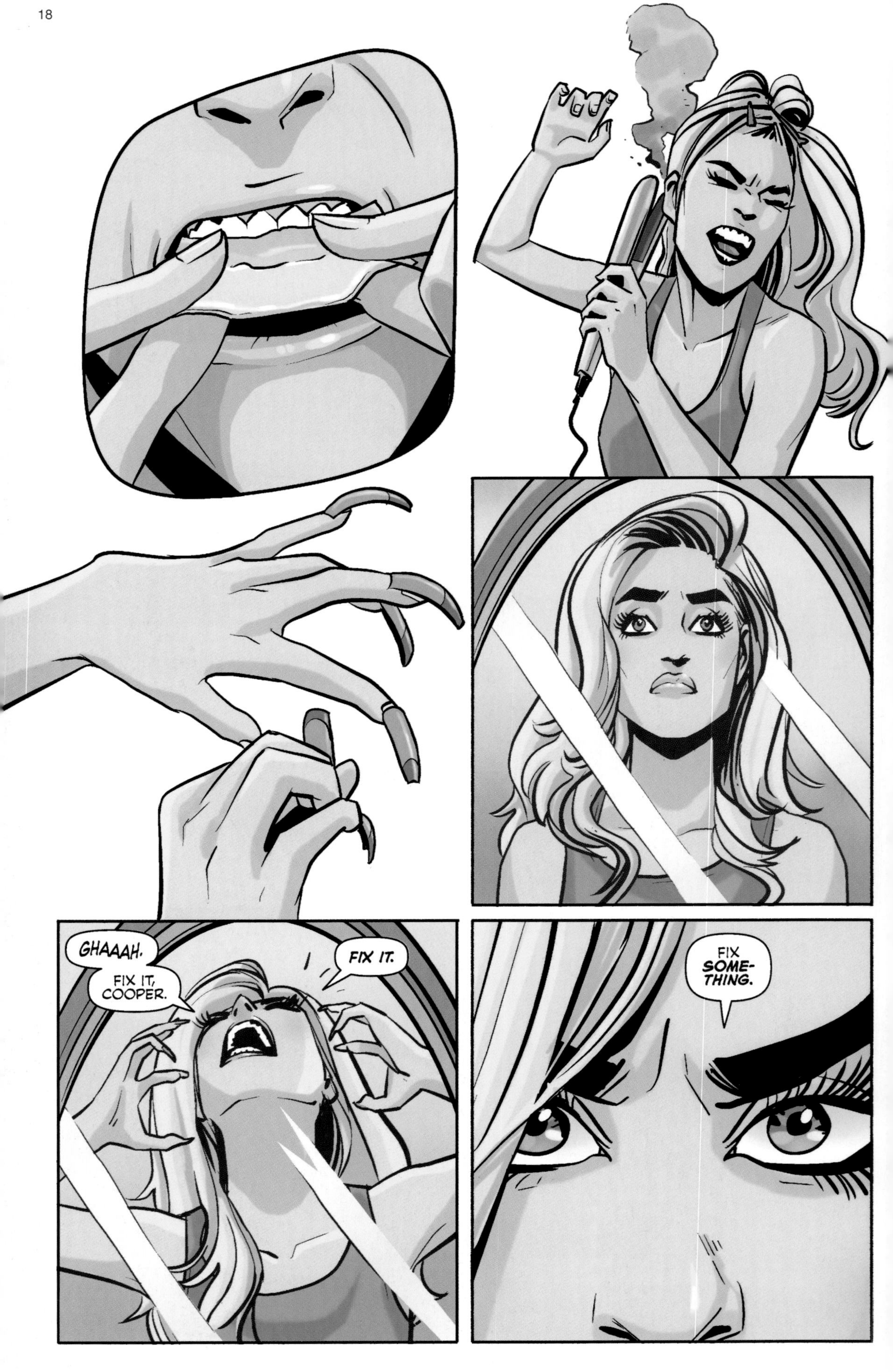
GHAAAH.
FIX IT, COOPER.
FIX IT.
FIX SOME-THING.

CHAPTER THREE: CAKEWALK

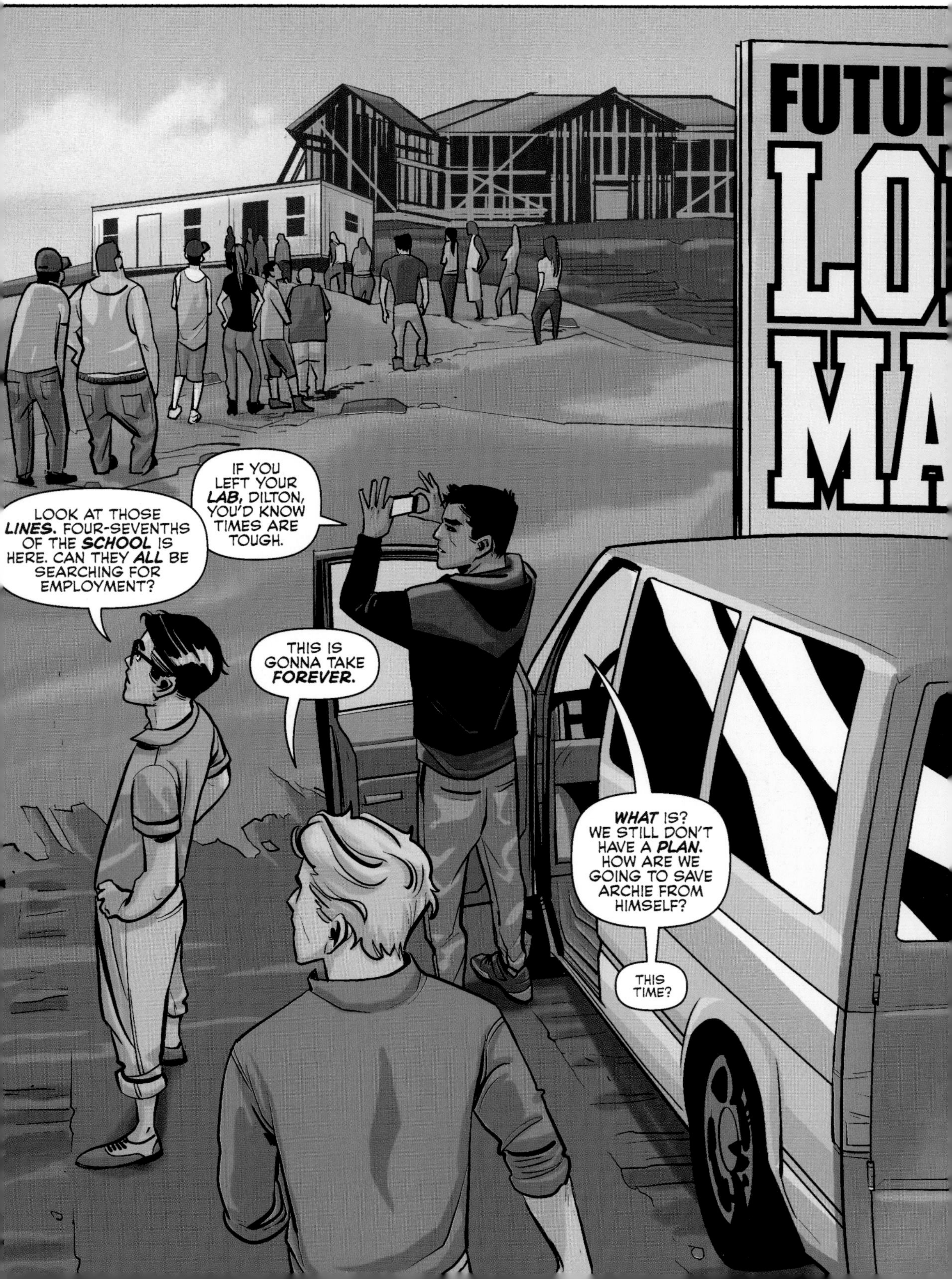
FUTUR
LO
MA
LOOK AT THOSE LINES. FOUR-SEVENTHS OF THE SCHOOL IS HERE. CAN THEY ALL BE SEARCHING FOR EMPLOYMENT?
IF YOU LEFT YOUR LAB, DILTON, YOU'D KNOW TIMES ARE TOUGH.
THIS IS GONNA TAKE FOREVER.
WHAT IS? WE STILL DON'T HAVE A PLAN. HOW ARE WE GOING TO SAVE ARCHIE FROM HIMSELF?
THIS TIME?

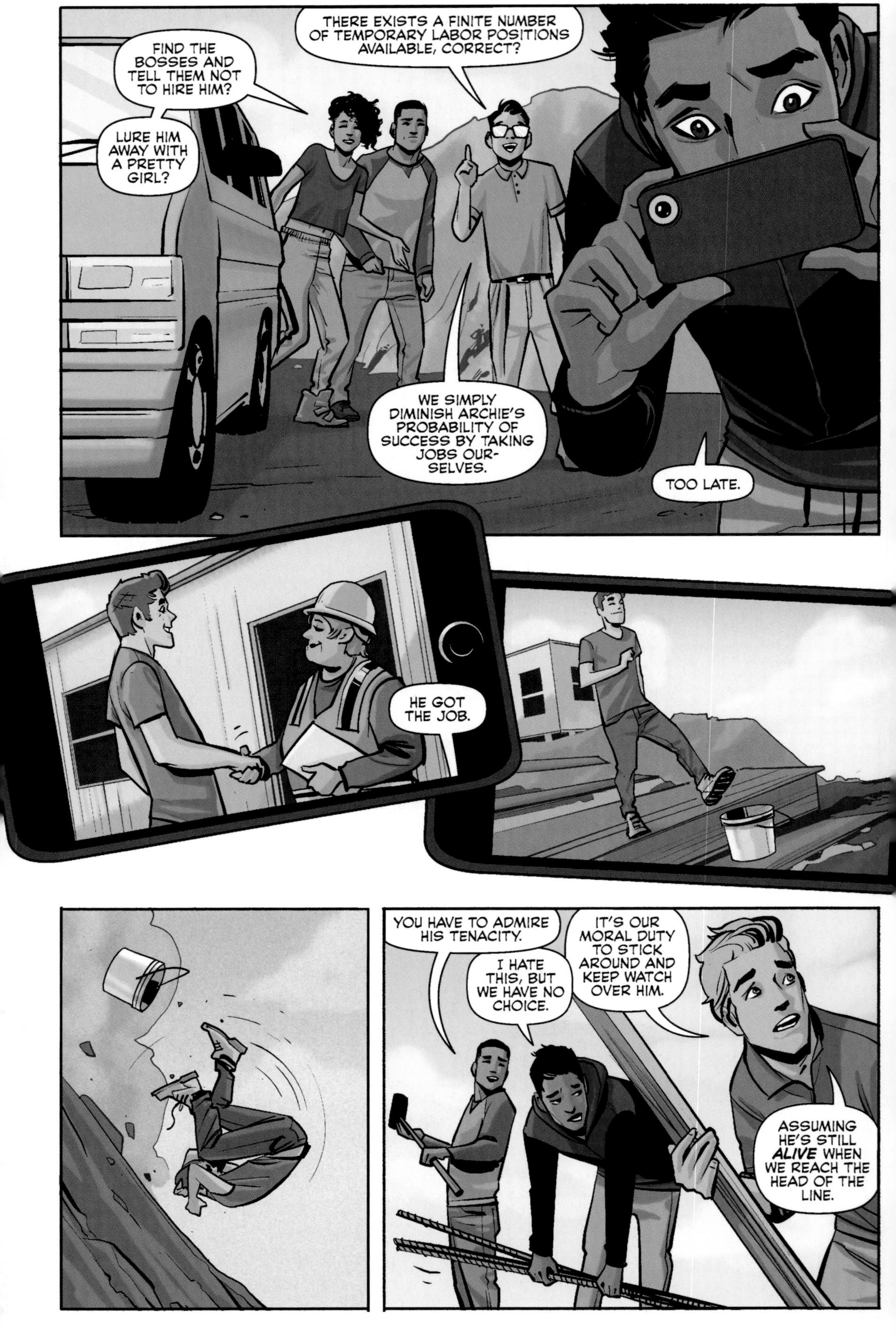

FIND THE BOSSES AND TELL THEM NOT TO HIRE HIM?
LURE HIM AWAY WITH A PRETTY GIRL?
THERE EXISTS A FINITE NUMBER OF TEMPORARY LABOR POSITIONS AVAILABLE, CORRECT?
WE SIMPLY DIMINISH ARCHIE'S PROBABILITY OF SUCCESS BY TAKING JOBS OUR-SELVES.
TOO LATE.
HE GOT THE JOB.
YOU HAVE TO ADMIRE HIS TENACITY.
I HATE THIS, BUT WE HAVE NO CHOICE.
IT'S OUR MORAL DUTY TO STICK AROUND AND KEEP WATCH OVER HIM.
ASSUMING HE'S STILL *ALIVE* WHEN WE REACH THE HEAD OF THE LINE.

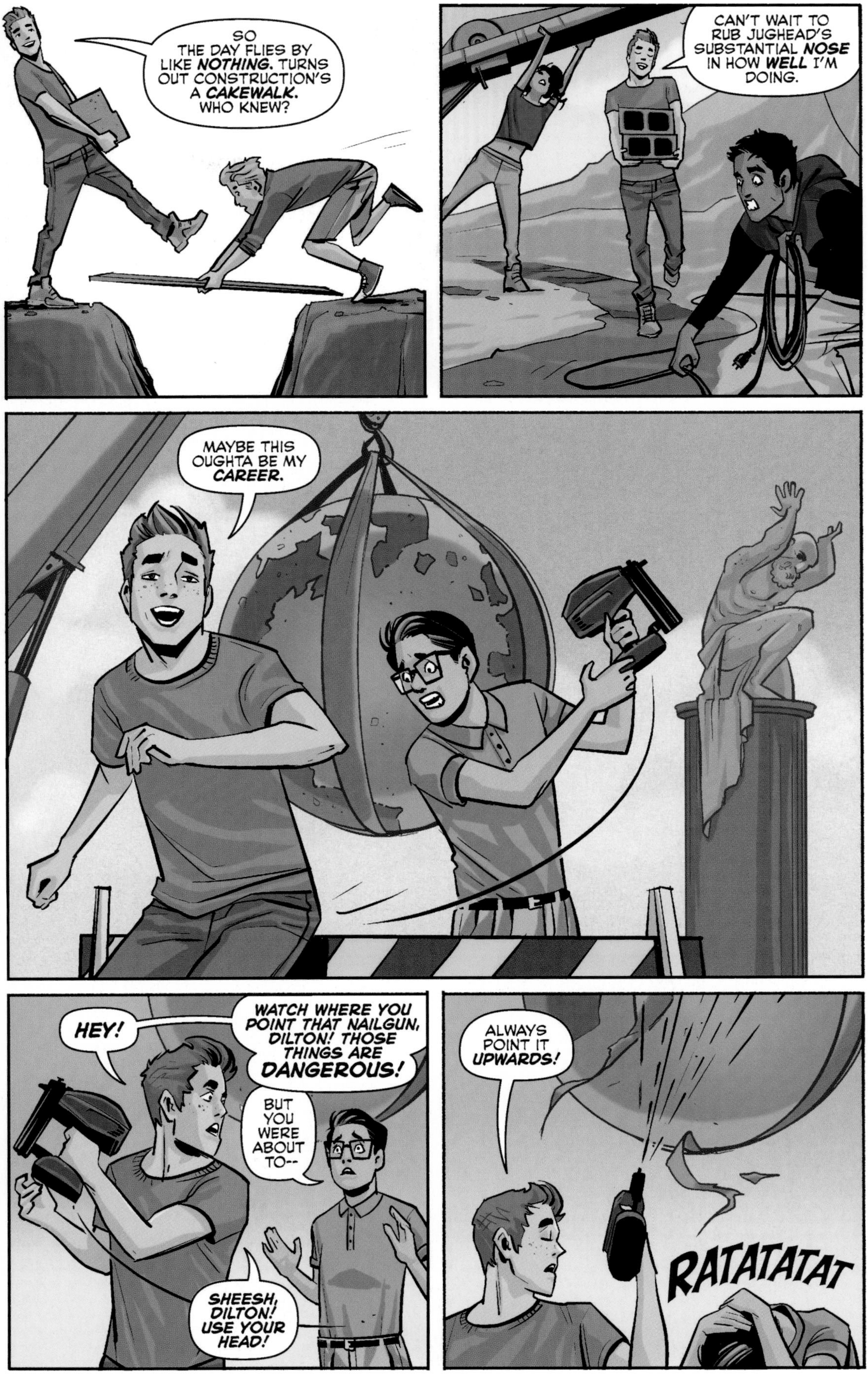

SO THE DAY FLIES BY LIKE **NOTHING.** TURNS OUT CONSTRUCTION'S A **CAKEWALK.** WHO KNEW?
CAN'T WAIT TO RUB JUGHEAD'S SUBSTANTIAL **NOSE** IN HOW **WELL** I'M DOING.
MAYBE THIS OUGHTA BE MY **CAREER.**
HEY!
WATCH WHERE YOU POINT THAT NAILGUN, DILTON! THOSE THINGS ARE DANGEROUS!
BUT YOU WERE ABOUT TO--
SHEESH, DILTON! USE YOUR HEAD!
ALWAYS POINT IT **UPWARDS!**
RATATATAT

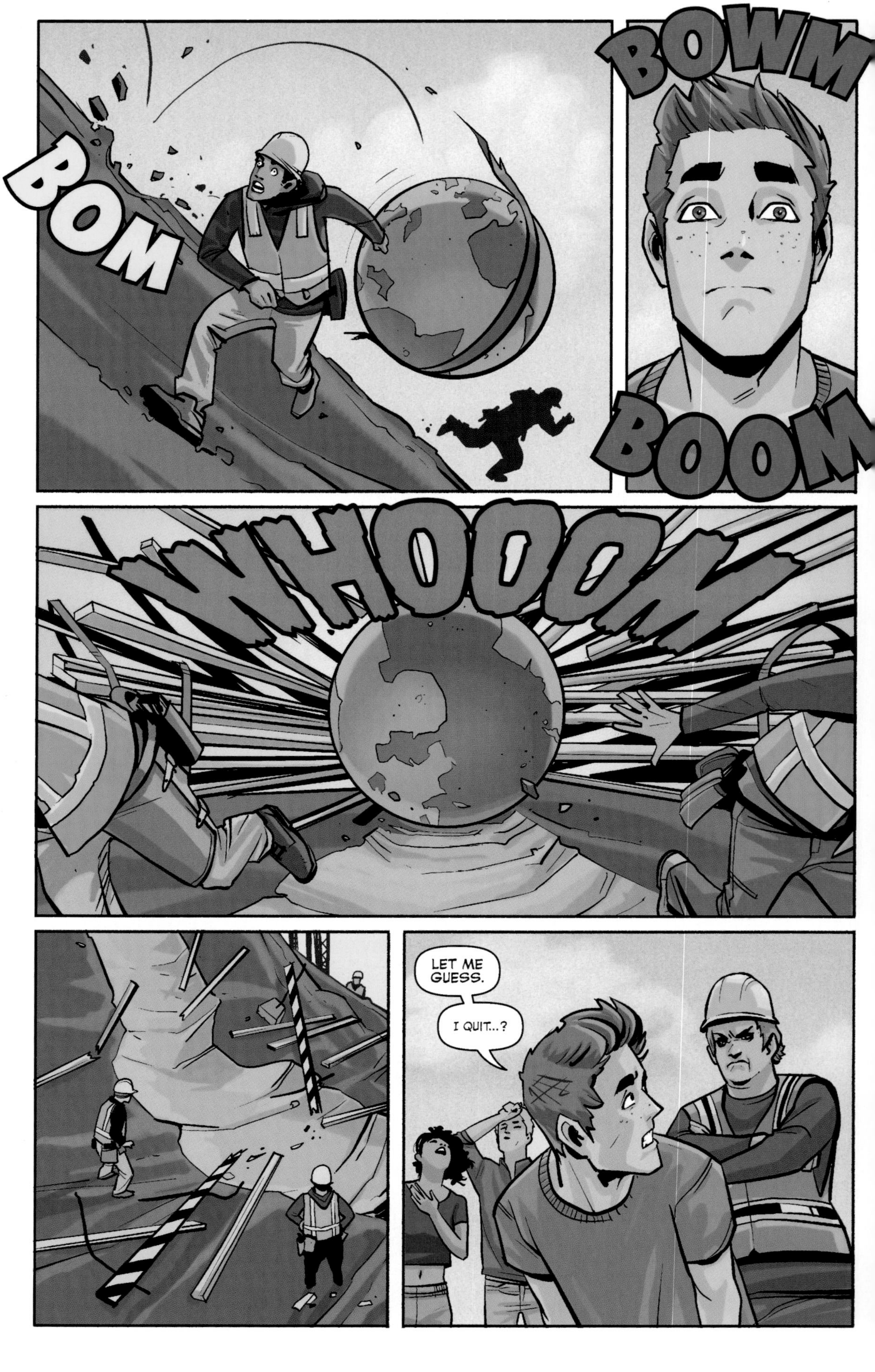
BOM
BOWM
BOOM
WHOOOM
LET ME GUESS.
I QUIT...?

CHAPTER FOUR: NOT MY SPECIAL TALENT

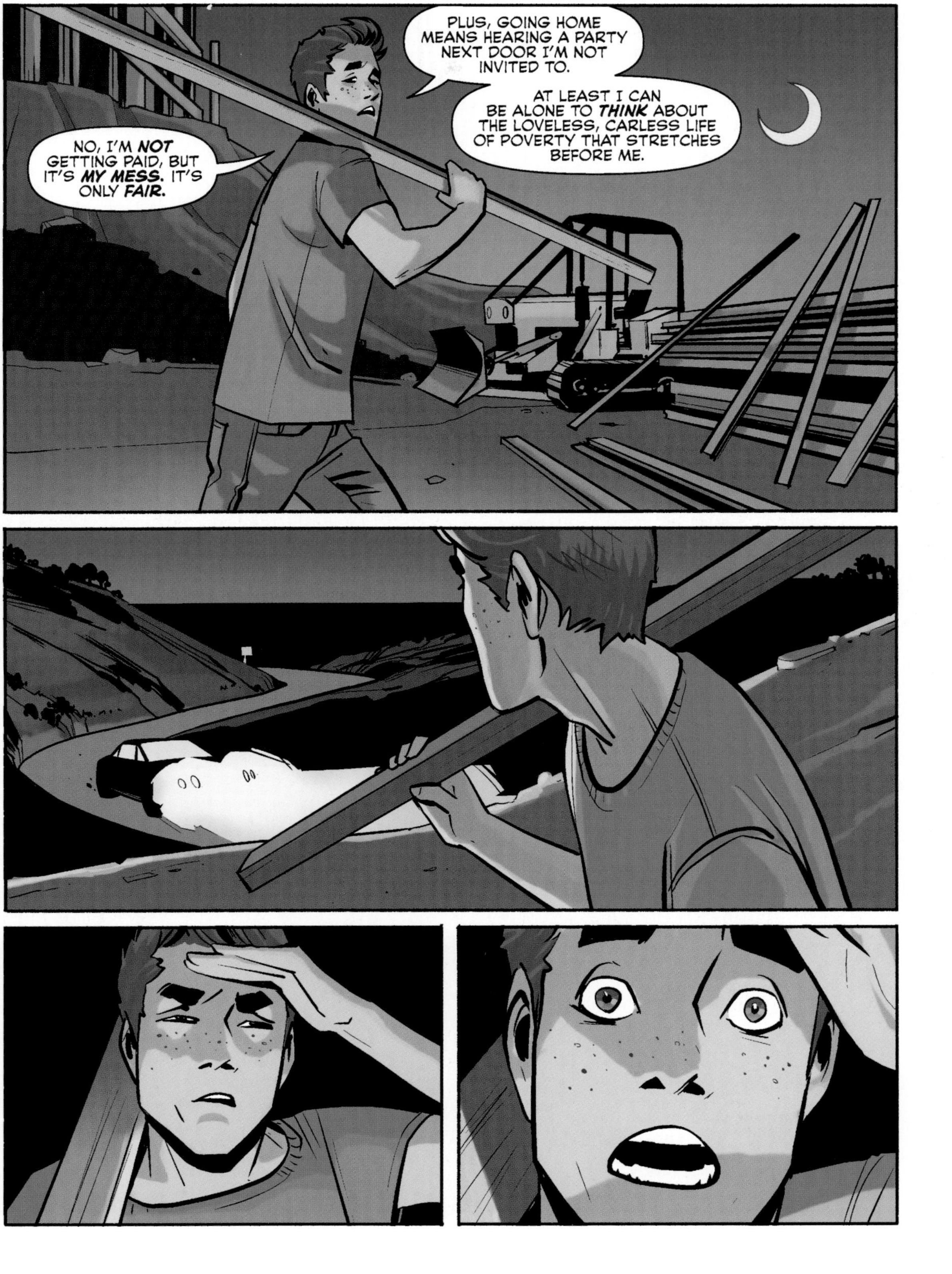
NO, I'M **NOT** GETTING PAID, BUT IT'S **MY MESS**. IT'S ONLY **FAIR**.
PLUS, GOING HOME MEANS HEARING A PARTY NEXT DOOR I'M NOT INVITED TO.
AT LEAST I CAN BE ALONE TO **THINK** ABOUT THE LOVELESS, CARLESS LIFE OF POVERTY THAT STRETCHES BEFORE ME.

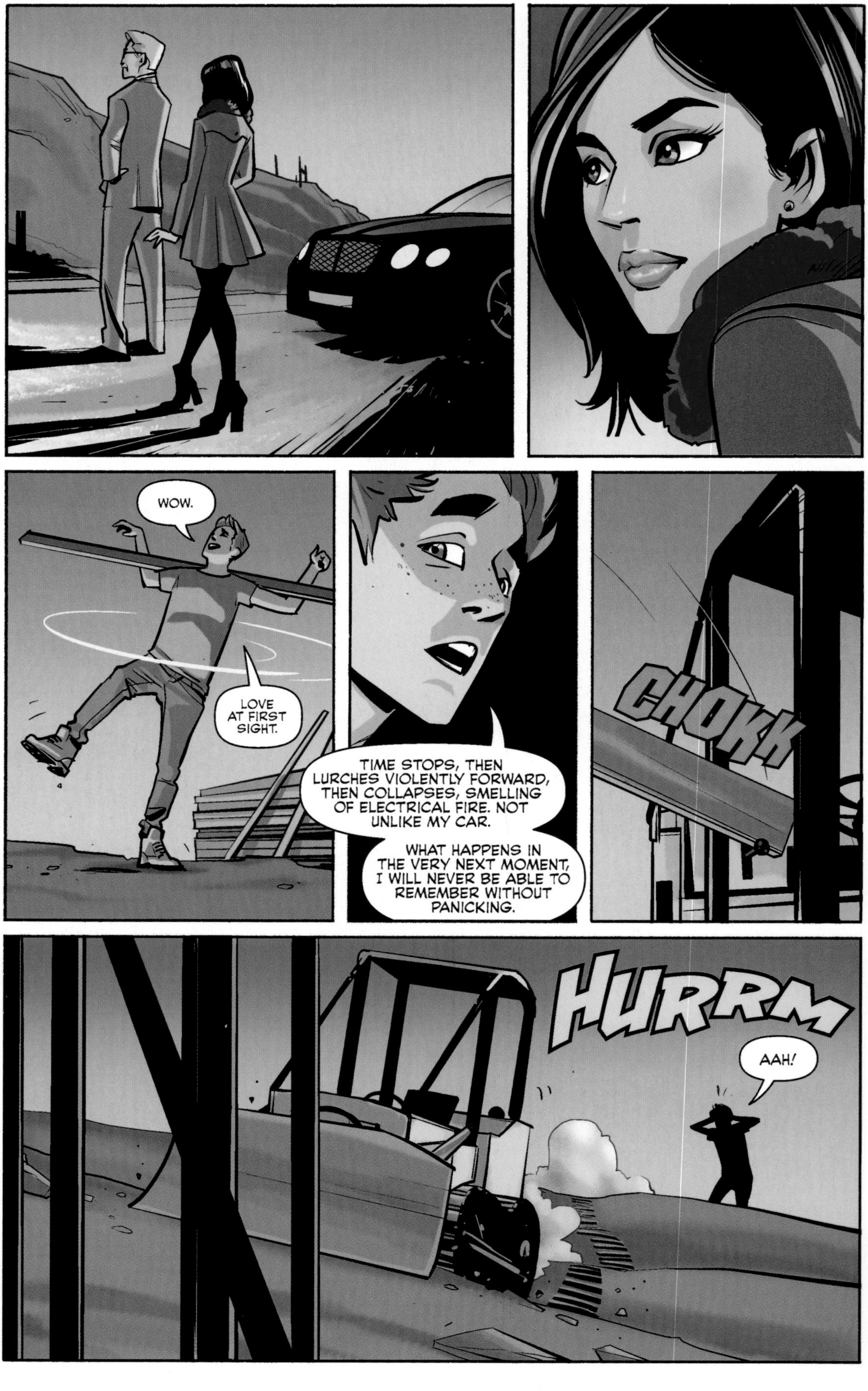
WOW.
LOVE AT FIRST SIGHT.
TIME STOPS, THEN LURCHES VIOLENTLY FORWARD, THEN COLLAPSES, SMELLING OF ELECTRICAL FIRE. NOT UNLIKE MY CAR.
WHAT HAPPENS IN THE VERY NEXT MOMENT, I WILL NEVER BE ABLE TO REMEMBER WITHOUT PANICKING.
CHOKK
HURRM
AAH!

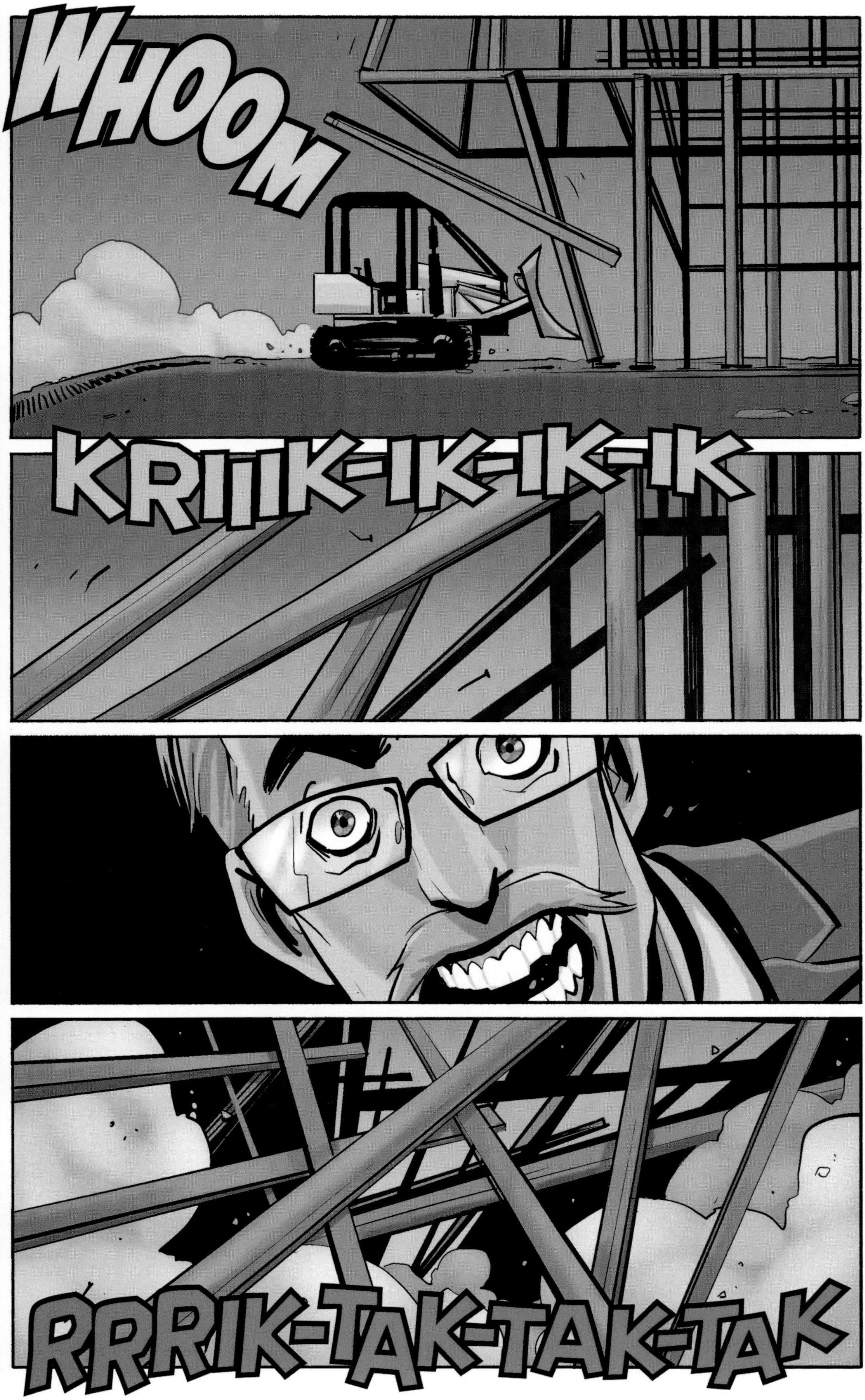
WHOOM
KRIIIK-IK-IK-IK
RRRIK-TAK-TAK-TAK

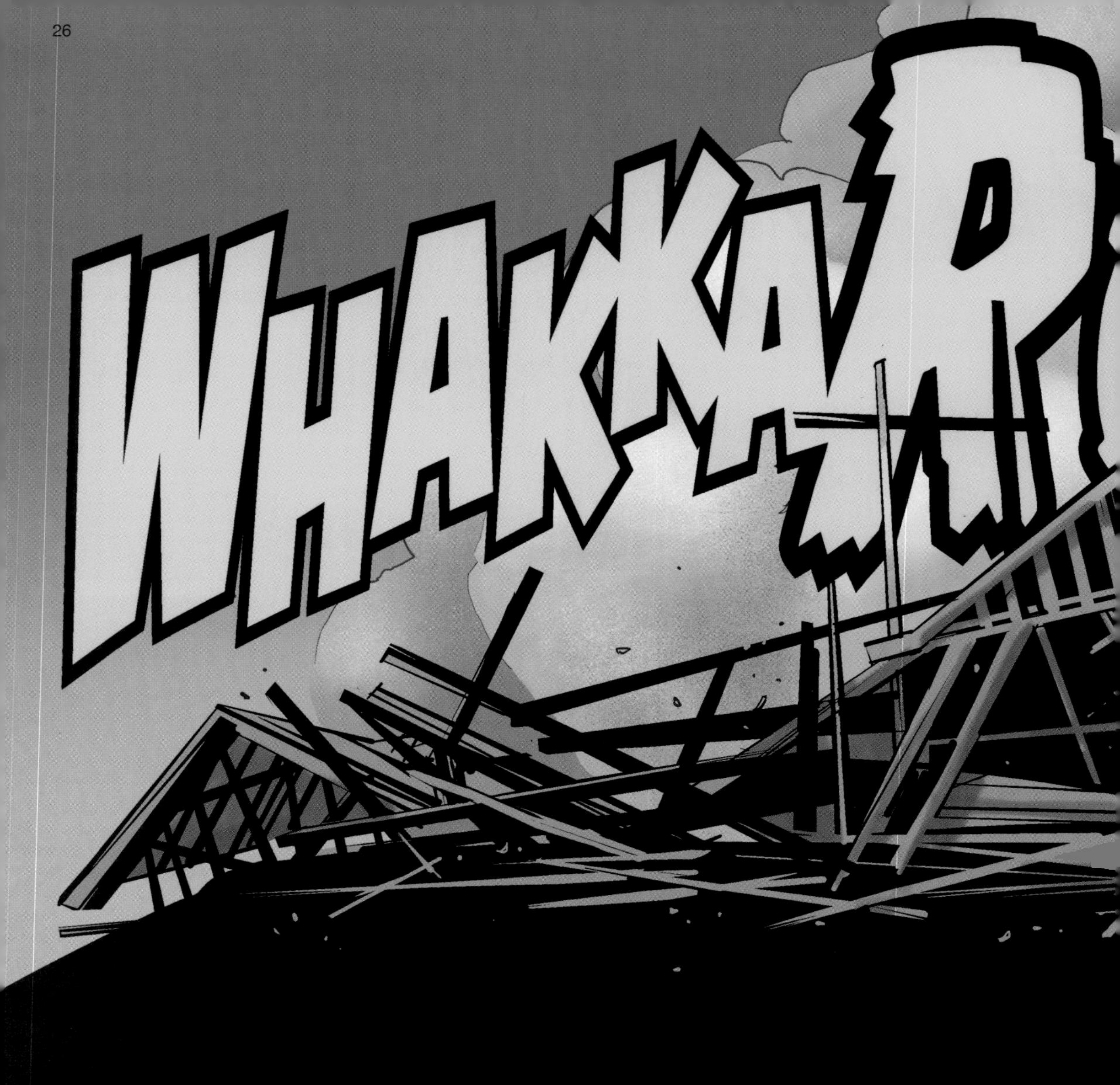
WHAKKA

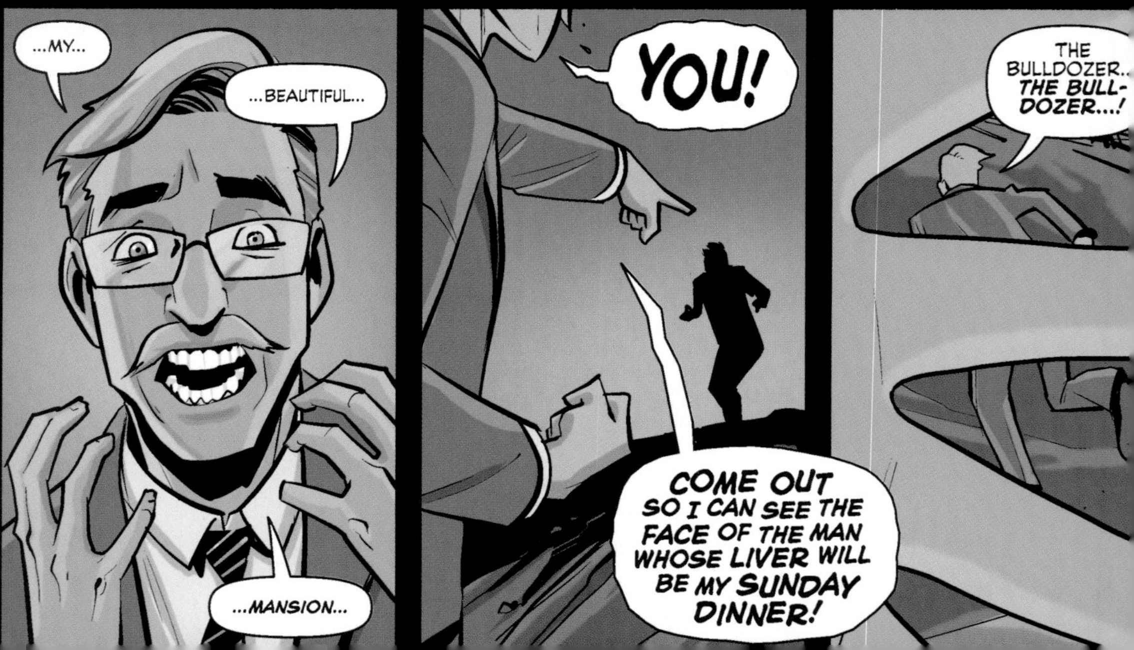
...MY...
...BEAUTIFUL...
...MANSION...
YOU!
COME OUT SO I CAN SEE THE FACE OF THE MAN WHOSE LIVER WILL BE MY SUNDAY DINNER!
THE BULLDOZER... THE BULL-DOZER...!

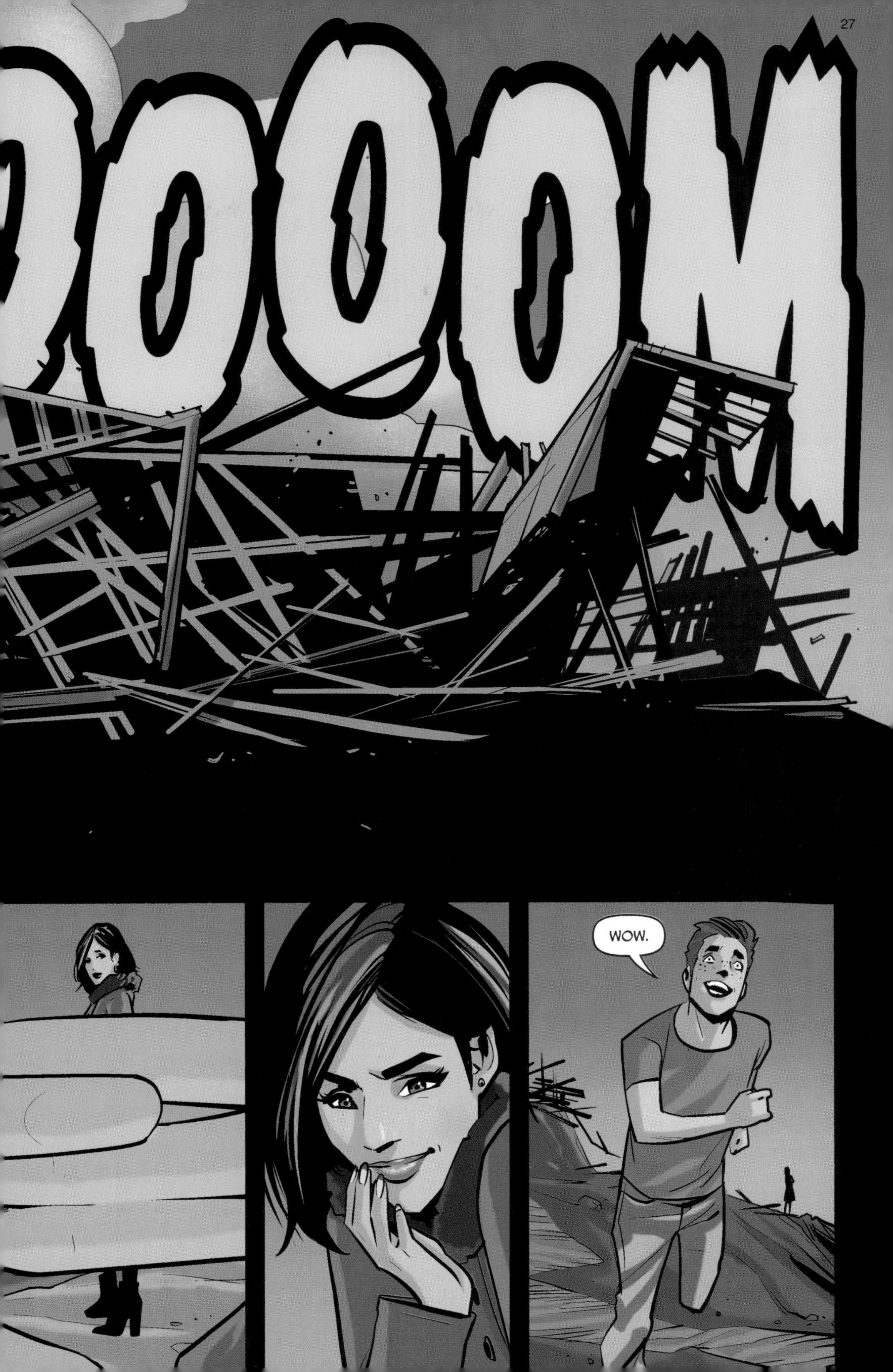
OOOM
WOW.

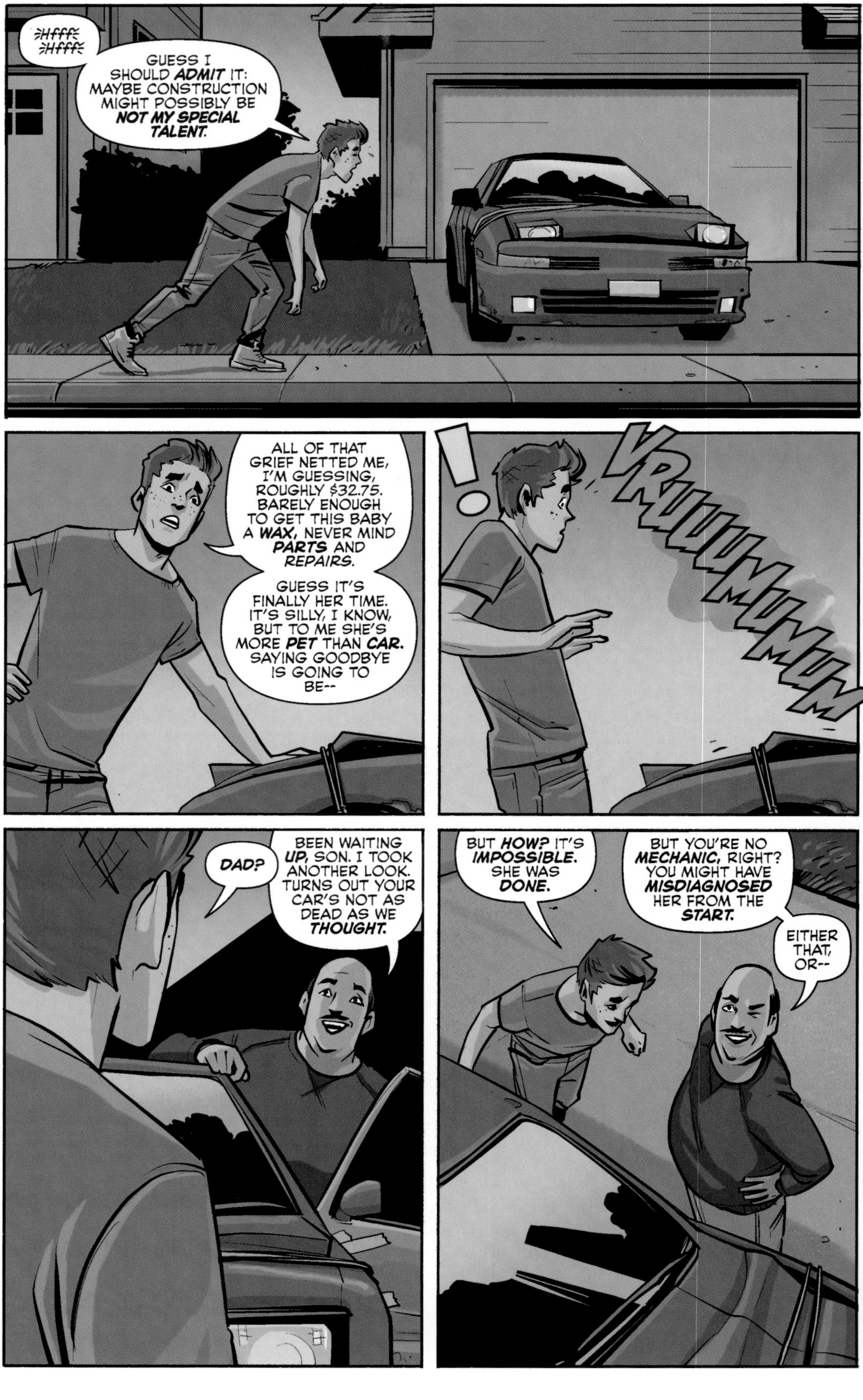
HFFF *HFFF*
GUESS I SHOULD **ADMIT** IT: MAYBE CONSTRUCTION MIGHT POSSIBLY BE ***NOT MY SPECIAL TALENT.***
ALL OF THAT GRIEF NETTED ME, I'M GUESSING, ROUGHLY $32.75. BARELY ENOUGH TO GET THIS BABY A ***WAX,*** NEVER MIND ***PARTS*** AND *REPAIRS.*
GUESS IT'S FINALLY HER TIME. IT'S SILLY, I KNOW, BUT TO ME SHE'S MORE ***PET*** THAN ***CAR.*** SAYING GOODBYE IS GOING TO BE--
!
VRUUUMUMUMUM
DAD?
BEEN WAITING ***UP,*** SON. I TOOK ANOTHER LOOK. TURNS OUT YOUR CAR'S NOT AS DEAD AS WE ***THOUGHT.***
BUT ***HOW?*** IT'S ***IMPOSSIBLE.*** SHE WAS ***DONE.***
BUT YOU'RE NO ***MECHANIC,*** RIGHT? YOU MIGHT HAVE ***MISDIAGNOSED*** HER FROM THE ***START.***
EITHER THAT, OR--

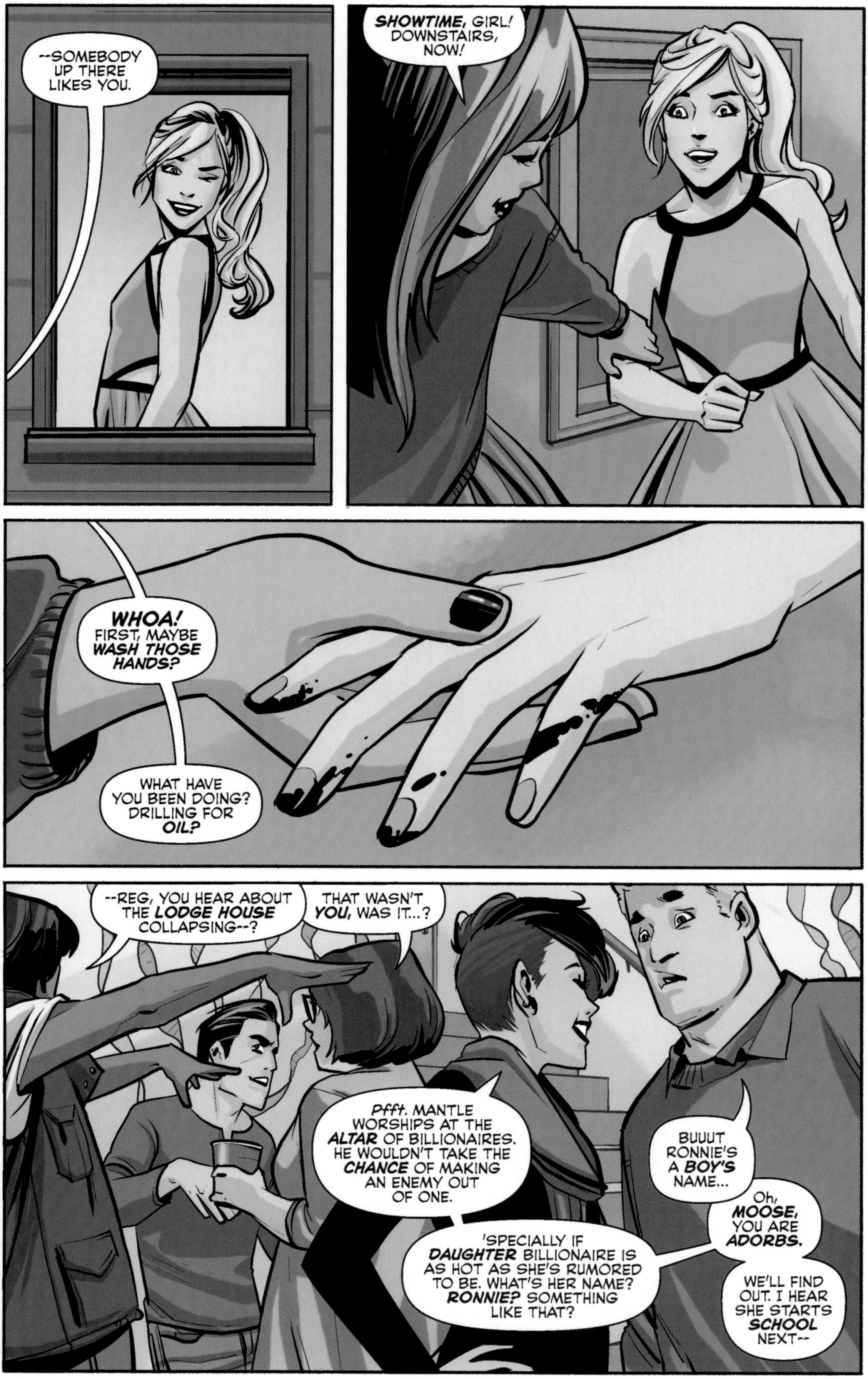
--SOMEBODY UP THERE LIKES YOU.
SHOWTIME, GIRL! DOWNSTAIRS, NOW!
WHOA! FIRST, MAYBE WASH THOSE HANDS?
WHAT HAVE YOU BEEN DOING? DRILLING FOR OIL?
--REG, YOU HEAR ABOUT THE LODGE HOUSE COLLAPSING--?
THAT WASN'T YOU, WAS IT...?
Pfft. MANTLE WORSHIPS AT THE ALTAR OF BILLIONAIRES. HE WOULDN'T TAKE THE CHANCE OF MAKING AN ENEMY OUT OF ONE.
'SPECIALLY IF DAUGHTER BILLIONAIRE IS AS HOT AS SHE'S RUMORED TO BE. WHAT'S HER NAME? RONNIE? SOMETHING LIKE THAT?
BUUUT RONNIE'S A BOY'S NAME...
Oh, MOOSE, YOU ARE ADORBS.
WE'LL FIND OUT. I HEAR SHE STARTS SCHOOL NEXT--

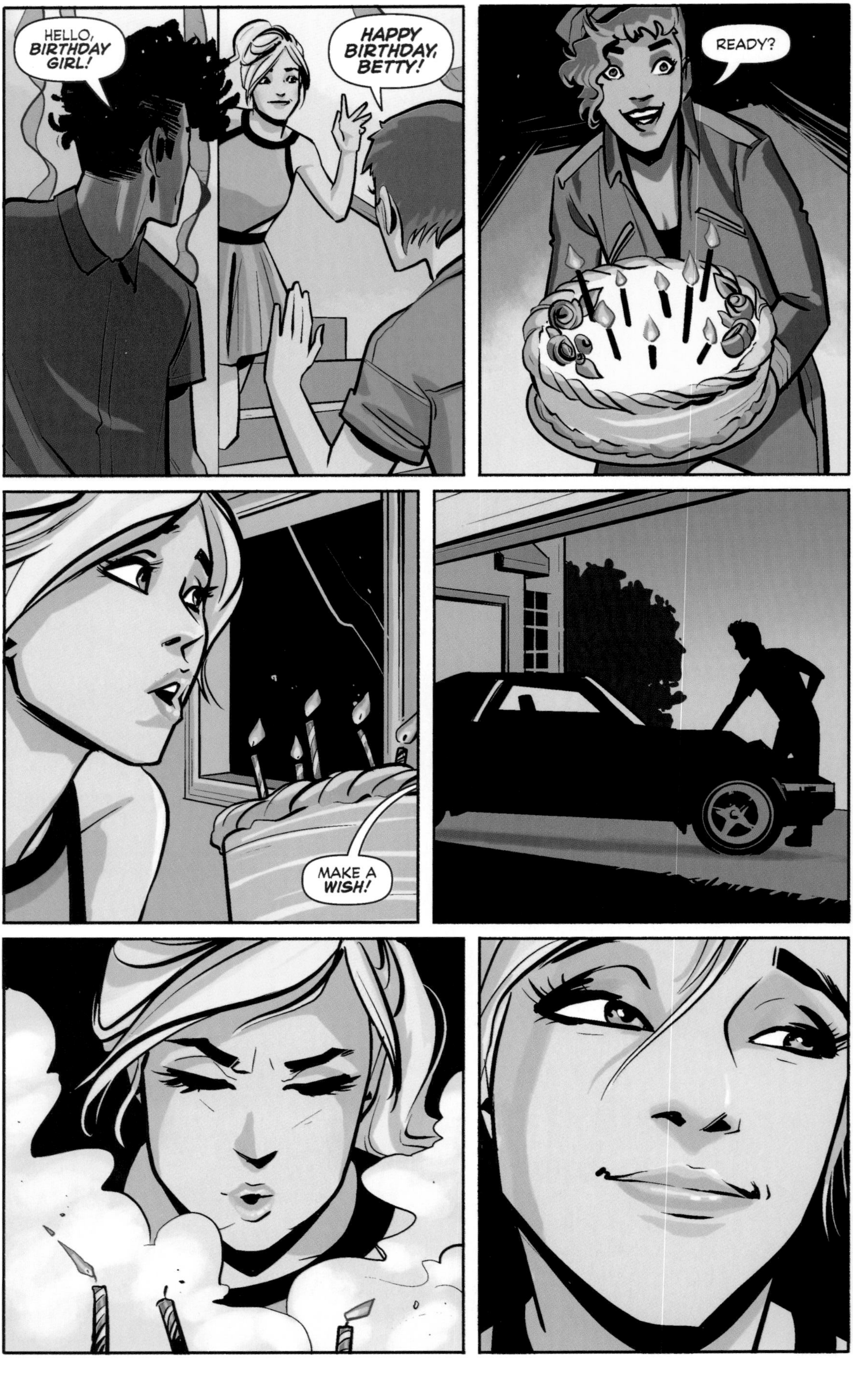
HELLO, BIRTHDAY GIRL!
HAPPY BIRTHDAY, BETTY!
READY?
MAKE A WISH!

CATCH UP WITH THE ONGOING
ARCHIE SERIES
ON SALE NOW!

Jughead

PREVIOUSLY IN THE TOWN OF RIVERDALE...

A travesty hit Riverdale High when the new principal, Mr. Stanger, outlawed burgers in the cafeteria. But Jughead's not one to sit idly by and let change happen that easily—ok, actually that's exactly what Jughead would do, but not this time! He found a loophole in the system and the new principal isn't standing for it.

Has Jughead become *public enemy #1*?

Or will he be the force of change that Riverdale High needs?

Either way, he's going to take a nap first.

STORY BY
CHIP ZDARSKY

ART BY
ERICA HENDERSON

LETTERING BY
JACK MORELLI

ROAD TO RIVERDALE®
JUGHEAD

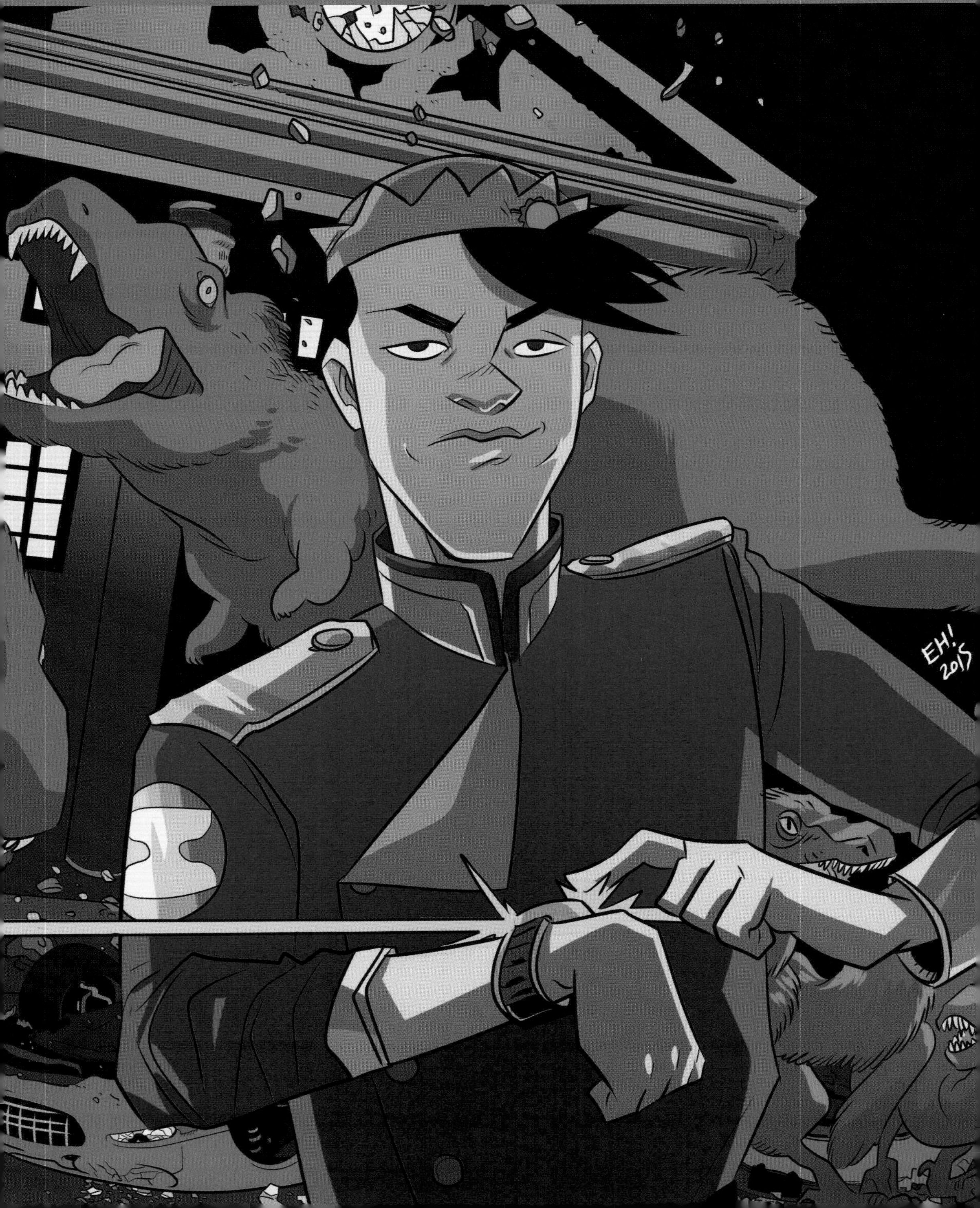
EH! 2015

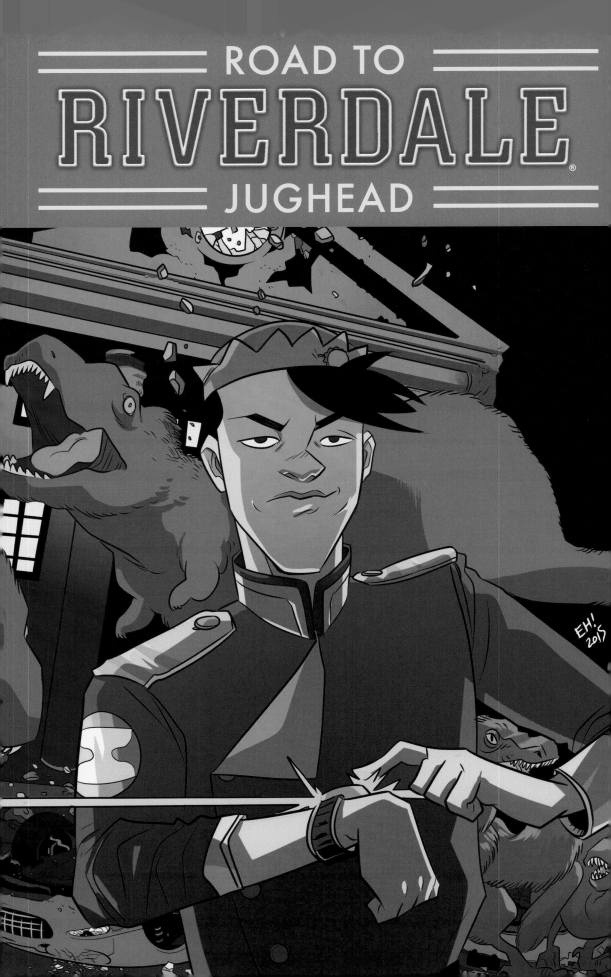

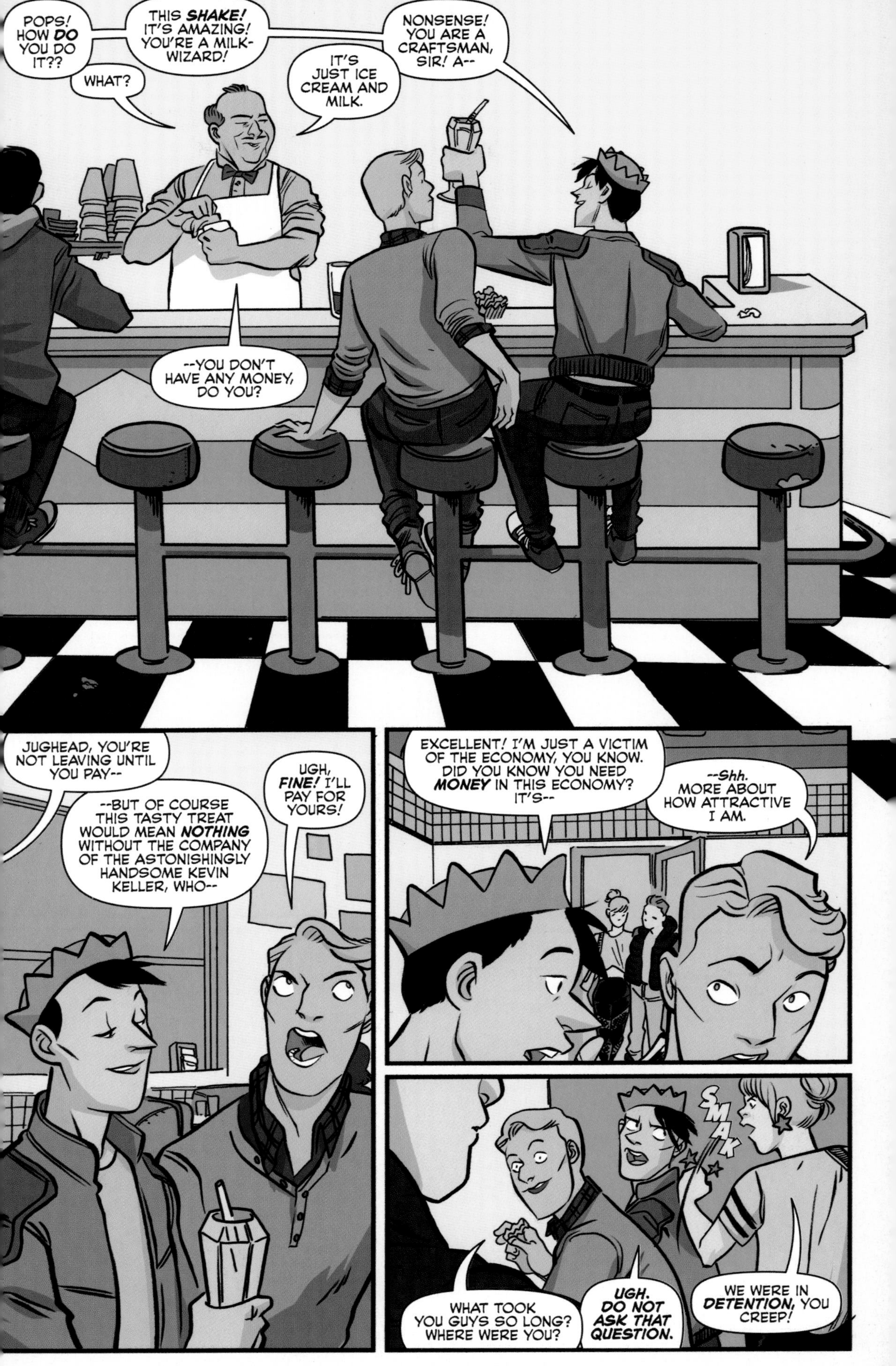
POPS! HOW DO YOU DO IT??
WHAT?
THIS SHAKE! IT'S AMAZING! YOU'RE A MILK-WIZARD!
IT'S JUST ICE CREAM AND MILK.
NONSENSE! YOU ARE A CRAFTSMAN, SIR! A--
--YOU DON'T HAVE ANY MONEY, DO YOU?
JUGHEAD, YOU'RE NOT LEAVING UNTIL YOU PAY--
--BUT OF COURSE THIS TASTY TREAT WOULD MEAN NOTHING WITHOUT THE COMPANY OF THE ASTONISHINGLY HANDSOME KEVIN KELLER, WHO--
UGH, FINE! I'LL PAY FOR YOURS!
EXCELLENT! I'M JUST A VICTIM OF THE ECONOMY, YOU KNOW. DID YOU KNOW YOU NEED MONEY IN THIS ECONOMY? IT'S--
--Shh. MORE ABOUT HOW ATTRACTIVE I AM.
SMAK
WHAT TOOK YOU GUYS SO LONG? WHERE WERE YOU?
UGH. DO NOT ASK THAT QUESTION.
WE WERE IN DETENTION, YOU CREEP!

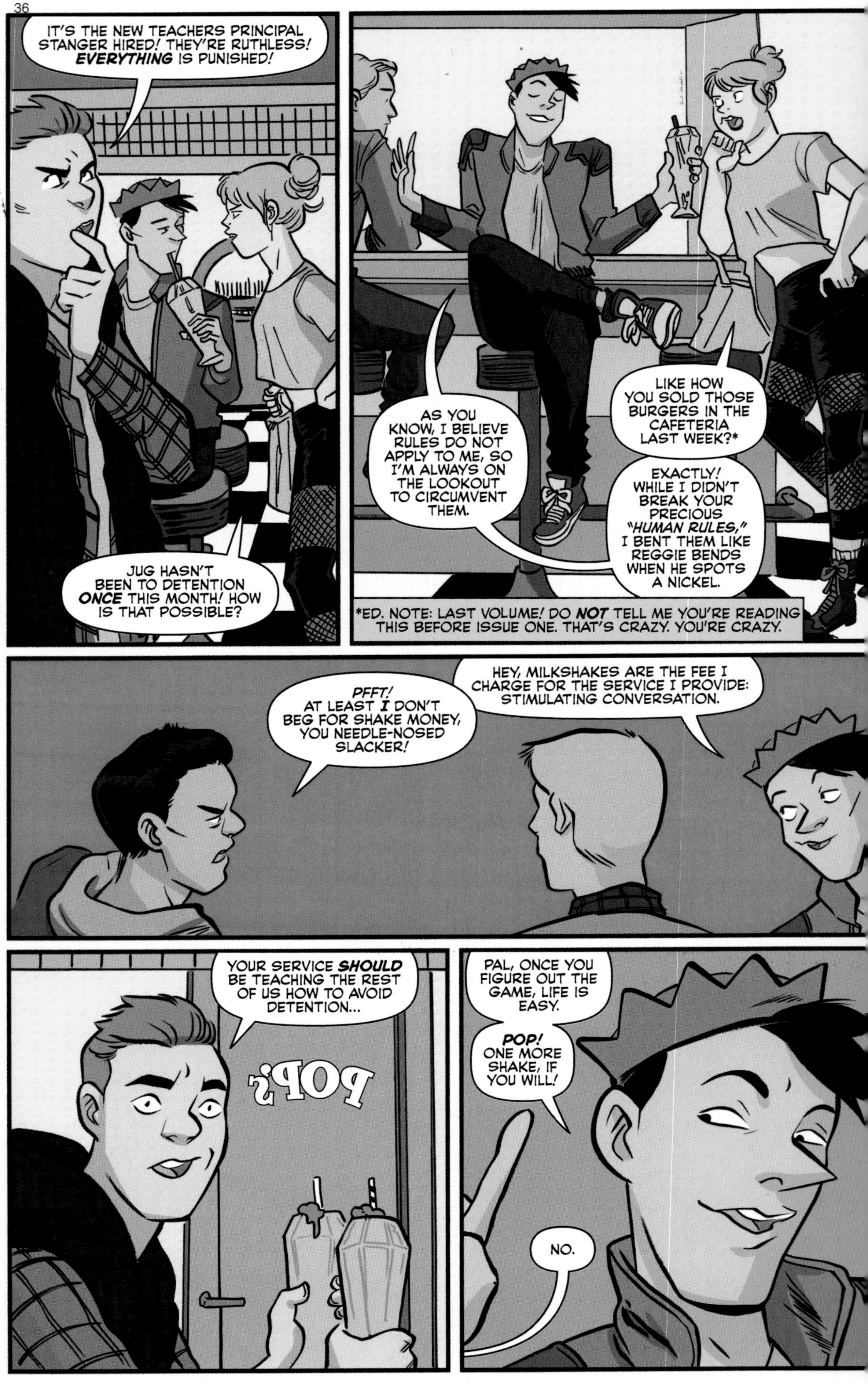
IT'S THE NEW TEACHERS PRINCIPAL STANGER HIRED! THEY'RE RUTHLESS! EVERYTHING IS PUNISHED!
JUG HASN'T BEEN TO DETENTION ONCE THIS MONTH! HOW IS THAT POSSIBLE?
AS YOU KNOW, I BELIEVE RULES DO NOT APPLY TO ME, SO I'M ALWAYS ON THE LOOKOUT TO CIRCUMVENT THEM.
LIKE HOW YOU SOLD THOSE BURGERS IN THE CAFETERIA LAST WEEK?*
EXACTLY! WHILE I DIDN'T BREAK YOUR PRECIOUS "HUMAN RULES," I BENT THEM LIKE REGGIE BENDS WHEN HE SPOTS A NICKEL.
*ED. NOTE: LAST VOLUME! DO NOT TELL ME YOU'RE READING THIS BEFORE ISSUE ONE. THAT'S CRAZY. YOU'RE CRAZY.
HEY, MILKSHAKES ARE THE FEE I CHARGE FOR THE SERVICE I PROVIDE: STIMULATING CONVERSATION.
PFFT! AT LEAST I DON'T BEG FOR SHAKE MONEY, YOU NEEDLE-NOSED SLACKER!
YOUR SERVICE SHOULD BE TEACHING THE REST OF US HOW TO AVOID DETENTION...
POP'S
PAL, ONCE YOU FIGURE OUT THE GAME, LIFE IS EASY.
POP! ONE MORE SHAKE, IF YOU WILL!
NO.

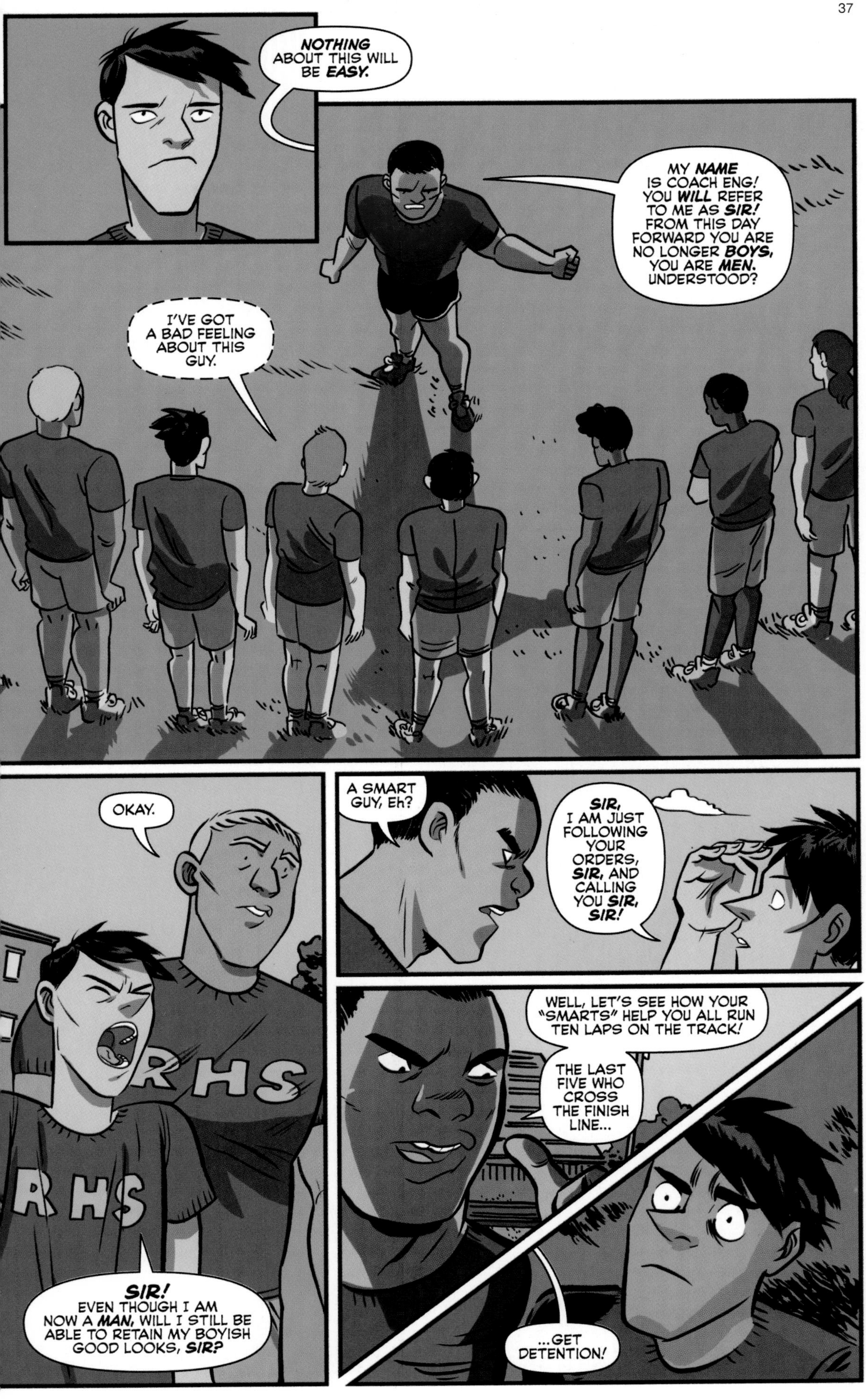
NOTHING ABOUT THIS WILL BE EASY.
MY NAME IS COACH ENG! YOU WILL REFER TO ME AS SIR! FROM THIS DAY FORWARD YOU ARE NO LONGER BOYS, YOU ARE MEN. UNDERSTOOD?
I'VE GOT A BAD FEELING ABOUT THIS GUY.
OKAY.
RHS
RHS
SIR! EVEN THOUGH I AM NOW A MAN, WILL I STILL BE ABLE TO RETAIN MY BOYISH GOOD LOOKS, SIR?
A SMART GUY, Eh?
SIR, I AM JUST FOLLOWING YOUR ORDERS, SIR, AND CALLING YOU SIR, SIR!
WELL, LET'S SEE HOW YOUR "SMARTS" HELP YOU ALL RUN TEN LAPS ON THE TRACK!
THE LAST FIVE WHO CROSS THE FINISH LINE...
...GET DETENTION!

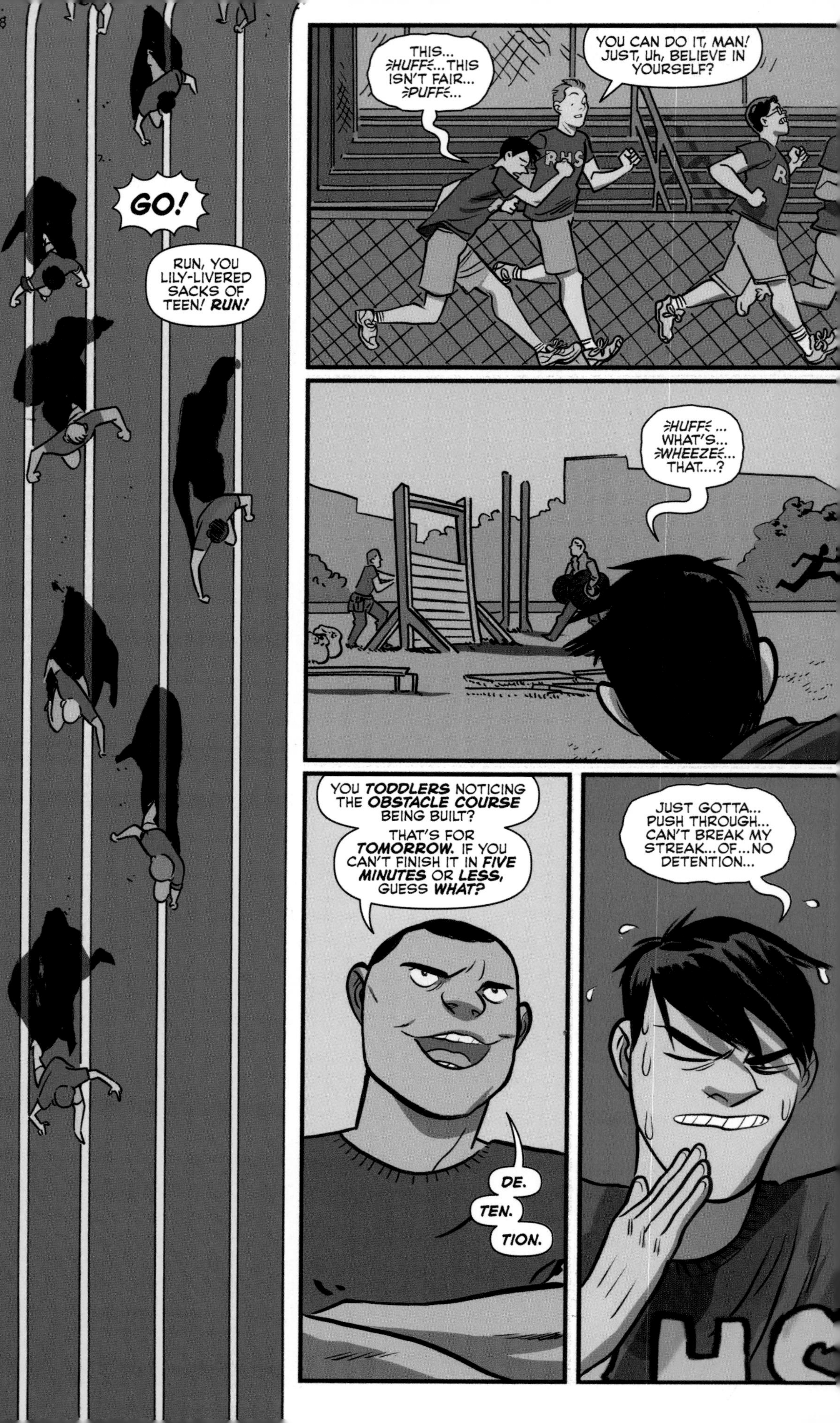
GO!
RUN, YOU LILY-LIVERED SACKS OF TEEN! RUN!
THIS... ≶HUFF≶... THIS ISN'T FAIR... ≶PUFF≶...
YOU CAN DO IT, MAN! JUST, UH, BELIEVE IN YOURSELF?
RHS
≶HUFF≶... WHAT'S... ≶WHEEZE≶... THAT...?
YOU TODDLERS NOTICING THE OBSTACLE COURSE BEING BUILT?
THAT'S FOR TOMORROW. IF YOU CAN'T FINISH IT IN FIVE MINUTES OR LESS, GUESS WHAT?
DE.
TEN.
TION.
JUST GOTTA... PUSH THROUGH... CAN'T BREAK MY STREAK...OF...NO DETENTION...

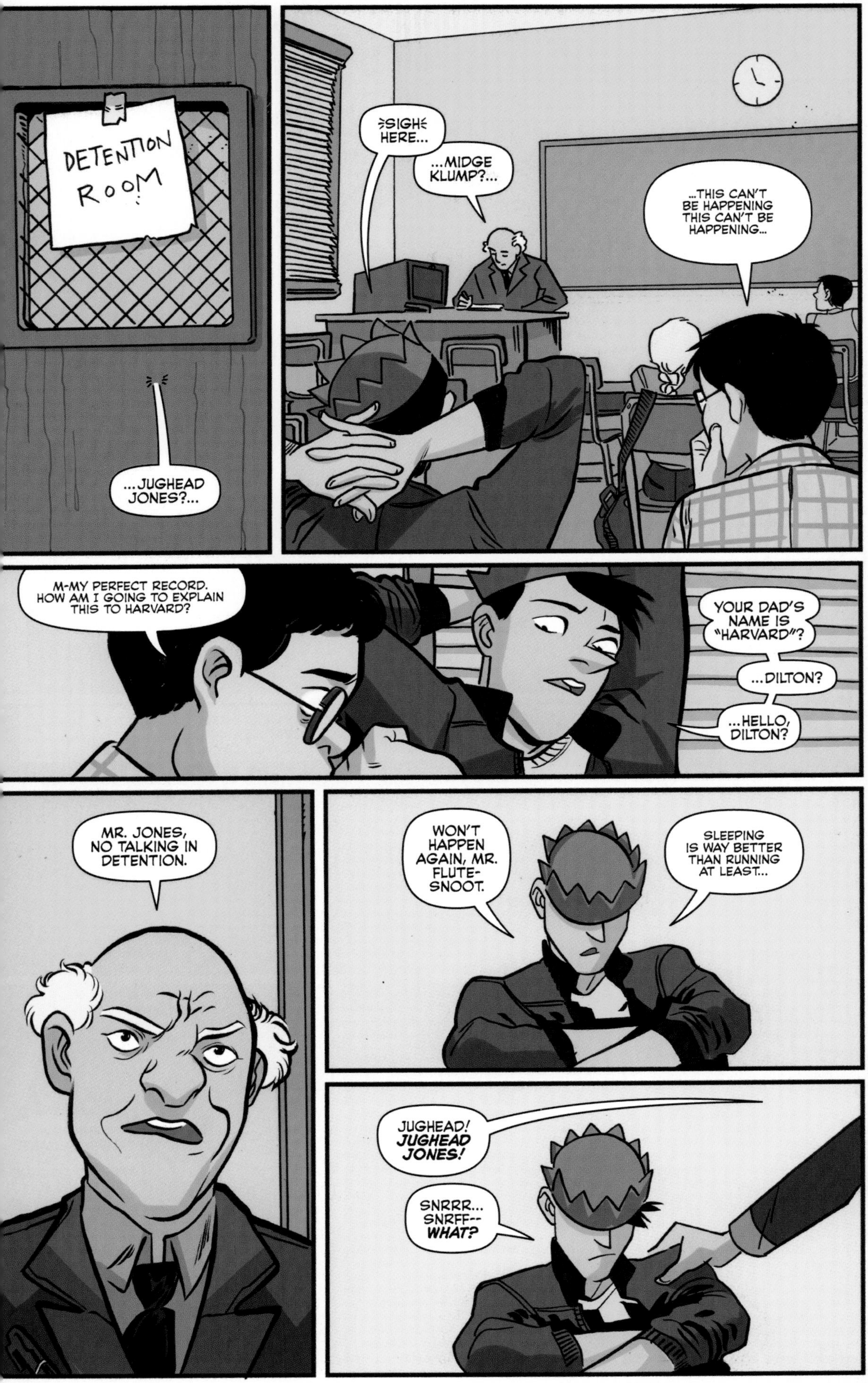
DETENTION ROOM
...JUGHEAD JONES?...
⪢SIGH⪡ HERE...
...MIDGE KLUMP?...
...THIS CAN'T BE HAPPENING THIS CAN'T BE HAPPENING...
M-MY PERFECT RECORD. HOW AM I GOING TO EXPLAIN THIS TO HARVARD?
YOUR DAD'S NAME IS "HARVARD"?
...DILTON?
...HELLO, DILTON?
MR. JONES, NO TALKING IN DETENTION.
WON'T HAPPEN AGAIN, MR. FLUTE-SNOOT.
SLEEPING IS WAY BETTER THAN RUNNING AT LEAST...
JUGHEAD! JUGHEAD JONES!
SNRRR... SNRFF-- WHAT?

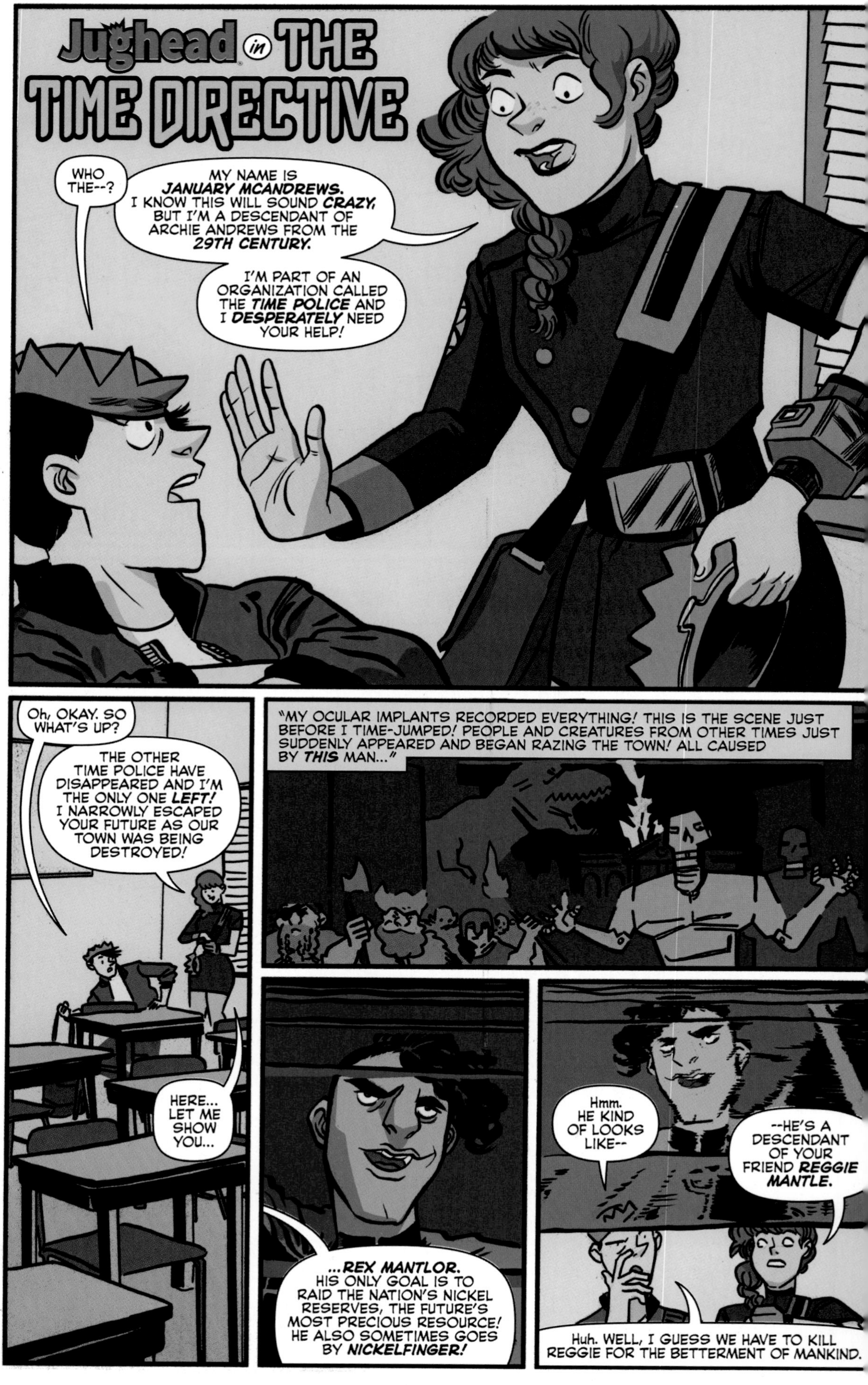
Jughead in THE TIME DIRECTIVE
WHO THE--?
MY NAME IS JANUARY MCANDREWS. I KNOW THIS WILL SOUND CRAZY, BUT I'M A DESCENDANT OF ARCHIE ANDREWS FROM THE 29TH CENTURY.
I'M PART OF AN ORGANIZATION CALLED THE TIME POLICE AND I DESPERATELY NEED YOUR HELP!
Oh, OKAY. SO WHAT'S UP?
THE OTHER TIME POLICE HAVE DISAPPEARED AND I'M THE ONLY ONE LEFT! I NARROWLY ESCAPED YOUR FUTURE AS OUR TOWN WAS BEING DESTROYED!
HERE... LET ME SHOW YOU...
"MY OCULAR IMPLANTS RECORDED EVERYTHING! THIS IS THE SCENE JUST BEFORE I TIME-JUMPED! PEOPLE AND CREATURES FROM OTHER TIMES JUST SUDDENLY APPEARED AND BEGAN RAZING THE TOWN! ALL CAUSED BY THIS MAN..."
...REX MANTLOR. HIS ONLY GOAL IS TO RAID THE NATION'S NICKEL RESERVES, THE FUTURE'S MOST PRECIOUS RESOURCE! HE ALSO SOMETIMES GOES BY NICKELFINGER!
Hmm. HE KIND OF LOOKS LIKE--
--HE'S A DESCENDANT OF YOUR FRIEND REGGIE MANTLE.
Huh. WELL, I GUESS WE HAVE TO KILL REGGIE FOR THE BETTERMENT OF MANKIND.

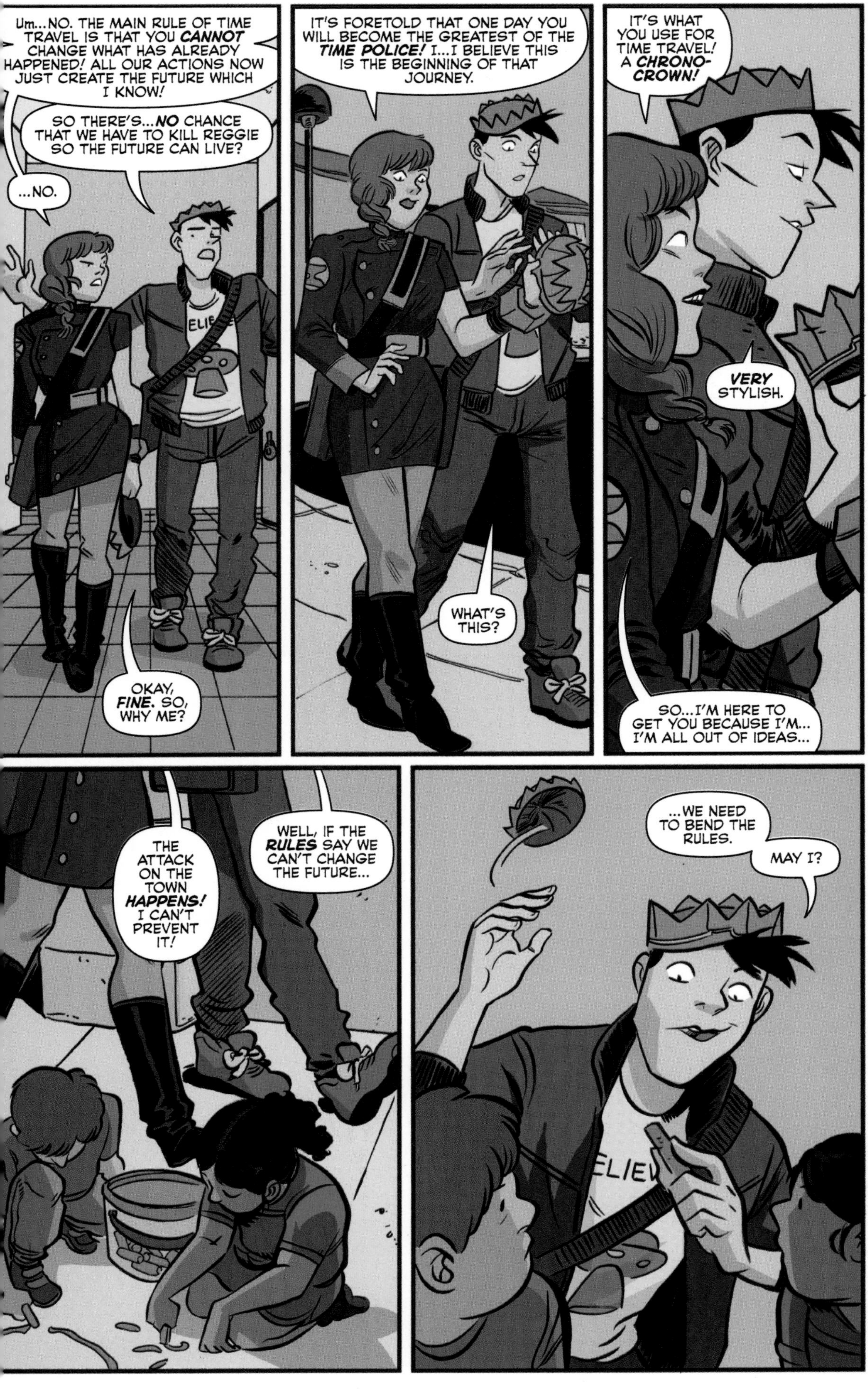
Um...NO. THE MAIN RULE OF TIME TRAVEL IS THAT YOU CANNOT CHANGE WHAT HAS ALREADY HAPPENED! ALL OUR ACTIONS NOW JUST CREATE THE FUTURE WHICH I KNOW!
SO THERE'S...NO CHANCE THAT WE HAVE TO KILL REGGIE SO THE FUTURE CAN LIVE?
...NO.
OKAY, FINE. SO, WHY ME?
IT'S FORETOLD THAT ONE DAY YOU WILL BECOME THE GREATEST OF THE TIME POLICE! I...I BELIEVE THIS IS THE BEGINNING OF THAT JOURNEY.
WHAT'S THIS?
IT'S WHAT YOU USE FOR TIME TRAVEL! A CHRONO-CROWN!
VERY STYLISH.
SO...I'M HERE TO GET YOU BECAUSE I'M... I'M ALL OUT OF IDEAS...
THE ATTACK ON THE TOWN HAPPENS! I CAN'T PREVENT IT!
WELL, IF THE RULES SAY WE CAN'T CHANGE THE FUTURE...
...WE NEED TO BEND THE RULES.
MAY I?

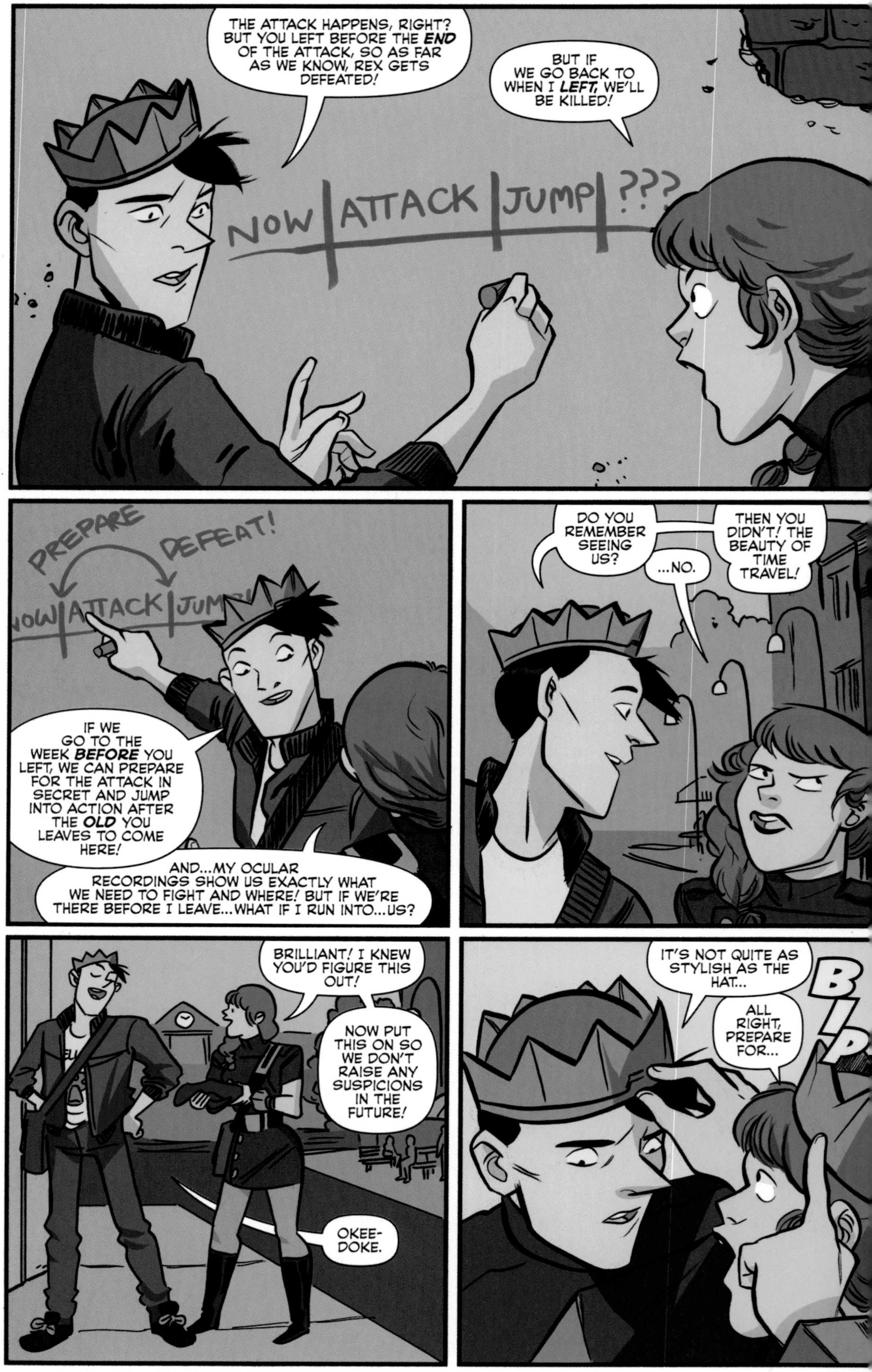
THE ATTACK HAPPENS, RIGHT? BUT YOU LEFT BEFORE THE **END** OF THE ATTACK, SO AS FAR AS WE KNOW, REX GETS DEFEATED!
BUT IF WE GO BACK TO WHEN I **LEFT**, WE'LL BE KILLED!
NOW ATTACK JUMP ???
PREPARE
DEFEAT!
NOW ATTACK JUM
IF WE GO TO THE WEEK **BEFORE** YOU LEFT, WE CAN PREPARE FOR THE ATTACK IN SECRET AND JUMP INTO ACTION AFTER THE **OLD** YOU LEAVES TO COME HERE!
AND...MY OCULAR RECORDINGS SHOW US EXACTLY WHAT WE NEED TO FIGHT AND WHERE! BUT IF WE'RE THERE BEFORE I LEAVE...WHAT IF I RUN INTO...US?
DO YOU REMEMBER SEEING US?
...NO.
THEN YOU DIDN'T! THE BEAUTY OF TIME TRAVEL!
BRILLIANT! I KNEW YOU'D FIGURE THIS OUT!
NOW PUT THIS ON SO WE DON'T RAISE ANY SUSPICIONS IN THE FUTURE!
OKEE-DOKE.
IT'S NOT QUITE AS STYLISH AS THE HAT...
ALL RIGHT, PREPARE FOR...
BLIP

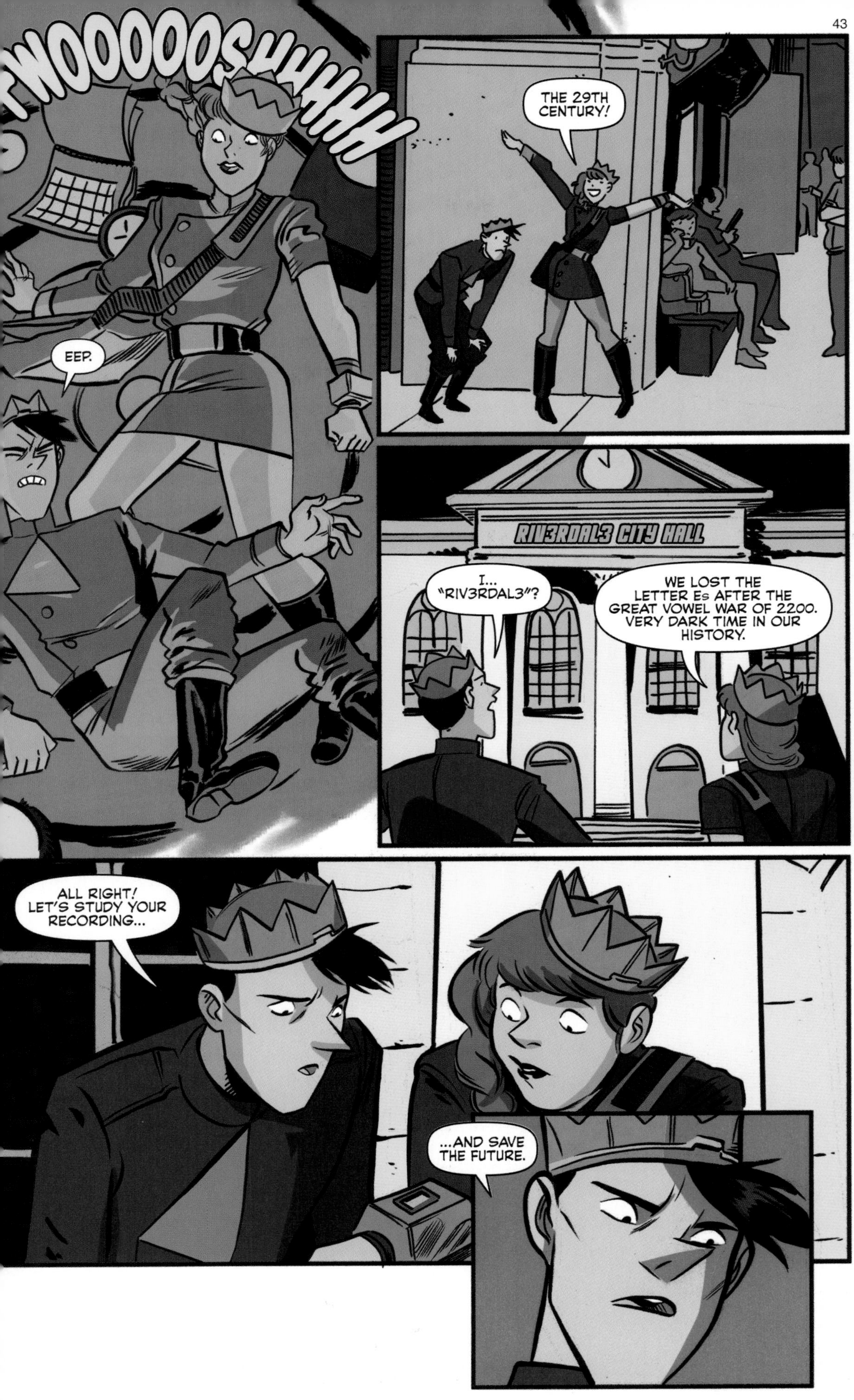
TWOOOOOSHHHHH
EEP.
THE 29TH CENTURY!
RIV3RDAL3 CITY HALL
I... "RIV3RDAL3"?
WE LOST THE LETTER Es AFTER THE GREAT VOWEL WAR OF 2200. VERY DARK TIME IN OUR HISTORY.
ALL RIGHT! LET'S STUDY YOUR RECORDING...
...AND SAVE THE FUTURE.

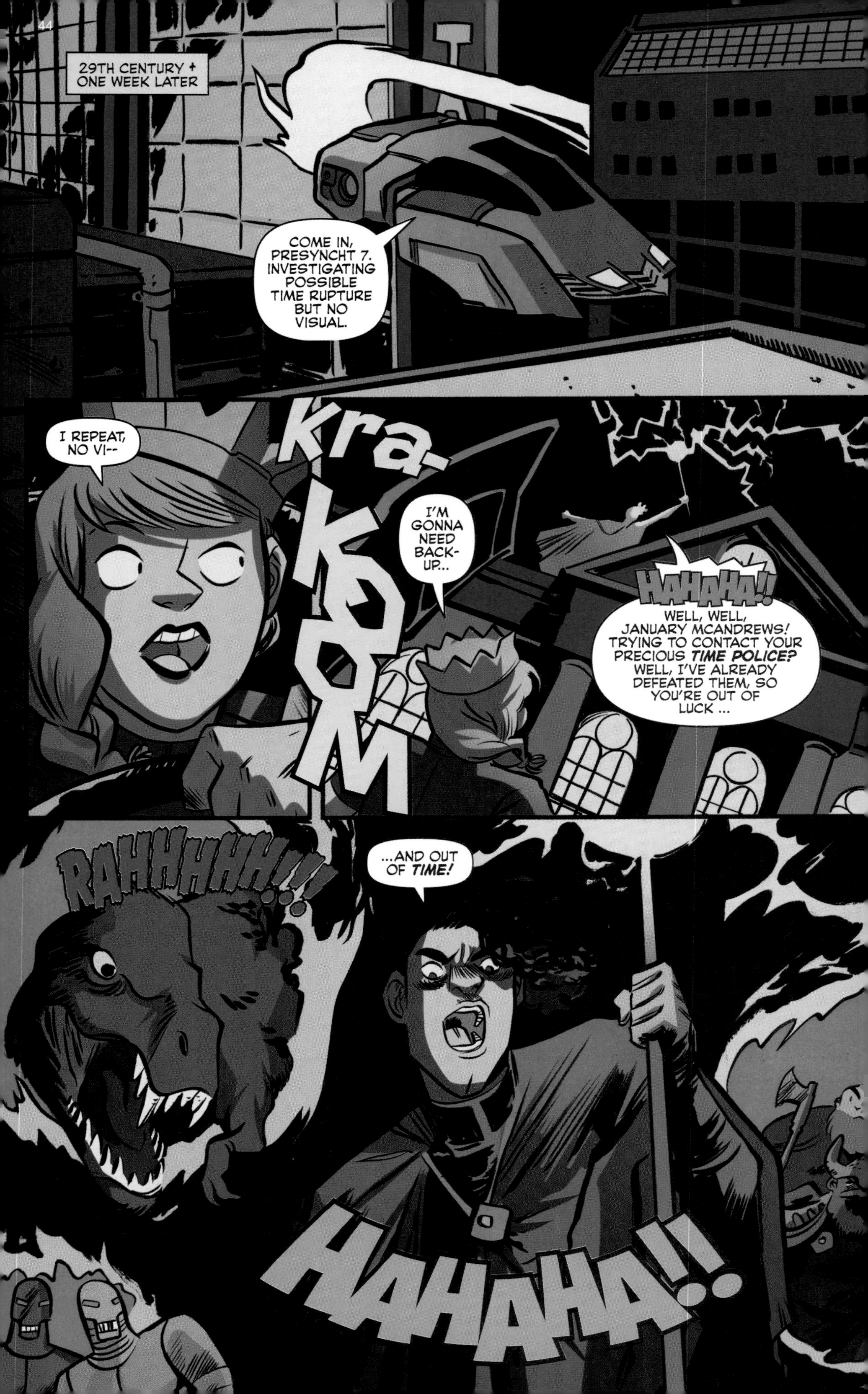
29TH CENTURY + ONE WEEK LATER
COME IN, PRESYNCHT 7. INVESTIGATING POSSIBLE TIME RUPTURE BUT NO VISUAL.
I REPEAT, NO VI--
KRA-KOOM
I'M GONNA NEED BACK-UP...
HAHAHA!!
WELL, WELL, JANUARY MCANDREWS! TRYING TO CONTACT YOUR PRECIOUS *TIME POLICE?* WELL, I'VE ALREADY DEFEATED THEM, SO YOU'RE OUT OF LUCK ...
RAHHHHHH!!!
...AND OUT OF *TIME!*
HAHAHA!!

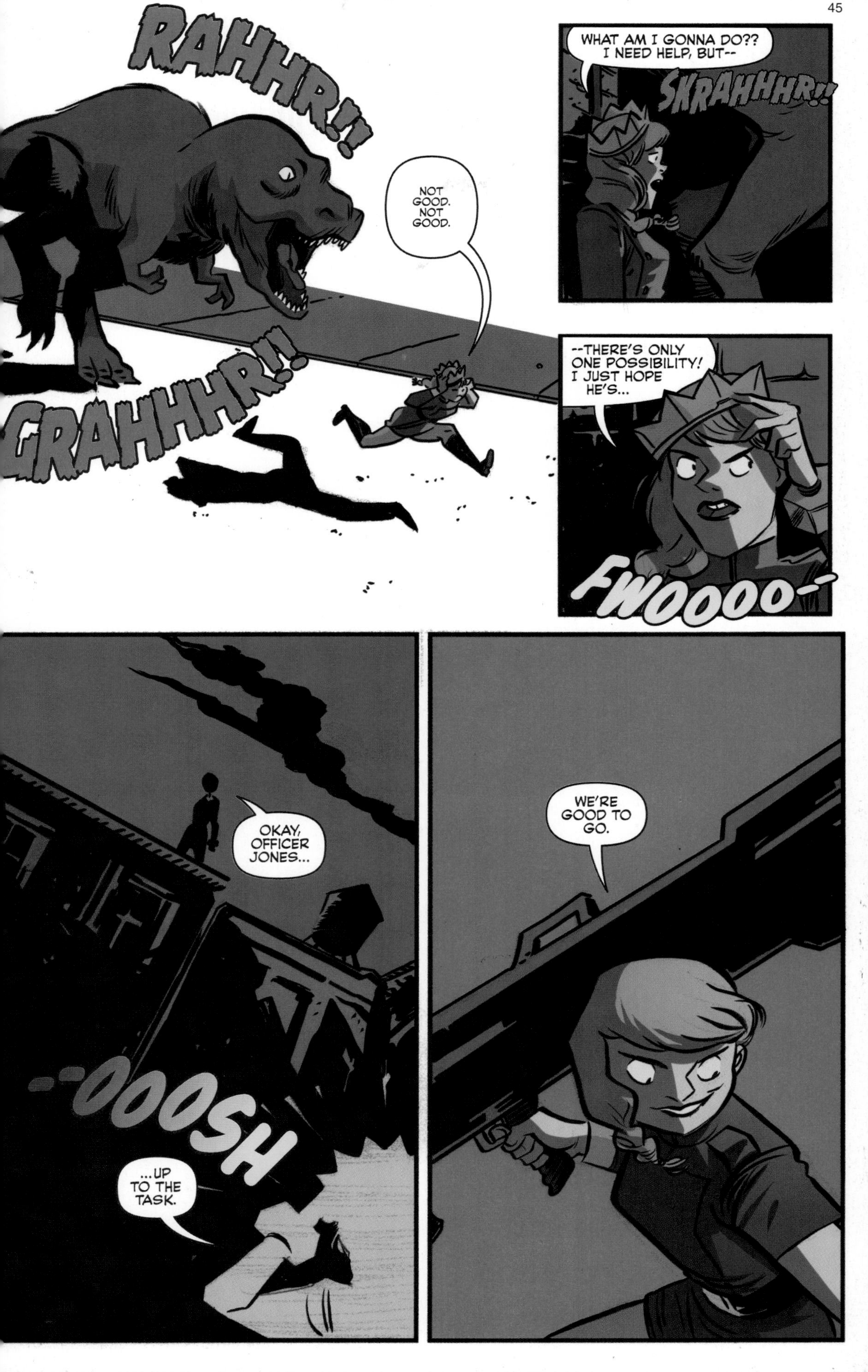
RAHHR!!
NOT GOOD. NOT GOOD.
GRAHHHR!!
WHAT AM I GONNA DO?? I NEED HELP, BUT--
SKRAHHHR!!
--THERE'S ONLY ONE POSSIBILITY! I JUST HOPE HE'S...
FWOOOO--
OKAY, OFFICER JONES...
--OOOSH
...UP TO THE TASK.
WE'RE GOOD TO GO.

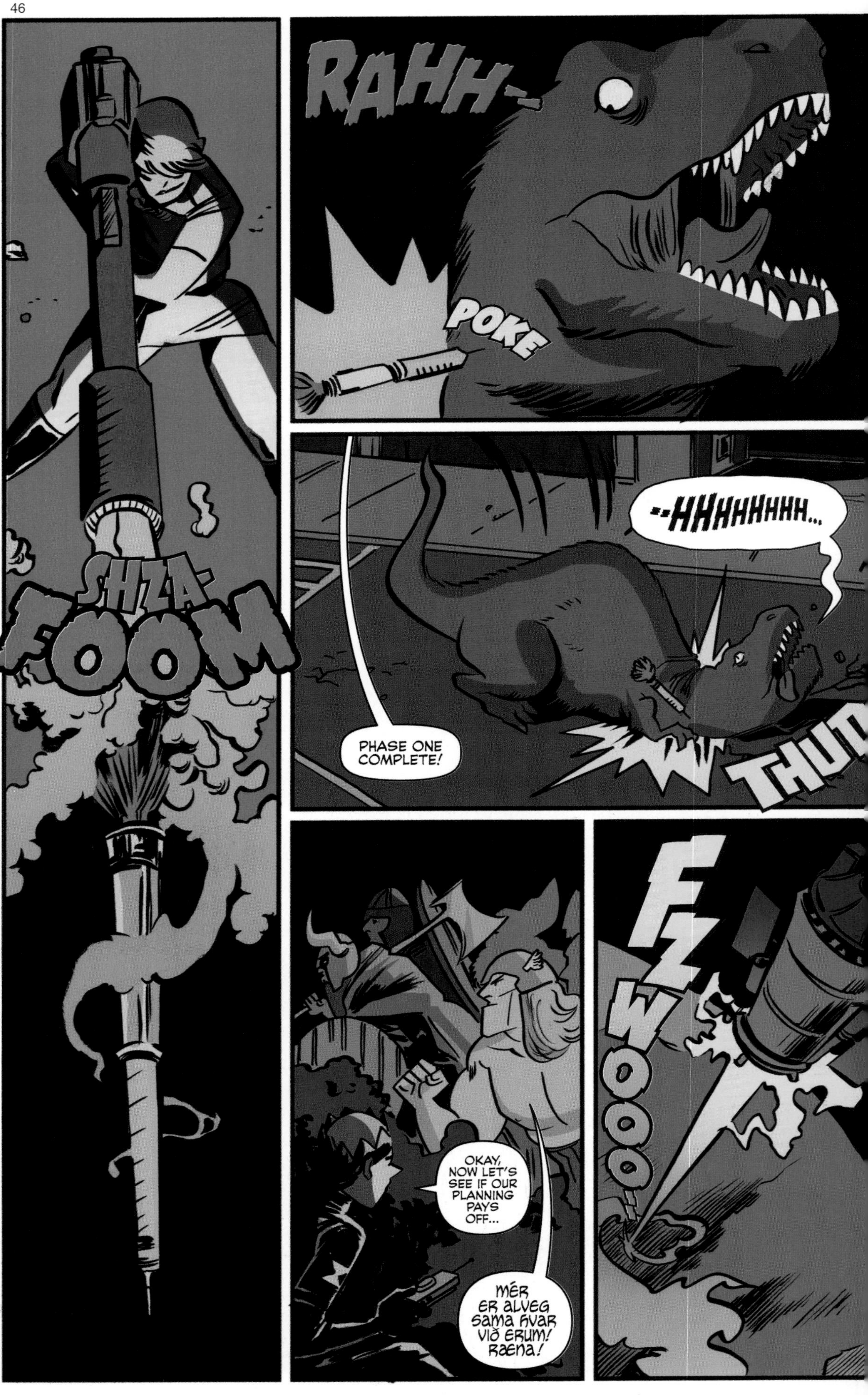
SHZA-
FOOM
RAHH-
POKE
--HHHHHHH...
PHASE ONE COMPLETE!
THUD
OKAY, NOW LET'S SEE IF OUR PLANNING PAYS OFF...
MÉR ER ALVEG SAMA HVAR VIÐ ERUM! RAENA!
FZWOOOO

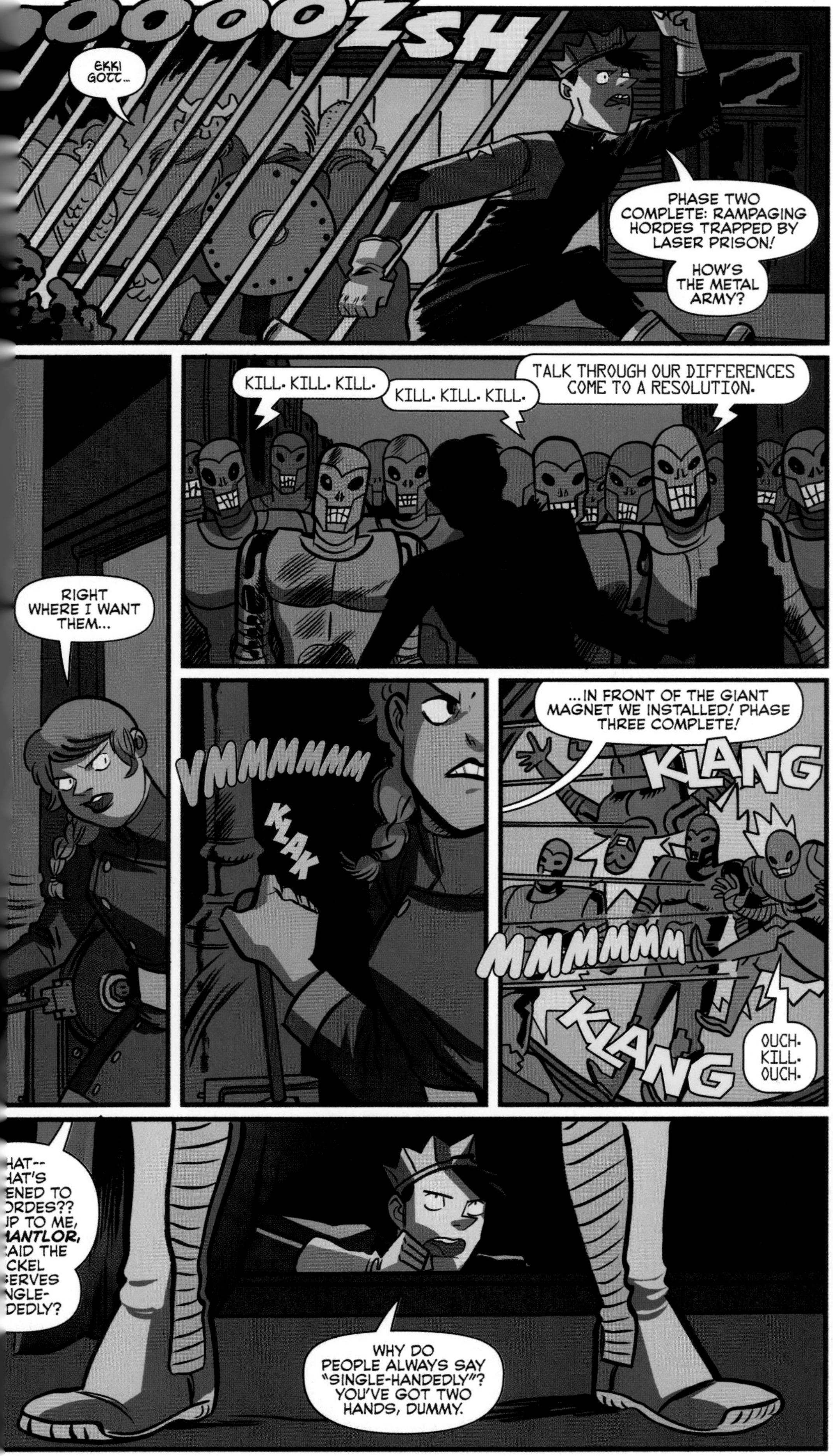
OOOOOOZSH
EKKI GOTT...
PHASE TWO COMPLETE: RAMPAGING HORDES TRAPPED BY LASER PRISON!
HOW'S THE METAL ARMY?
KILL. KILL. KILL.
KILL. KILL. KILL.
TALK THROUGH OUR DIFFERENCES COME TO A RESOLUTION.
RIGHT WHERE I WANT THEM...
VMMMMMM
KLAK
...IN FRONT OF THE GIANT MAGNET WE INSTALLED! PHASE THREE COMPLETE!
KLANG
MMMMMM
KLANG
OUCH. KILL. OUCH.
WHY DO PEOPLE ALWAYS SAY "SINGLE-HANDEDLY"? YOU'VE GOT TWO HANDS, DUMMY.

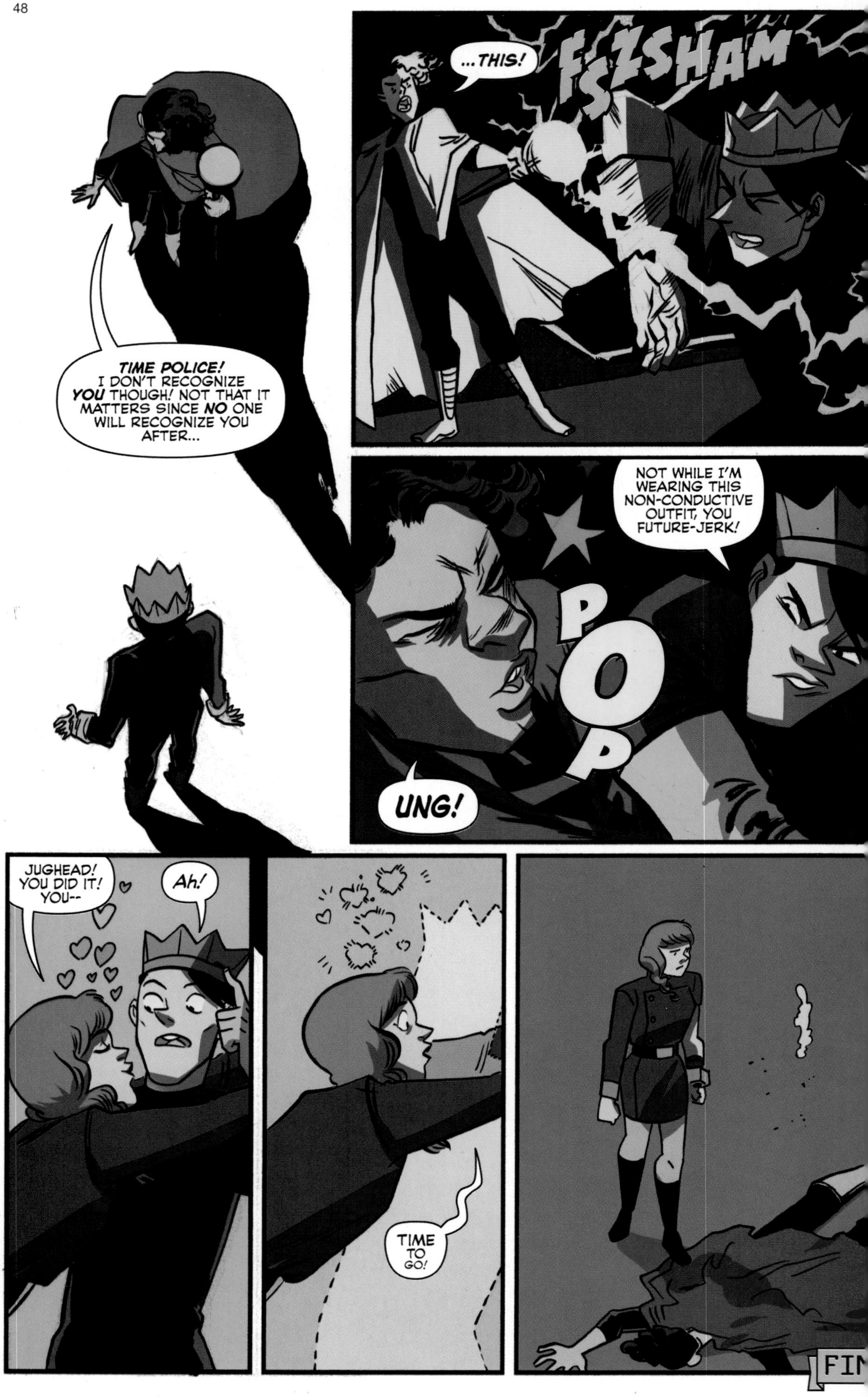
TIME POLICE! I DON'T RECOGNIZE YOU THOUGH! NOT THAT IT MATTERS SINCE NO ONE WILL RECOGNIZE YOU AFTER...
...THIS!
FSZSHAM
NOT WHILE I'M WEARING THIS NON-CONDUCTIVE OUTFIT, YOU FUTURE-JERK!
POP
UNG!
JUGHEAD! YOU DID IT! YOU--
Ah!
TIME TO GO!
FIN

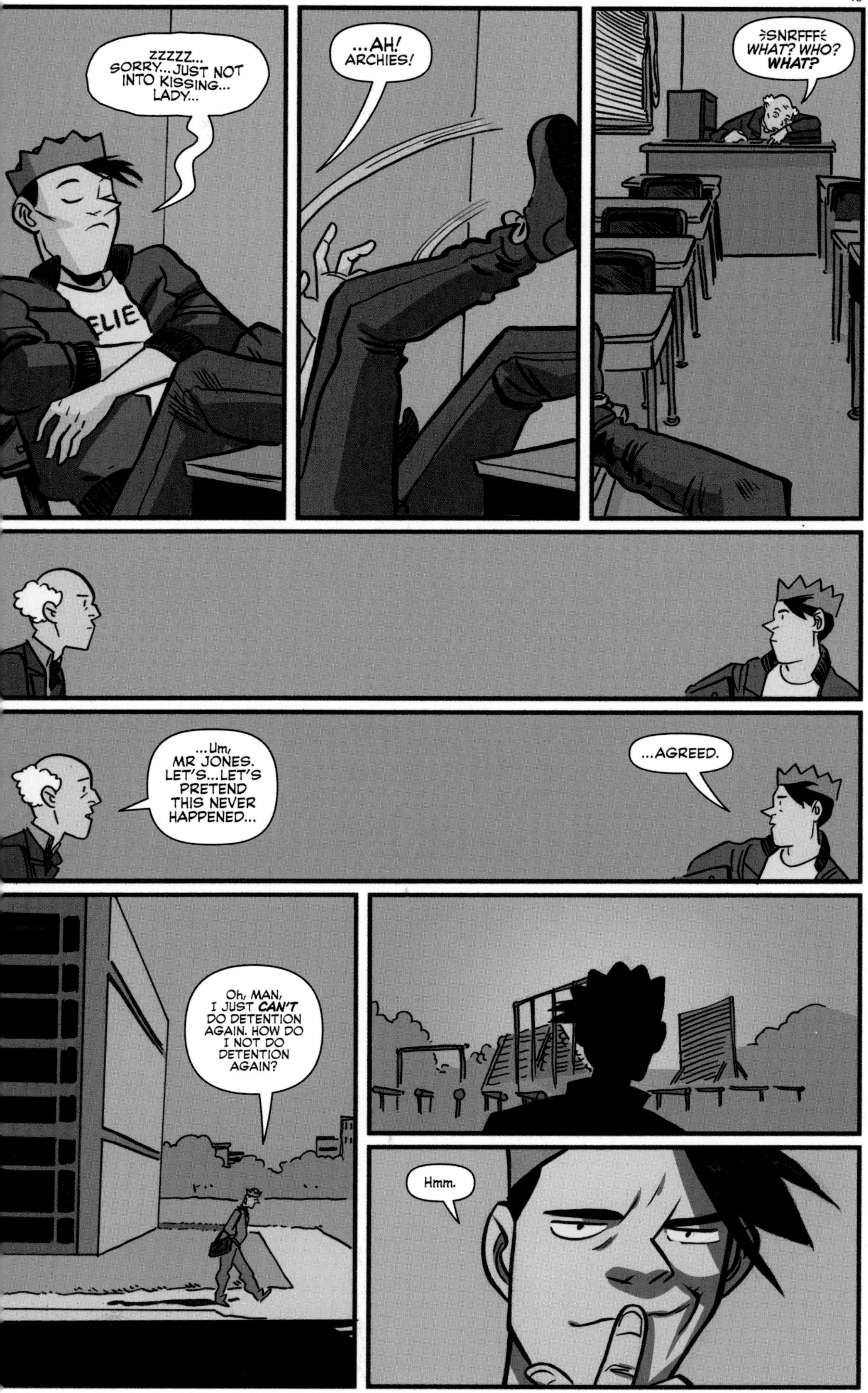
ZZZZZ... SORRY... JUST NOT INTO KISSING... LADY...
ELIE
...AH! ARCHIES!
SNRFFF WHAT? WHO? WHAT?
...Um, MR JONES. LET'S...LET'S PRETEND THIS NEVER HAPPENED...
...AGREED.
Oh, MAN, I JUST CAN'T DO DETENTION AGAIN. HOW DO I NOT DO DETENTION AGAIN?
Hmm.

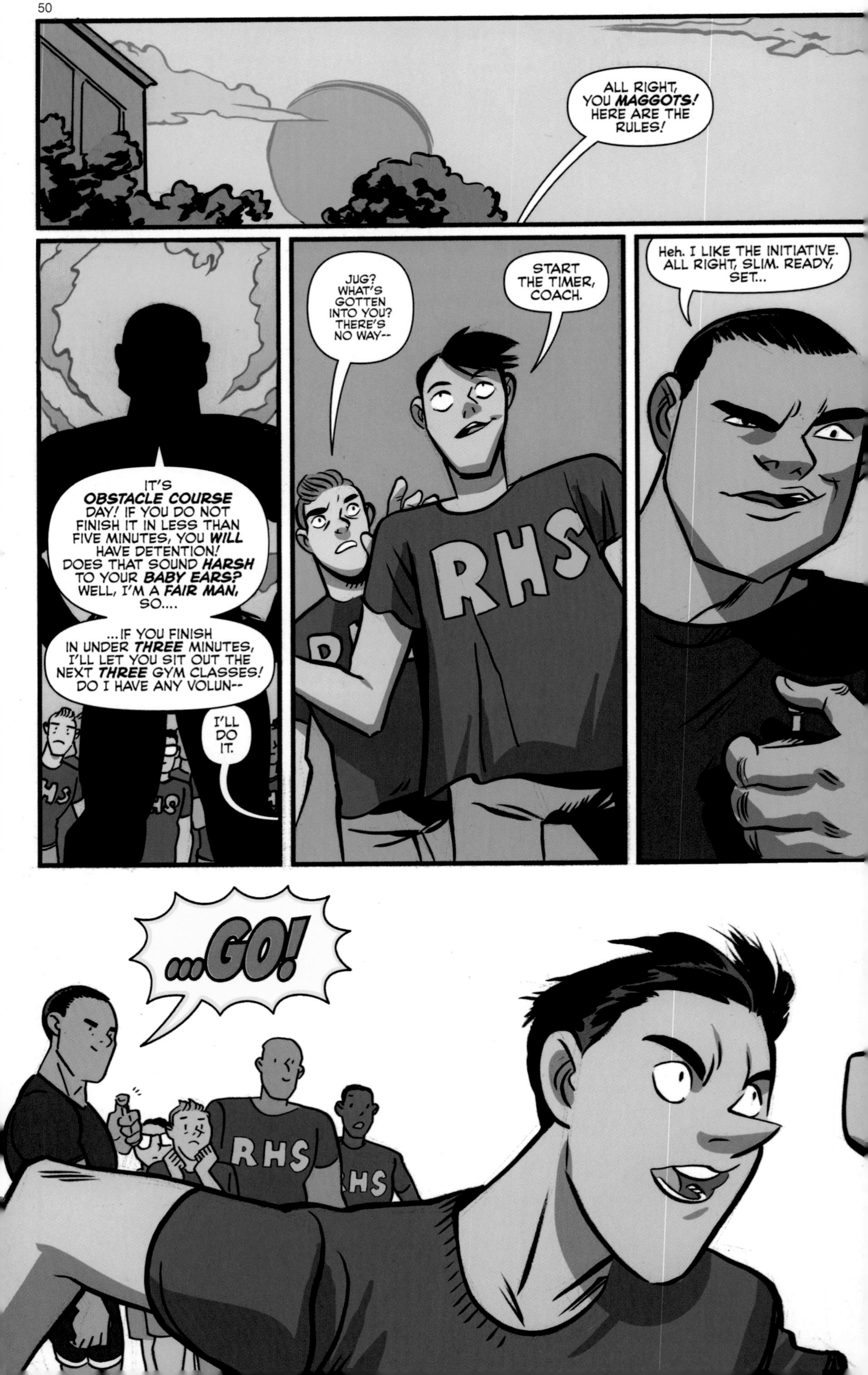
ALL RIGHT, YOU MAGGOTS! HERE ARE THE RULES!
IT'S OBSTACLE COURSE DAY! IF YOU DO NOT FINISH IT IN LESS THAN FIVE MINUTES, YOU WILL HAVE DETENTION! DOES THAT SOUND HARSH TO YOUR BABY EARS? WELL, I'M A FAIR MAN, SO....
...IF YOU FINISH IN UNDER THREE MINUTES, I'LL LET YOU SIT OUT THE NEXT THREE GYM CLASSES! DO I HAVE ANY VOLUN--
I'LL DO IT.
JUG? WHAT'S GOTTEN INTO YOU? THERE'S NO WAY--
START THE TIMER, COACH.
Heh. I LIKE THE INITIATIVE. ALL RIGHT, SLIM. READY, SET...
...GO!

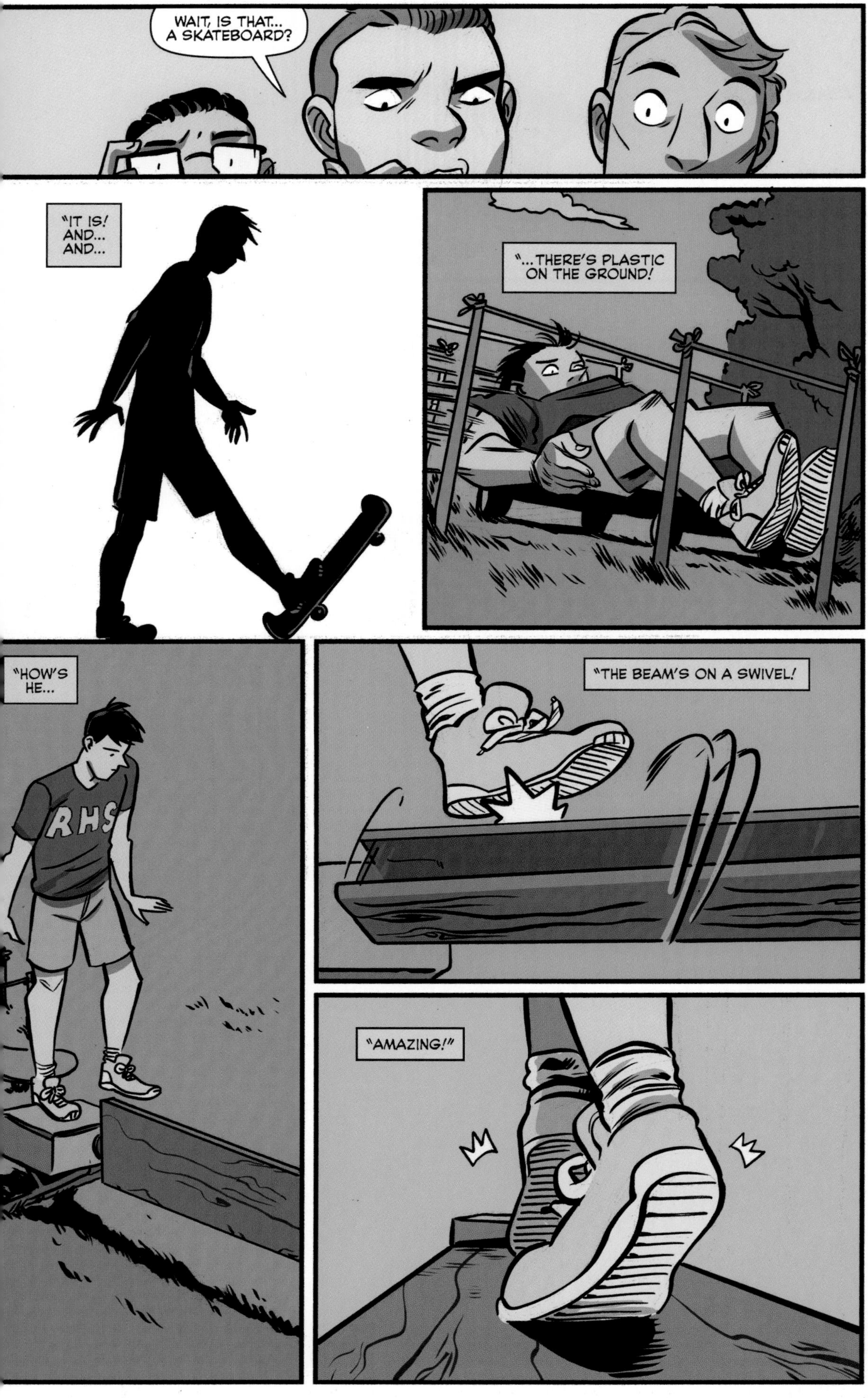
WAIT, IS THAT... A SKATEBOARD?
"IT IS! AND... AND...
"...THERE'S PLASTIC ON THE GROUND!
"HOW'S HE...
"THE BEAM'S ON A SWIVEL!
"AMAZING!"

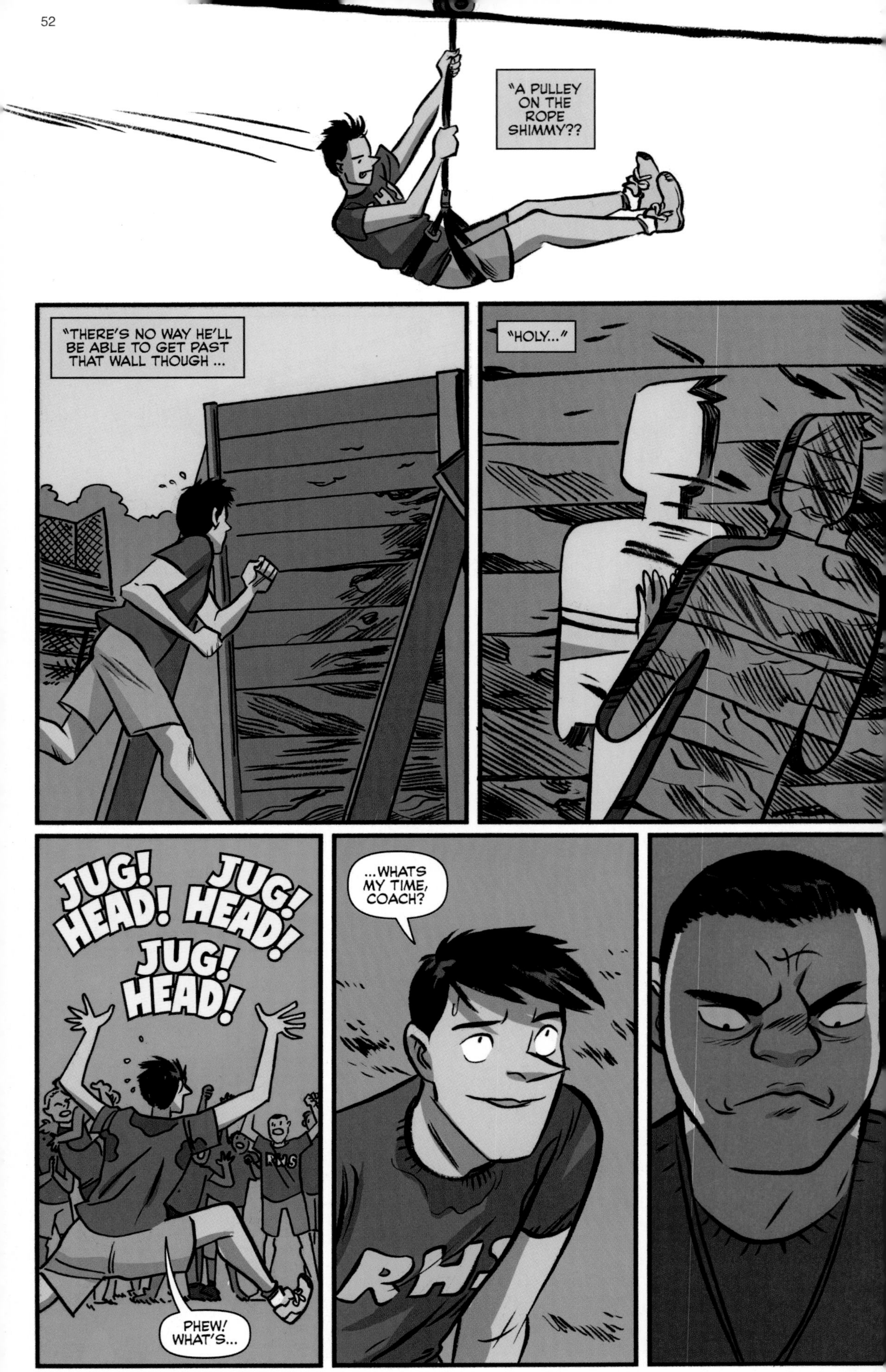
"A PULLEY ON THE ROPE SHIMMY??
"THERE'S NO WAY HE'LL BE ABLE TO GET PAST THAT WALL THOUGH ...
"HOLY..."
JUG! HEAD! JUG! HEAD! JUG! HEAD!
PHEW! WHAT'S...
...WHATS MY TIME, COACH?

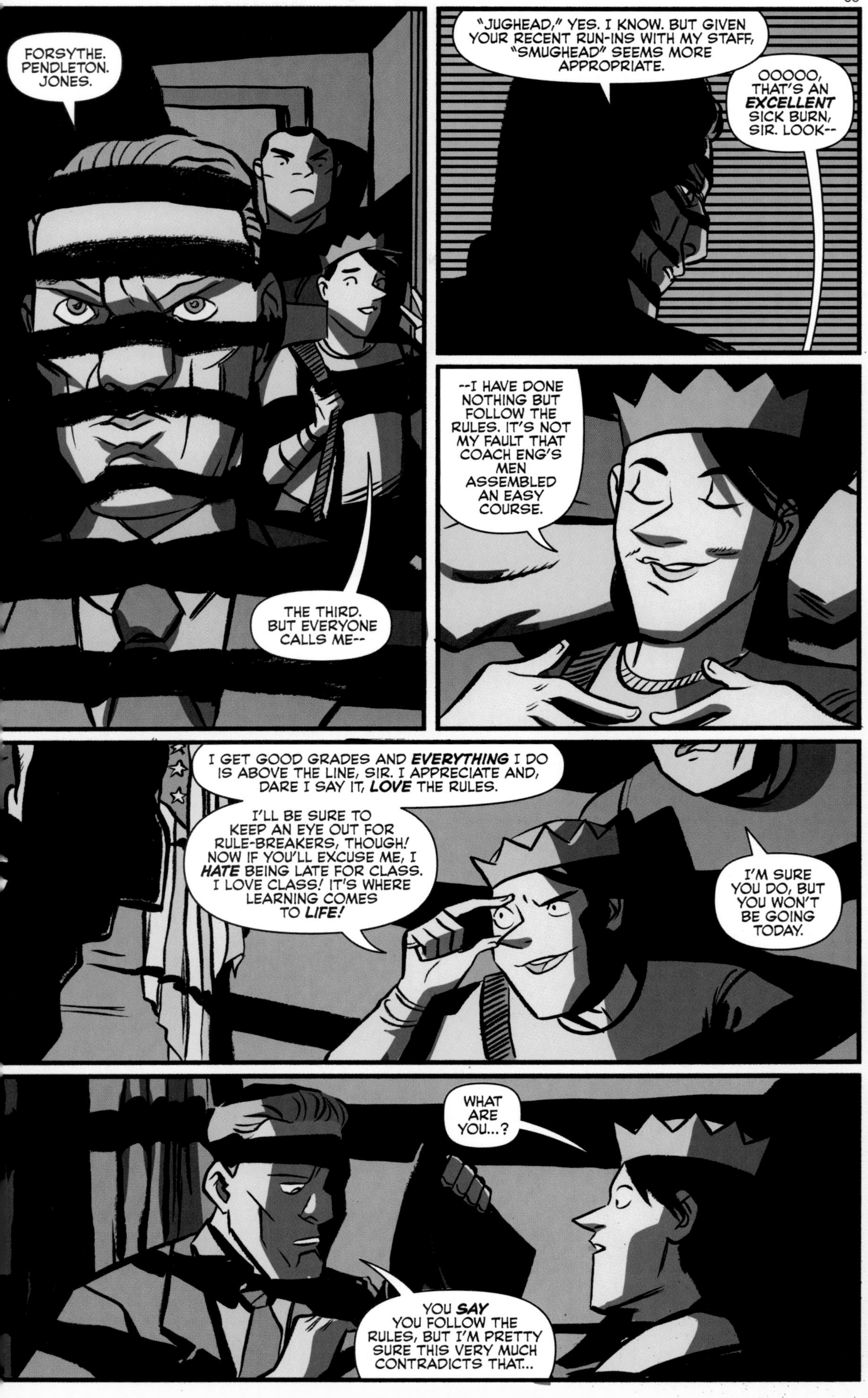
FORSYTHE. PENDLETON. JONES.
THE THIRD. BUT EVERYONE CALLS ME--
"JUGHEAD," YES. I KNOW. BUT GIVEN YOUR RECENT RUN-INS WITH MY STAFF, "SMUGHEAD" SEEMS MORE APPROPRIATE.
OOOOO, THAT'S AN **EXCELLENT** SICK BURN, SIR. LOOK--
--I HAVE DONE NOTHING BUT FOLLOW THE RULES. IT'S NOT MY FAULT THAT COACH ENG'S MEN ASSEMBLED AN EASY COURSE.
I GET GOOD GRADES AND **EVERYTHING** I DO IS ABOVE THE LINE, SIR. I APPRECIATE AND, DARE I SAY IT, **LOVE** THE RULES.
I'LL BE SURE TO KEEP AN EYE OUT FOR RULE-BREAKERS, THOUGH! NOW IF YOU'LL EXCUSE ME, I **HATE** BEING LATE FOR CLASS. I LOVE CLASS! IT'S WHERE LEARNING COMES TO **LIFE!**
I'M SURE YOU DO, BUT YOU WON'T BE GOING TODAY.
WHAT ARE YOU...?
YOU **SAY** YOU FOLLOW THE RULES, BUT I'M PRETTY SURE THIS VERY MUCH CONTRADICTS THAT...

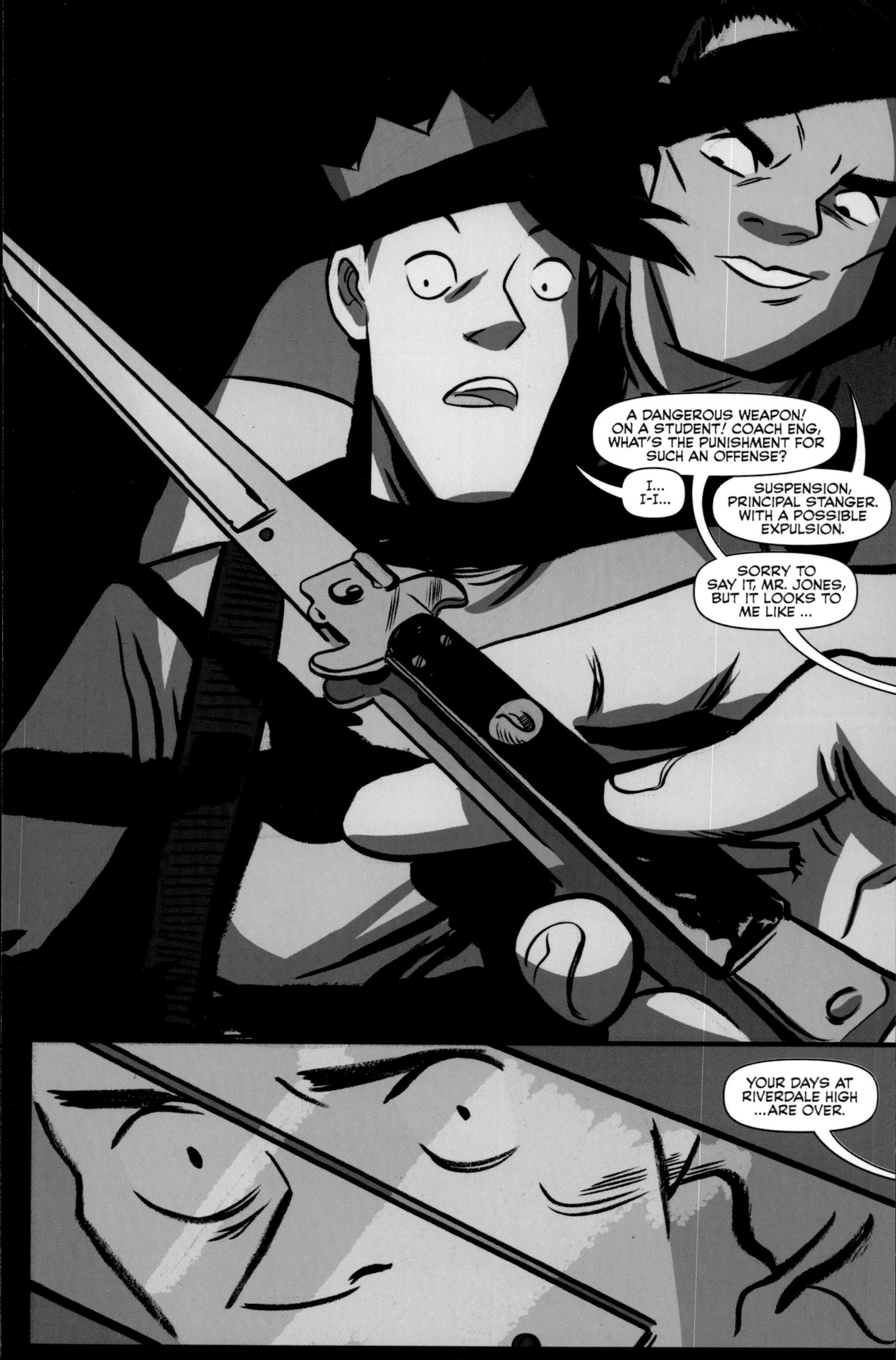
A DANGEROUS WEAPON! ON A STUDENT! COACH ENG, WHAT'S THE PUNISHMENT FOR SUCH AN OFFENSE?
I... I-I...
SUSPENSION, PRINCIPAL STANGER. WITH A POSSIBLE EXPULSION.
SORRY TO SAY IT, MR. JONES, BUT IT LOOKS TO ME LIKE ...
YOUR DAYS AT RIVERDALE HIGH ...ARE OVER.

CATCH UP WITH THE ONGOING
JUGHEAD SERIES
ON SALE NOW!

BETTY & VERONICA

PREVIOUSLY IN THE TOWN OF RIVERDALE...

One word (if you want to call it a "word"). Three letters. It's the first thing that comes to mind when most people hear the names BETTY AND VERONICA: "BFF." So what could possibly make these two gorgeous gal pals turn against each other? Two words. One man: POP TATE (betcha didn't see that one comin'!).

When Pop's Chocklit Shoppe is threatened to close to make way for a high-end coffee chain, Betty Cooper rallies the troops to save his shop and restore the local culture that's made Riverdale a welcoming town for everyone. But one person is missing from her efforts: Veronica Lodge. And that's no coincidence—Lodge Industries owns the coffee chain set to take over Pop's!

Now it's BETTY VS. VERONICA in a throwdown showdown set to rattle the entire town of Riverdale!

LET'S GET READY TO RUMBLE!

STORY & ART BY
ADAM HUGHES

COLORING BY
JOSÉ VILLARRUBIA

LETTERING BY
JACK MORELLI

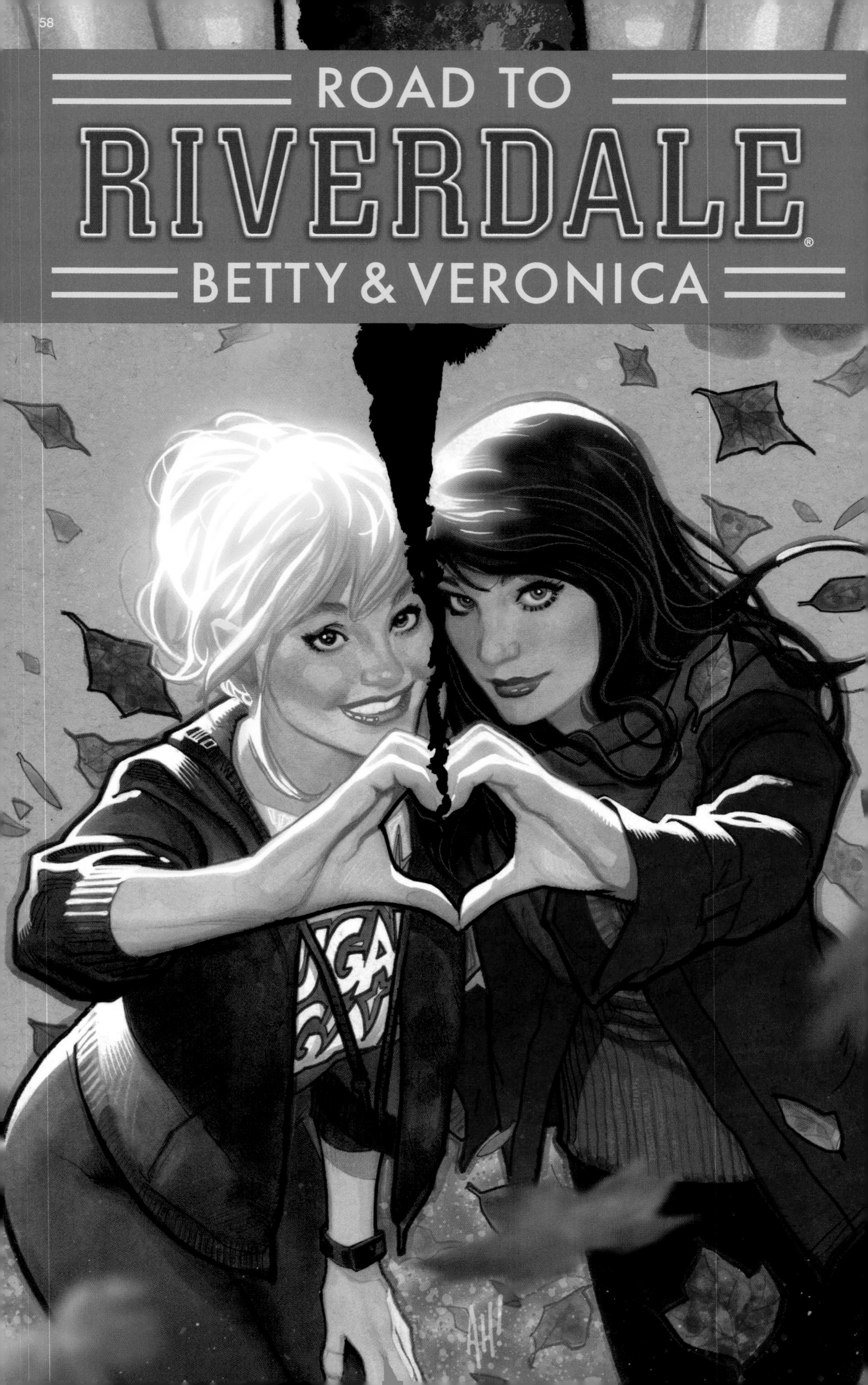
ROAD TO
RIVERDALE®
BETTY & VERONICA

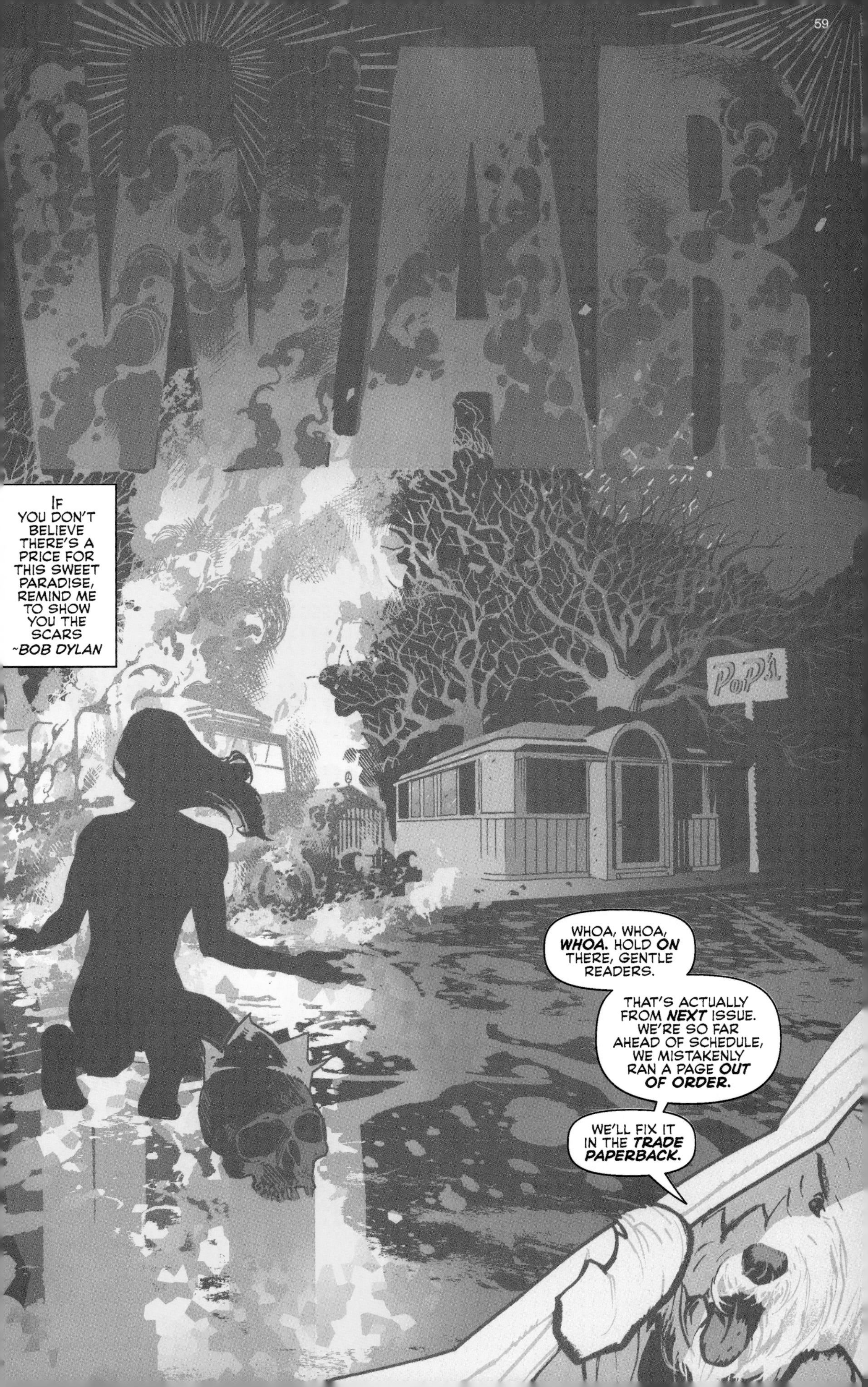
WAR
IF YOU DON'T BELIEVE THERE'S A PRICE FOR THIS SWEET PARADISE, REMIND ME TO SHOW YOU THE SCARS ~BOB DYLAN
POP'S
WHOA, WHOA, WHOA. HOLD ON THERE, GENTLE READERS.
THAT'S ACTUALLY FROM NEXT ISSUE. WE'RE SO FAR AHEAD OF SCHEDULE, WE MISTAKENLY RAN A PAGE OUT OF ORDER.
WE'LL FIX IT IN THE TRADE PAPERBACK.

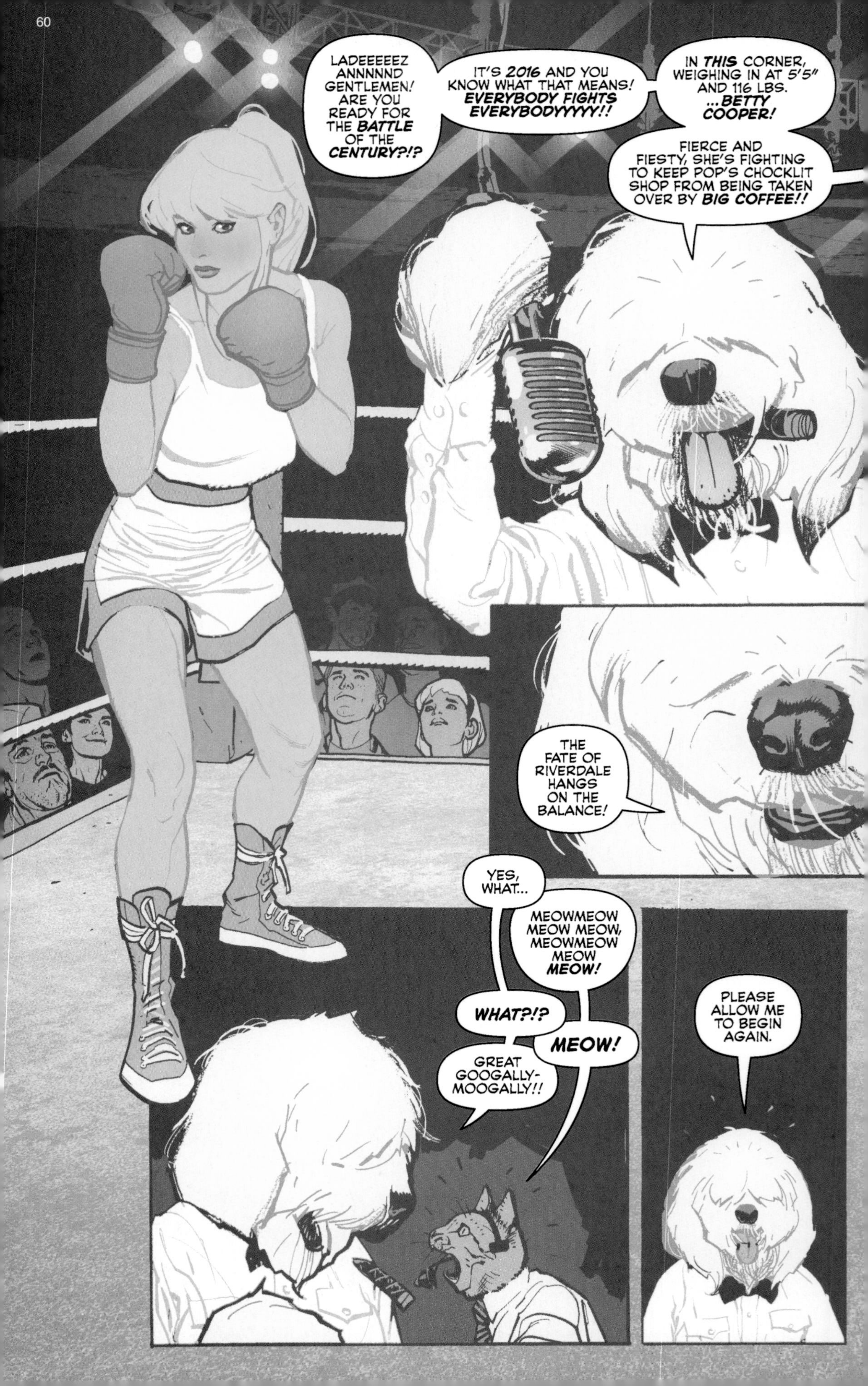
LADEEEEEZ ANNNNND GENTLEMEN! ARE YOU READY FOR THE BATTLE OF THE CENTURY?!?
IT'S 2016 AND YOU KNOW WHAT THAT MEANS! EVERYBODY FIGHTS EVERYBODYYYYY!!
IN THIS CORNER, WEIGHING IN AT 5'5" AND 116 LBS. ...BETTY COOPER!
FIERCE AND FIESTY, SHE'S FIGHTING TO KEEP POP'S CHOCKLIT SHOP FROM BEING TAKEN OVER BY BIG COFFEE!!
THE FATE OF RIVERDALE HANGS ON THE BALANCE!
YES, WHAT...
MEOWMEOW MEOW MEOW, MEOWMEOW MEOW MEOW!
WHAT?!?
MEOW!
GREAT GOOGALLY-MOOGALLY!!
PLEASE ALLOW ME TO BEGIN AGAIN.

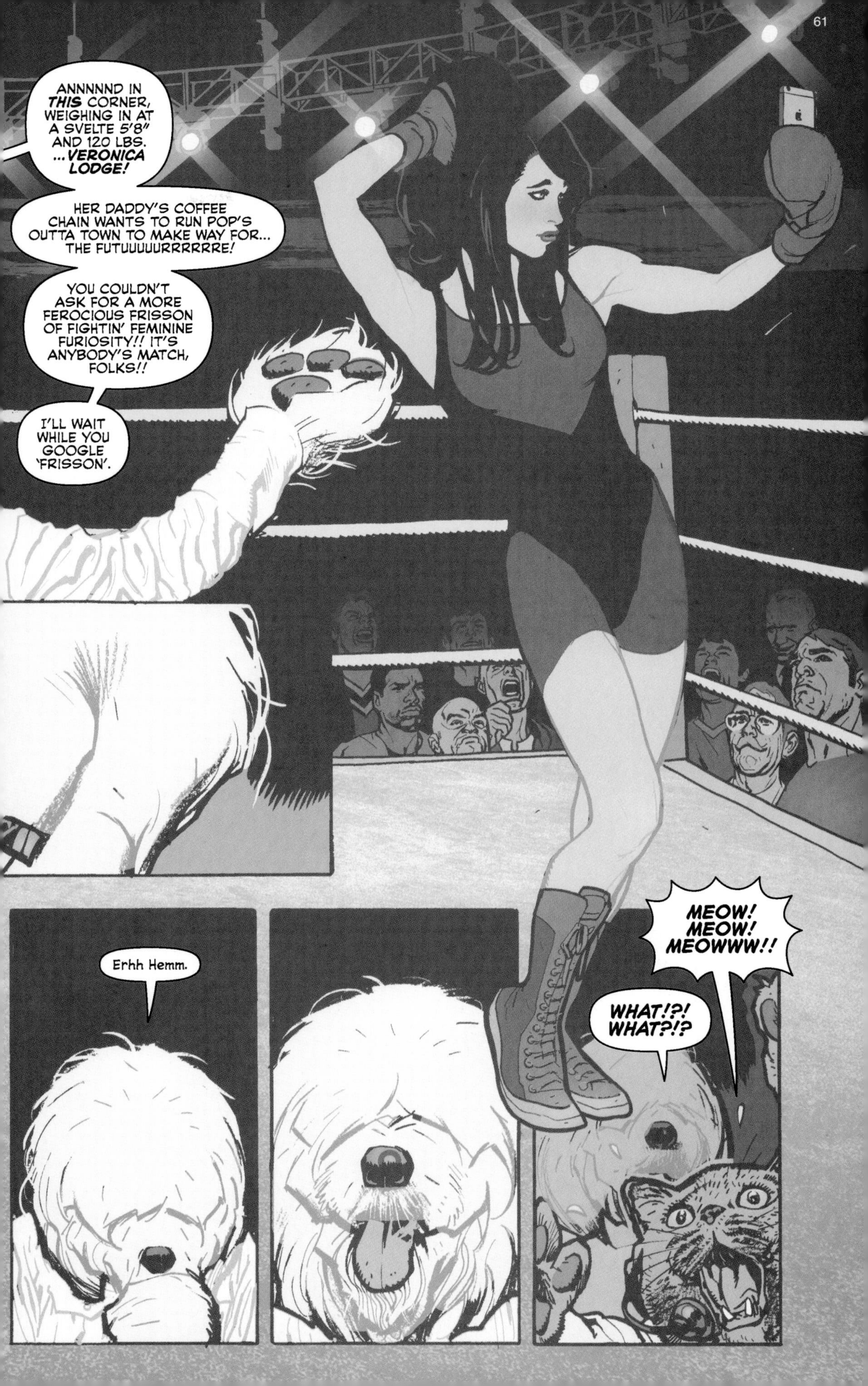
ANNNNND IN THIS CORNER, WEIGHING IN AT A SVELTE 5'8" AND 120 LBS. ...VERONICA LODGE!
HER DADDY'S COFFEE CHAIN WANTS TO RUN POP'S OUTTA TOWN TO MAKE WAY FOR... THE FUTUUUUURRRRRE!
YOU COULDN'T ASK FOR A MORE FEROCIOUS FRISSON OF FIGHTIN' FEMININE FURIOSITY!! IT'S ANYBODY'S MATCH, FOLKS!!
I'LL WAIT WHILE YOU GOOGLE 'FRISSON'.
Erhh Hemm.
MEOW! MEOW! MEOWWW!!
WHAT!?! WHAT?!?

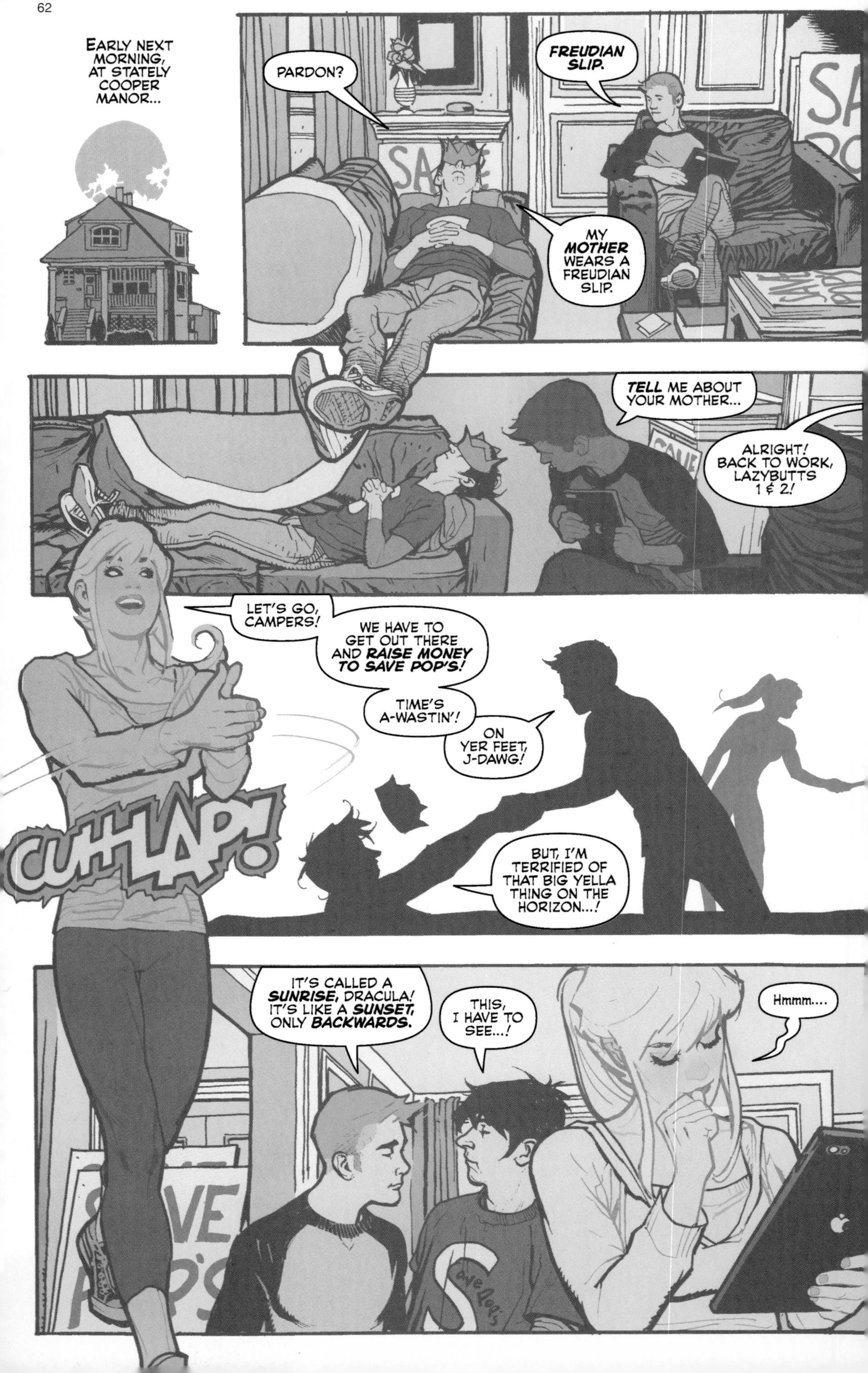
EARLY NEXT MORNING, AT STATELY COOPER MANOR...
PARDON?
FREUDIAN SLIP.
MY MOTHER WEARS A FREUDIAN SLIP.
TELL ME ABOUT YOUR MOTHER...
ALRIGHT! BACK TO WORK, LAZYBUTTS 1 & 2!
LET'S GO, CAMPERS!
WE HAVE TO GET OUT THERE AND RAISE MONEY TO SAVE POP'S!
TIME'S A-WASTIN'!
ON YER FEET, J-DAWG!
CUHLAP!
BUT, I'M TERRIFIED OF THAT BIG YELLA THING ON THE HORIZON...!
IT'S CALLED A SUNRISE, DRACULA! IT'S LIKE A SUNSET, ONLY BACKWARDS.
THIS, I HAVE TO SEE...!
Hmmm....
SAVE POP'S

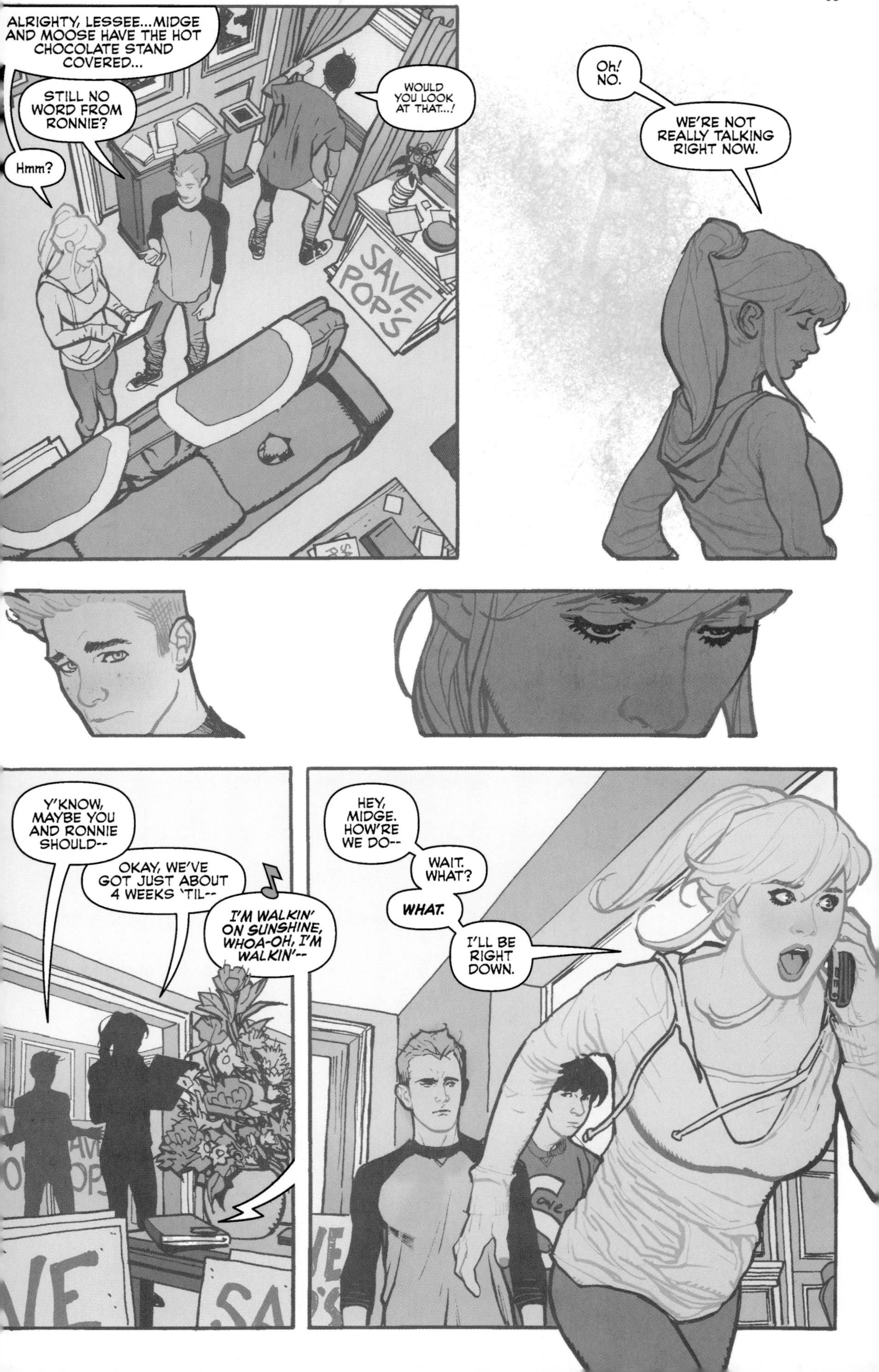
ALRIGHTY, LESSEE...MIDGE AND MOOSE HAVE THE HOT CHOCOLATE STAND COVERED...
STILL NO WORD FROM RONNIE?
Hmm?
WOULD YOU LOOK AT THAT...!
SAVE POP'S
Oh! NO.
WE'RE NOT REALLY TALKING RIGHT NOW.
Y'KNOW, MAYBE YOU AND RONNIE SHOULD--
OKAY, WE'VE GOT JUST ABOUT 4 WEEKS 'TIL--
I'M WALKIN' ON SUNSHINE, WHOA-OH, I'M WALKIN'--
HEY, MIDGE. HOW'RE WE DO--
WAIT. WHAT?
WHAT.
I'LL BE RIGHT DOWN.

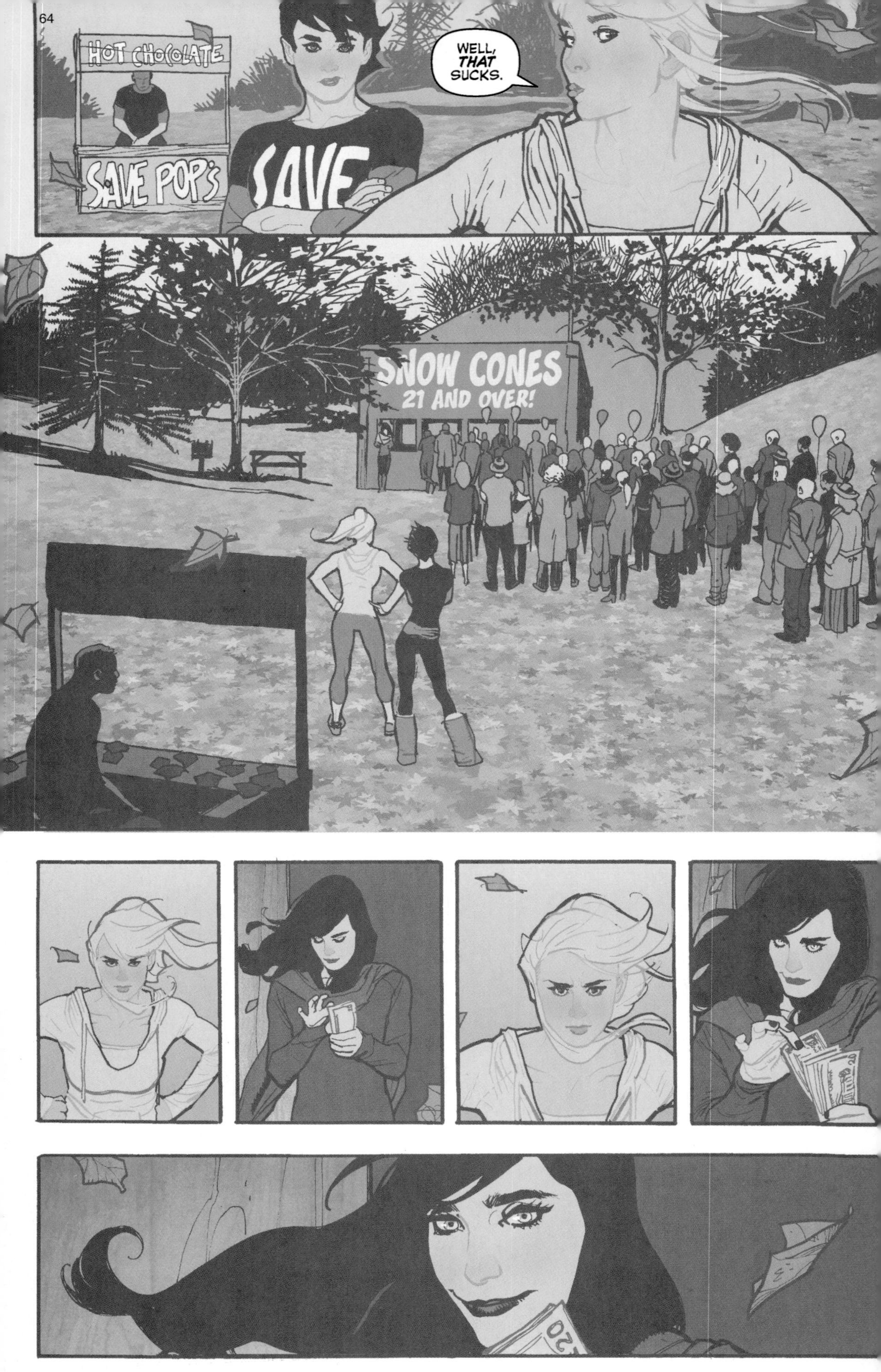
HOT CHOCOLATE
SAVE POP's
SAVE
WELL, THAT SUCKS.
SNOW CONES
21 AND OVER!

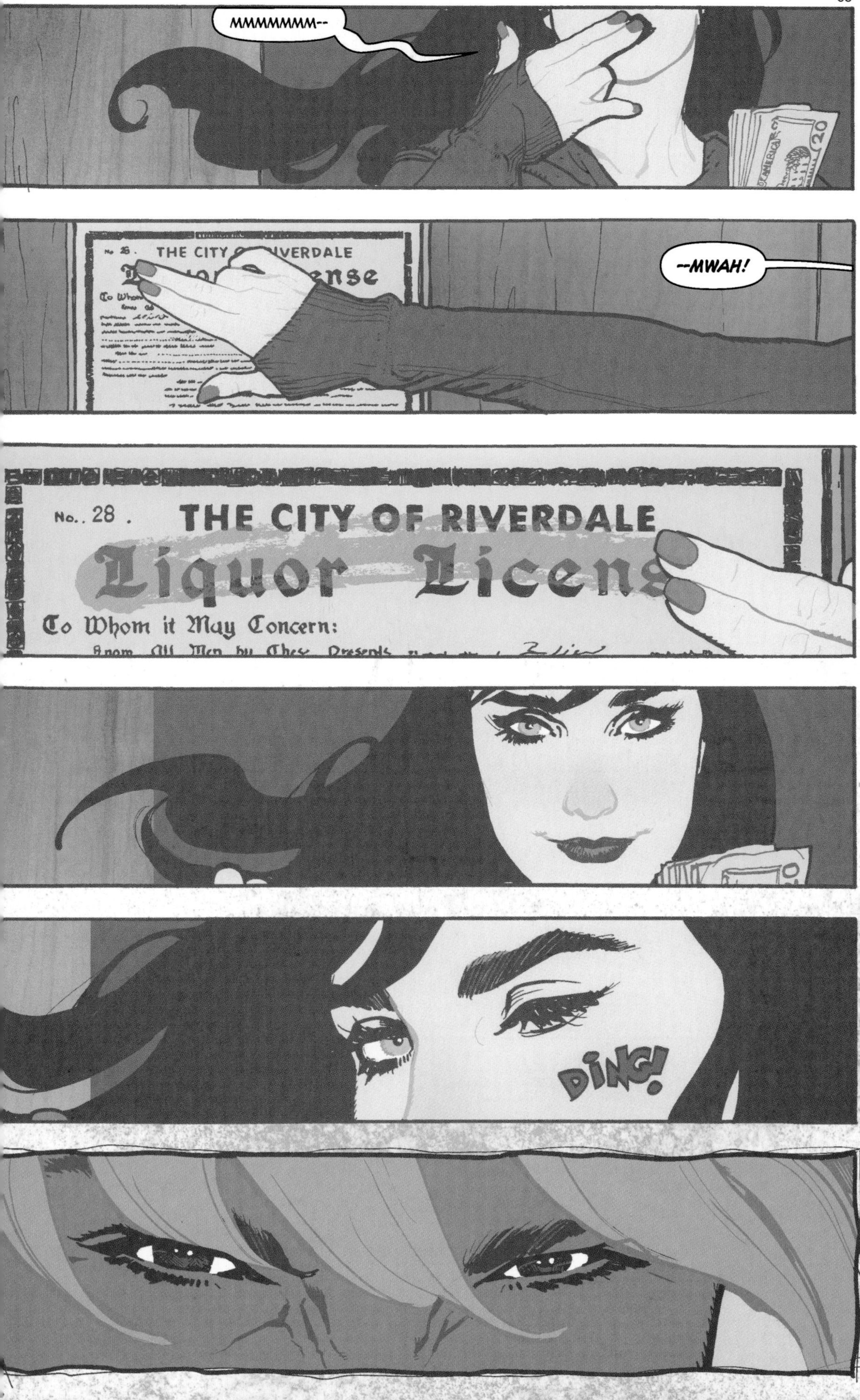
MMMMMMM--
--MWAH!
No.. 28 .
THE CITY OF RIVERDALE
Liquor Licens
To Whom it May Concern:
DING!

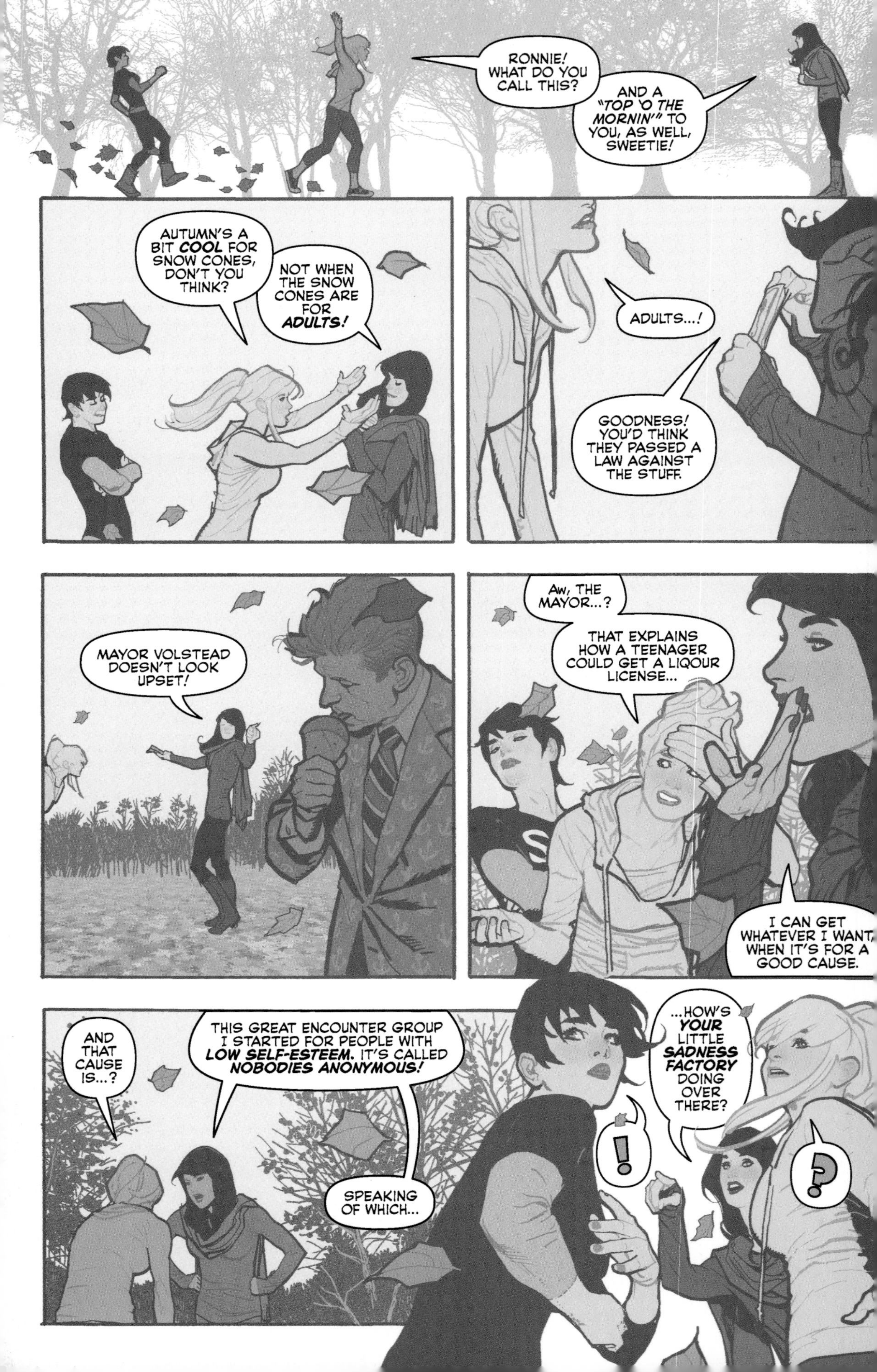
RONNIE! WHAT DO YOU CALL THIS?
AND A "TOP 'O THE MORNIN'" TO YOU, AS WELL, SWEETIE!
AUTUMN'S A BIT COOL FOR SNOW CONES, DON'T YOU THINK?
NOT WHEN THE SNOW CONES ARE FOR ADULTS!
ADULTS...!
GOODNESS! YOU'D THINK THEY PASSED A LAW AGAINST THE STUFF.
MAYOR VOLSTEAD DOESN'T LOOK UPSET!
Aw, THE MAYOR...?
THAT EXPLAINS HOW A TEENAGER COULD GET A LIQOUR LICENSE...
I CAN GET WHATEVER I WANT, WHEN IT'S FOR A GOOD CAUSE.
AND THAT CAUSE IS...?
THIS GREAT ENCOUNTER GROUP I STARTED FOR PEOPLE WITH LOW SELF-ESTEEM. IT'S CALLED NOBODIES ANONYMOUS!
SPEAKING OF WHICH...
...HOW'S YOUR LITTLE SADNESS FACTORY DOING OVER THERE?
!
?

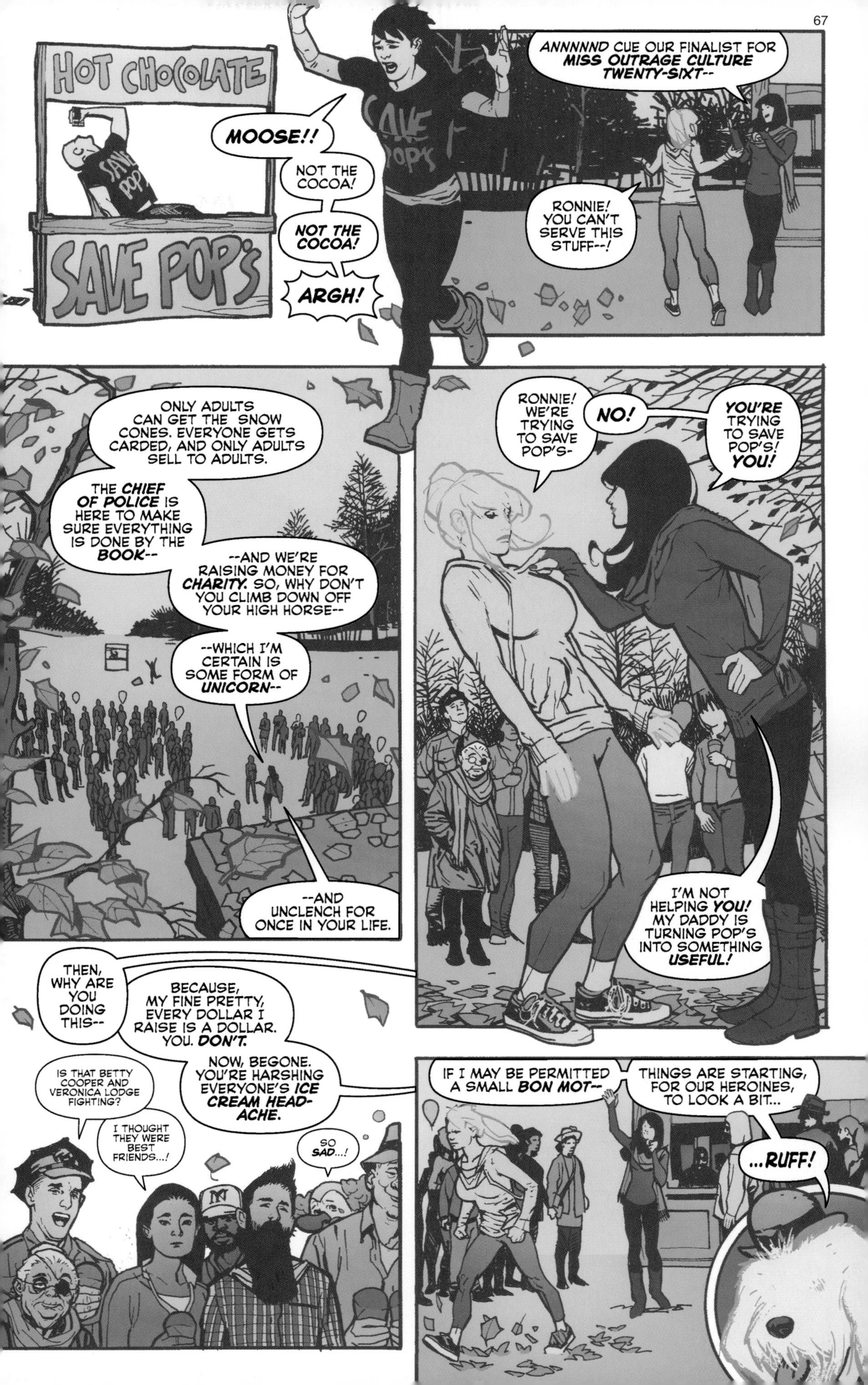
HOT CHOCOLATE
SAVE POP'S
MOOSE!!
NOT THE COCOA!
NOT THE COCOA!
ARGH!
ANNNNND CUE OUR FINALIST FOR MISS OUTRAGE CULTURE TWENTY-SIXT--
RONNIE! YOU CAN'T SERVE THIS STUFF--!
ONLY ADULTS CAN GET THE SNOW CONES. EVERYONE GETS CARDED, AND ONLY ADULTS SELL TO ADULTS.
THE CHIEF OF POLICE IS HERE TO MAKE SURE EVERYTHING IS DONE BY THE BOOK--
--AND WE'RE RAISING MONEY FOR CHARITY. SO, WHY DON'T YOU CLIMB DOWN OFF YOUR HIGH HORSE--
--WHICH I'M CERTAIN IS SOME FORM OF UNICORN--
--AND UNCLENCH FOR ONCE IN YOUR LIFE.
RONNIE! WE'RE TRYING TO SAVE POP'S-
NO!
YOU'RE TRYING TO SAVE POP'S! YOU!
I'M NOT HELPING YOU! MY DADDY IS TURNING POP'S INTO SOMETHING USEFUL!
THEN, WHY ARE YOU DOING THIS--
BECAUSE, MY FINE PRETTY, EVERY DOLLAR I RAISE IS A DOLLAR. YOU. DON'T.
NOW, BEGONE. YOU'RE HARSHING EVERYONE'S ICE CREAM HEAD-ACHE.
IS THAT BETTY COOPER AND VERONICA LODGE FIGHTING?
I THOUGHT THEY WERE BEST FRIENDS...!
SO SAD...!
IF I MAY BE PERMITTED A SMALL BON MOT--
THINGS ARE STARTING, FOR OUR HEROINES, TO LOOK A BIT...
...RUFF!

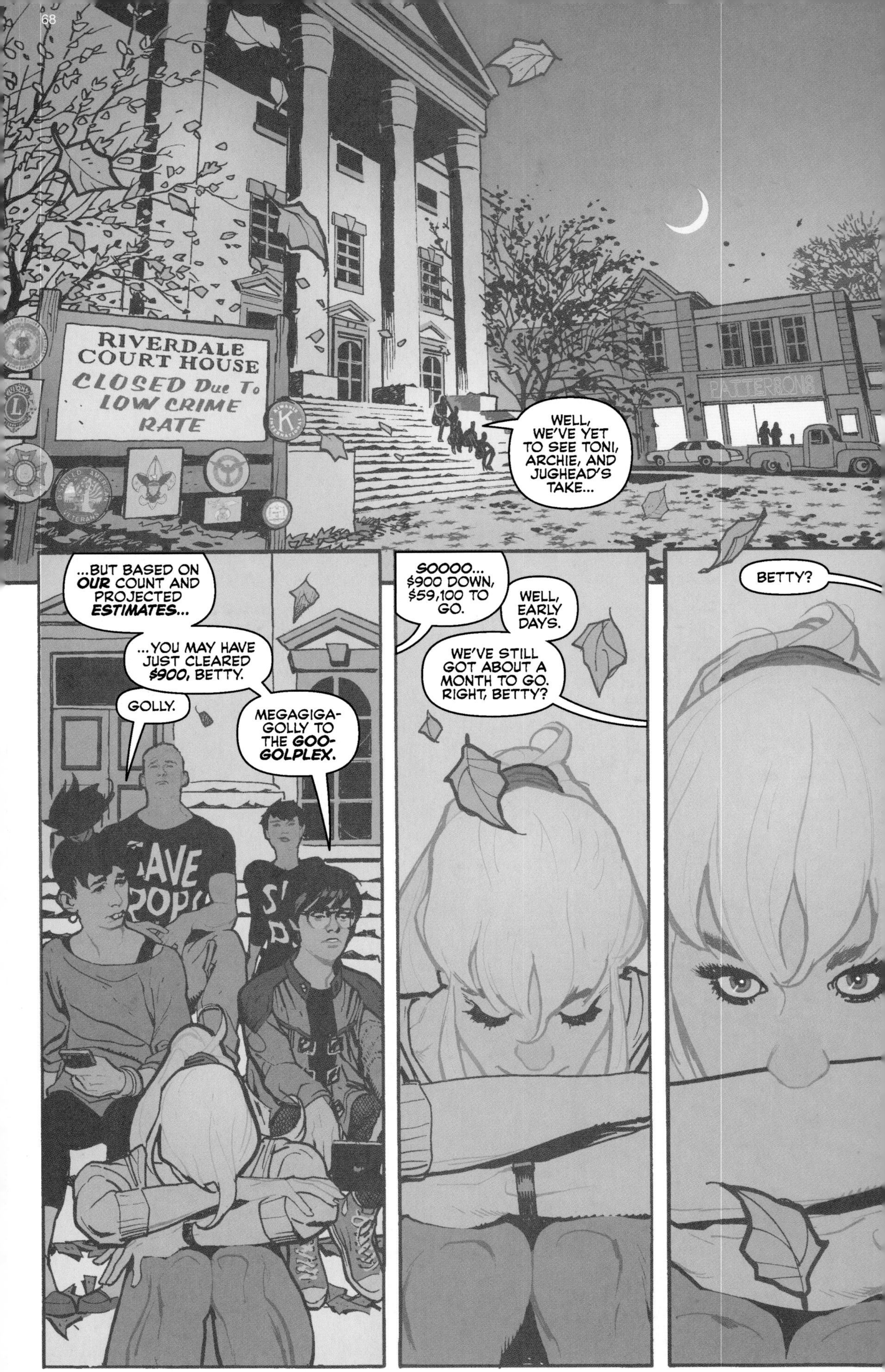
RIVERDALE COURT HOUSE
CLOSED Due To LOW CRIME RATE
PATTERSONS
WELL, WE'VE YET TO SEE TONI, ARCHIE, AND JUGHEAD'S TAKE...
...BUT BASED ON OUR COUNT AND PROJECTED ESTIMATES...
...YOU MAY HAVE JUST CLEARED $900, BETTY.
GOLLY.
MEGAGIGA-GOLLY TO THE GOO-GOLPLEX.
SOOOO... $900 DOWN, $59,100 TO GO.
WELL, EARLY DAYS.
WE'VE STILL GOT ABOUT A MONTH TO GO. RIGHT, BETTY?
BETTY?

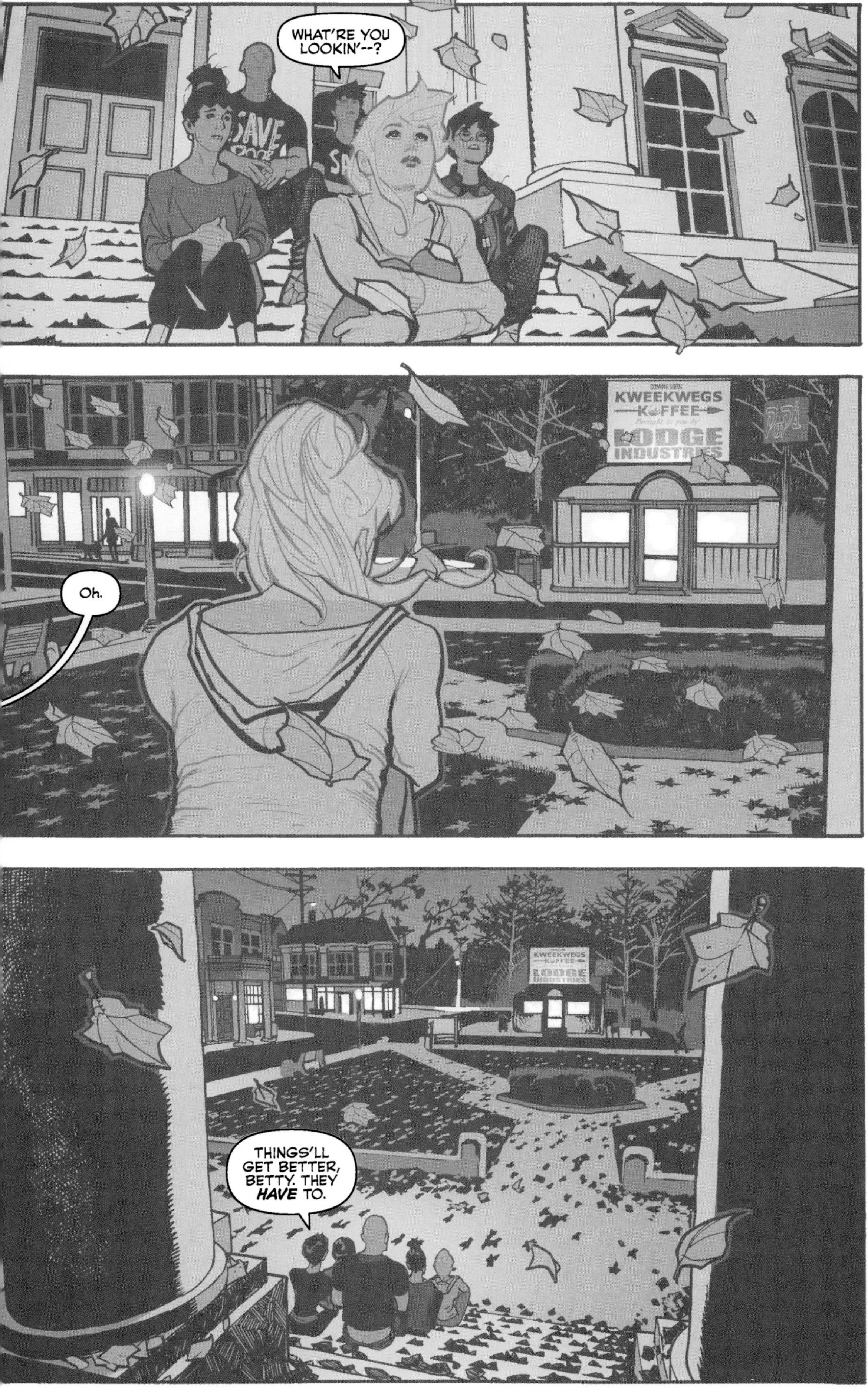
WHAT'RE YOU LOOKIN'--?
COMING SOON
KWEEKWEGS KOFFEE
Brought to you by
LODGE INDUSTRIES
Oh.
KWEEKWEGS KOFFEE
LODGE INDUSTRIES
THINGS'LL GET BETTER, BETTY. THEY *HAVE* TO.

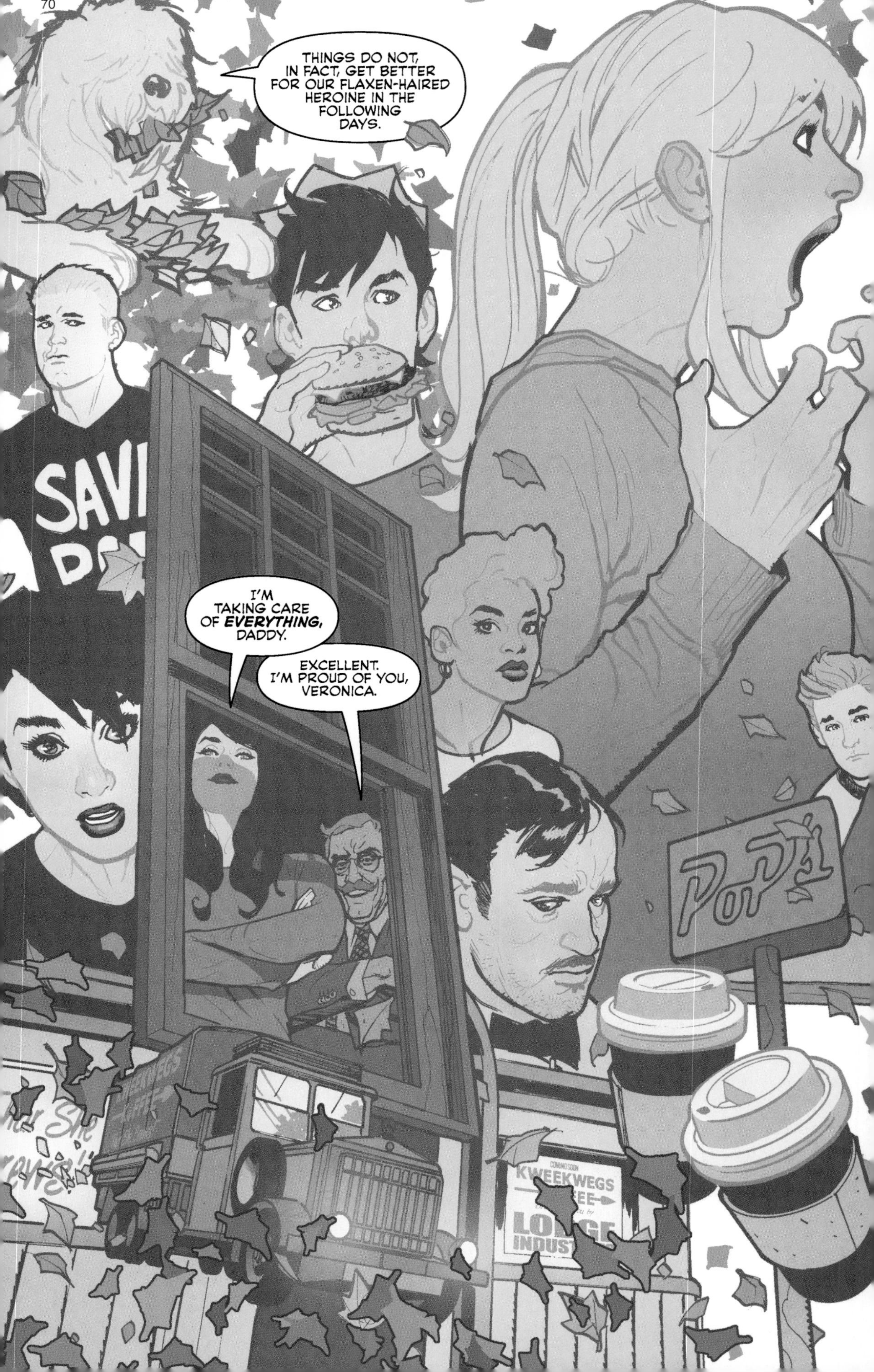
THINGS DO NOT, IN FACT, GET BETTER FOR OUR FLAXEN-HAIRED HEROINE IN THE FOLLOWING DAYS.
I'M TAKING CARE OF *EVERYTHING,* DADDY.
EXCELLENT. I'M PROUD OF YOU, VERONICA.
POP'S
KWEEKWEGS COFFEE
LODGE INDUST

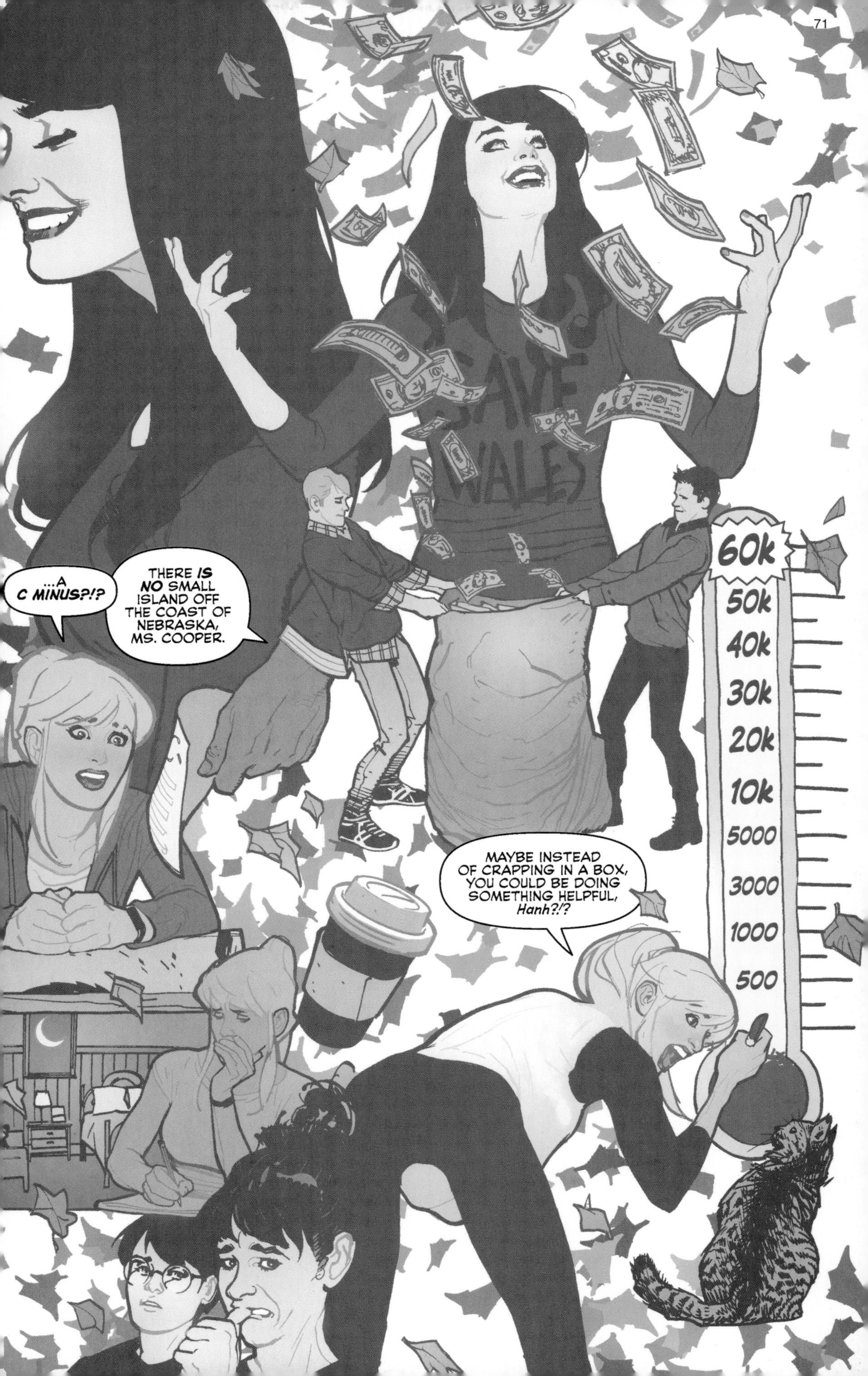

SAVE WALES
...A C MINUS?!?
THERE IS NO SMALL ISLAND OFF THE COAST OF NEBRASKA, MS. COOPER.
60k
50k
40k
30k
20k
10k
5000
3000
1000
500
MAYBE INSTEAD OF CRAPPING IN A BOX, YOU COULD BE DOING SOMETHING HELPFUL, Hanh?!?

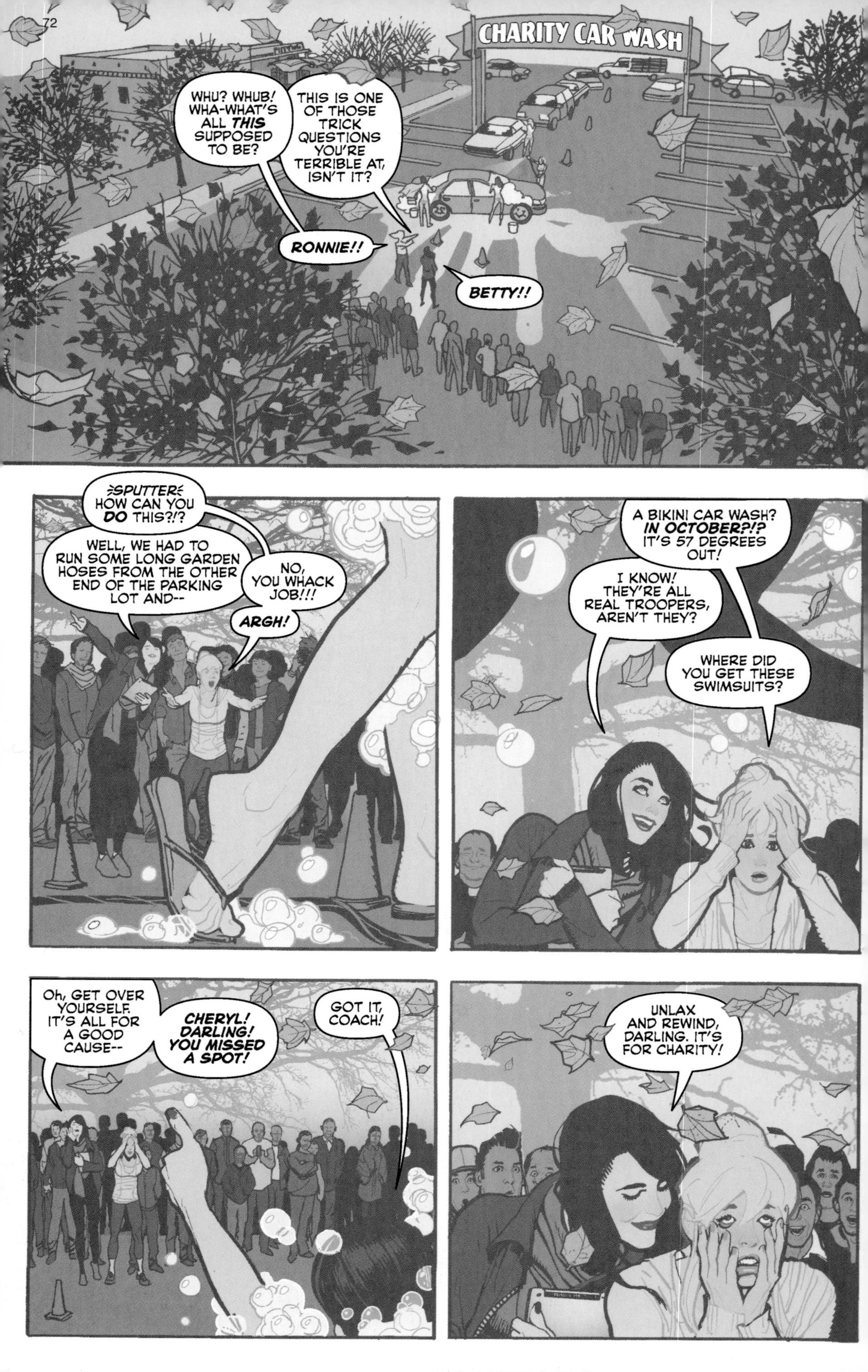
CHARITY CAR WASH
WHU? WHUB! WHA-WHAT'S ALL THIS SUPPOSED TO BE?
THIS IS ONE OF THOSE TRICK QUESTIONS YOU'RE TERRIBLE AT, ISN'T IT?
RONNIE!!
BETTY!!
≶SPUTTER≷ HOW CAN YOU DO THIS?!?
WELL, WE HAD TO RUN SOME LONG GARDEN HOSES FROM THE OTHER END OF THE PARKING LOT AND--
NO, YOU WHACK JOB!!!
ARGH!
A BIKINI CAR WASH? IN OCTOBER?!? IT'S 57 DEGREES OUT!
I KNOW! THEY'RE ALL REAL TROOPERS, AREN'T THEY?
WHERE DID YOU GET THESE SWIMSUITS?
Oh, GET OVER YOURSELF. IT'S ALL FOR A GOOD CAUSE--
CHERYL! DARLING! YOU MISSED A SPOT!
GOT IT, COACH!
UNLAX AND REWIND, DARLING. IT'S FOR CHARITY!

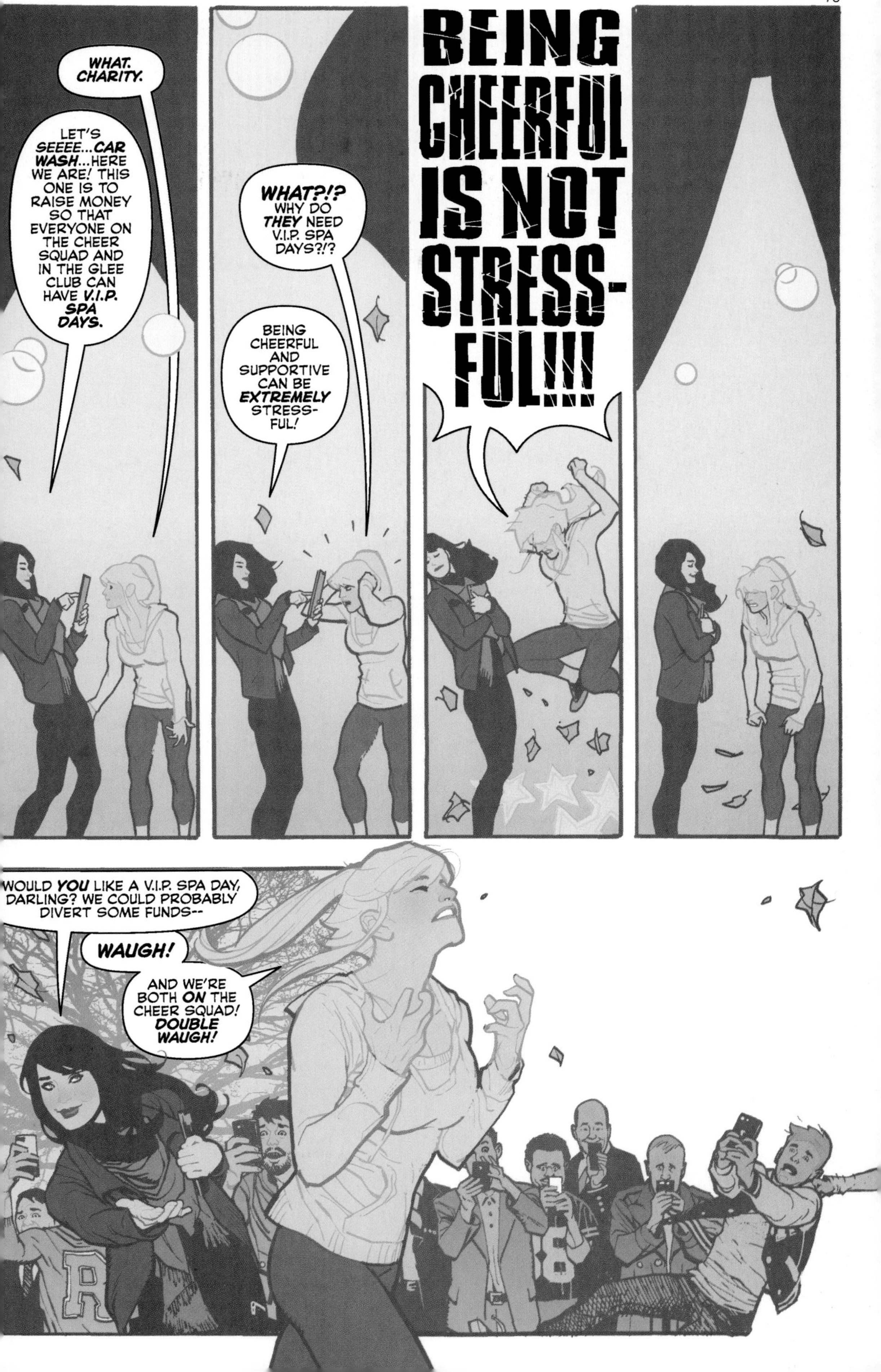
WHAT. CHARITY.
LET'S SEEEE...CAR WASH...HERE WE ARE! THIS ONE IS TO RAISE MONEY SO THAT EVERYONE ON THE CHEER SQUAD AND IN THE GLEE CLUB CAN HAVE V.I.P. SPA DAYS.
WHAT?!? WHY DO THEY NEED V.I.P. SPA DAYS?!?
BEING CHEERFUL AND SUPPORTIVE CAN BE EXTREMELY STRESS-FUL!
BEING CHEERFUL IS NOT STRESS-FUL!!!
WOULD YOU LIKE A V.I.P. SPA DAY, DARLING? WE COULD PROBABLY DIVERT SOME FUNDS--
WAUGH!
AND WE'RE BOTH ON THE CHEER SQUAD! DOUBLE WAUGH!

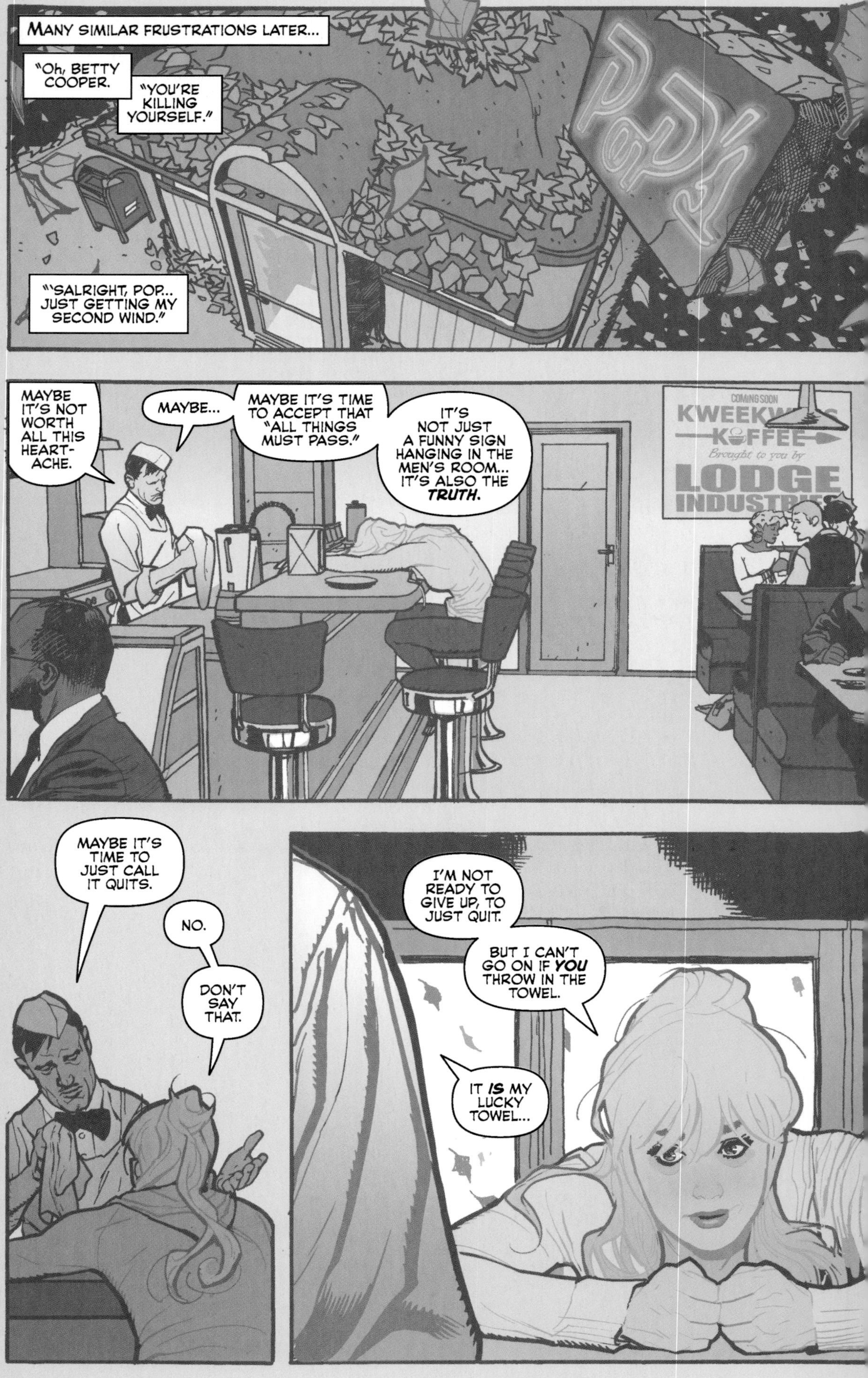
MANY SIMILAR FRUSTRATIONS LATER...
"Oh, BETTY COOPER.
"YOU'RE KILLING YOURSELF."
"'SALRIGHT, POP... JUST GETTING MY SECOND WIND."
Pop's
MAYBE IT'S NOT WORTH ALL THIS HEART-ACHE.
MAYBE...
MAYBE IT'S TIME TO ACCEPT THAT "ALL THINGS MUST PASS."
IT'S NOT JUST A FUNNY SIGN HANGING IN THE MEN'S ROOM... IT'S ALSO THE *TRUTH*.
COMING SOON
KWEEKW
KOFFEE
Brought to you by
LODGE
INDUSTRI
MAYBE IT'S TIME TO JUST CALL IT QUITS.
NO.
DON'T SAY THAT.
I'M NOT READY TO GIVE UP, TO JUST QUIT.
BUT I CAN'T GO ON IF *YOU* THROW IN THE TOWEL.
IT *IS* MY LUCKY TOWEL...

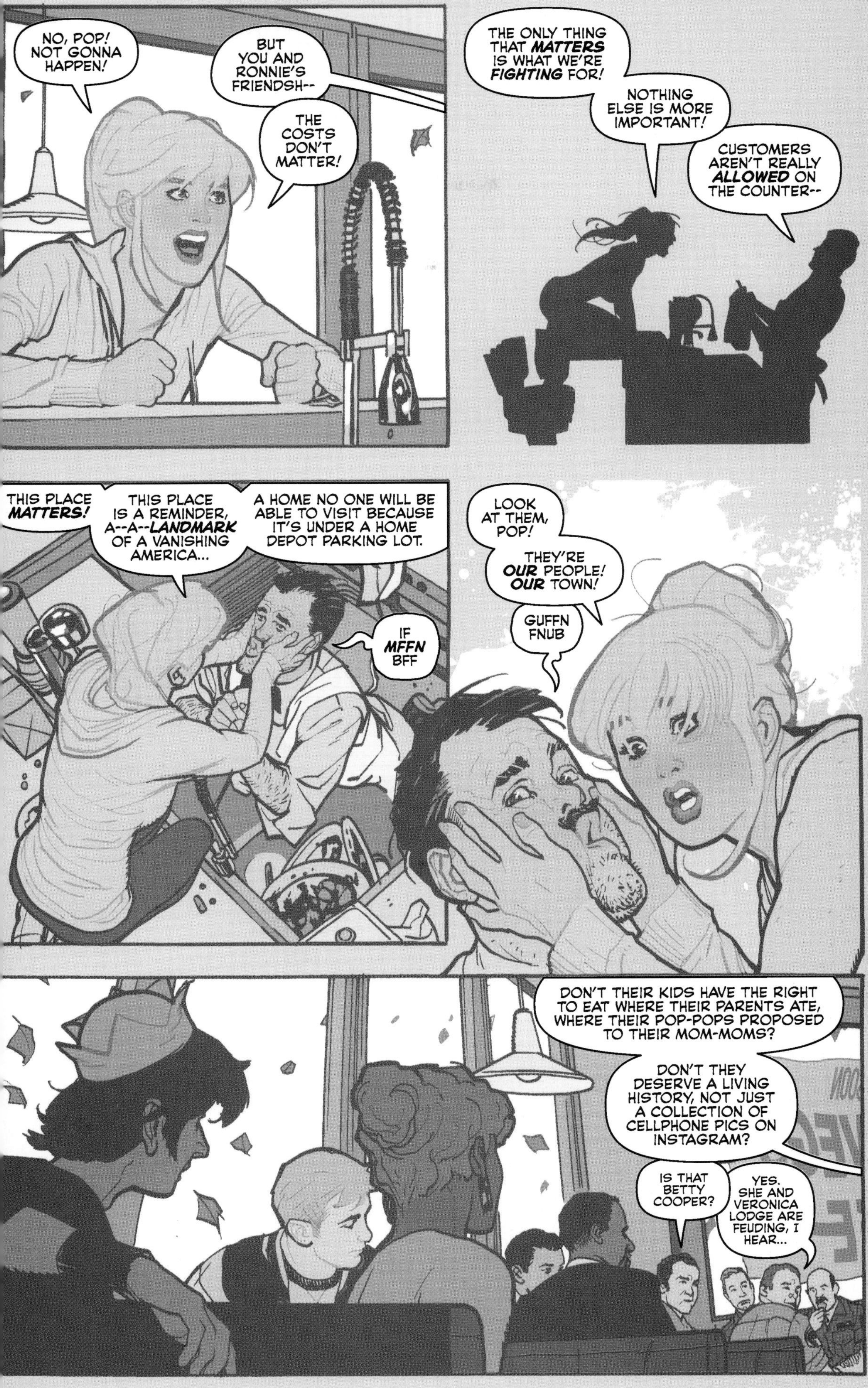
NO, POP! NOT GONNA HAPPEN!
BUT YOU AND RONNIE'S FRIENDSH--
THE COSTS DON'T MATTER!
THE ONLY THING THAT MATTERS IS WHAT WE'RE FIGHTING FOR!
NOTHING ELSE IS MORE IMPORTANT!
CUSTOMERS AREN'T REALLY ALLOWED ON THE COUNTER--
THIS PLACE MATTERS!
THIS PLACE IS A REMINDER, A--A--LANDMARK OF A VANISHING AMERICA...
A HOME NO ONE WILL BE ABLE TO VISIT BECAUSE IT'S UNDER A HOME DEPOT PARKING LOT.
IF MFFN BFF
LOOK AT THEM, POP!
THEY'RE OUR PEOPLE! OUR TOWN!
GUFFN FNUB
DON'T THEIR KIDS HAVE THE RIGHT TO EAT WHERE THEIR PARENTS ATE, WHERE THEIR POP-POPS PROPOSED TO THEIR MOM-MOMS?
DON'T THEY DESERVE A LIVING HISTORY, NOT JUST A COLLECTION OF CELLPHONE PICS ON INSTAGRAM?
IS THAT BETTY COOPER?
YES. SHE AND VERONICA LODGE ARE FEUDING, I HEAR...

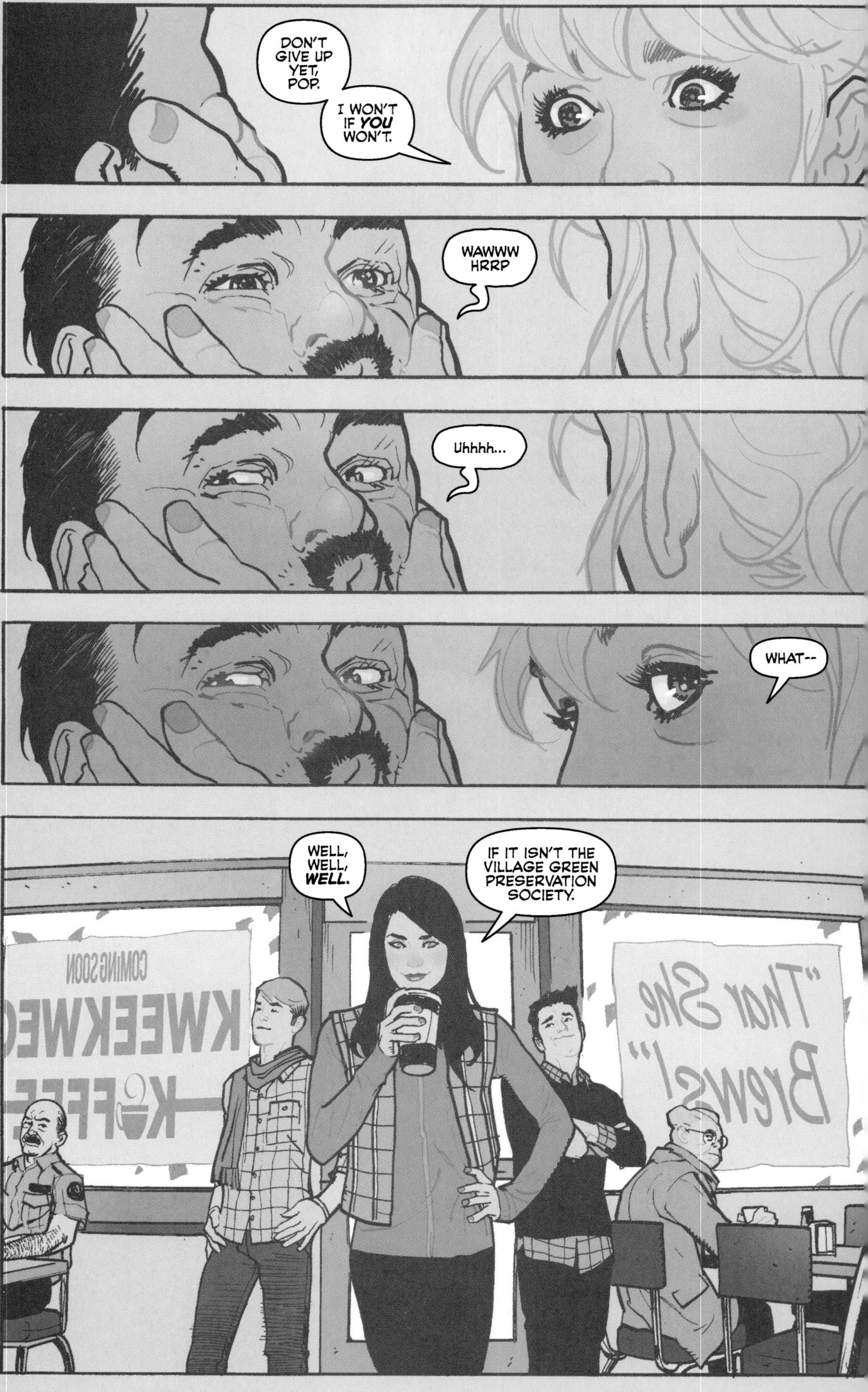
DON'T GIVE UP YET, POP.
I WON'T IF ***YOU*** WON'T.
WAWWW HRRP
Uhhhh...
WHAT--
WELL, WELL, ***WELL.***
IF IT ISN'T THE VILLAGE GREEN PRESERVATION SOCIETY.

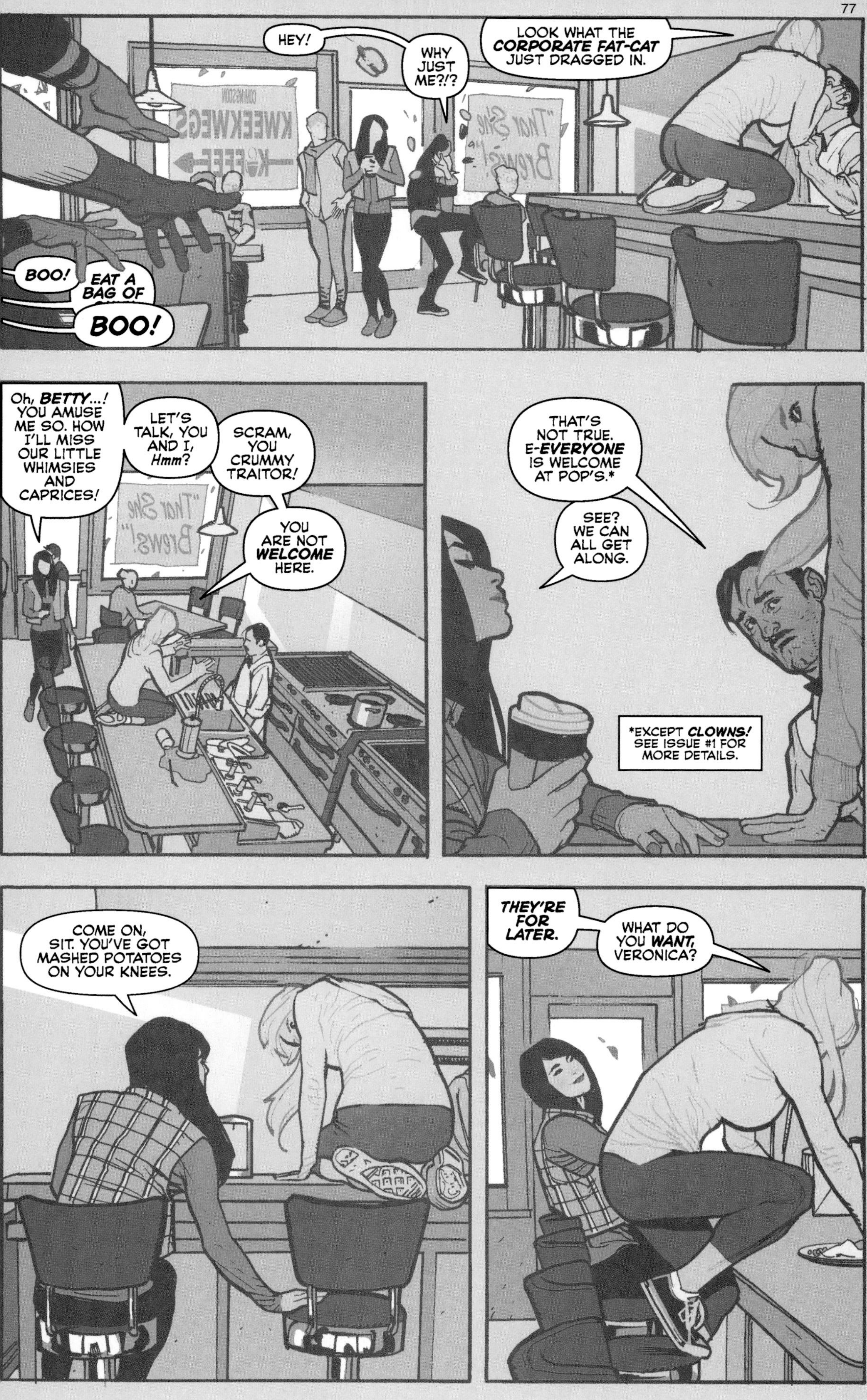
HEY!
WHY JUST ME?!?
LOOK WHAT THE **CORPORATE FAT-CAT** JUST DRAGGED IN.
COMING SOON KWEEKWEGS KOFFEE
"Thar She Brews!"
BOO!
EAT A BAG OF
BOO!
Oh, **BETTY**...! YOU AMUSE ME SO. HOW I'LL MISS OUR LITTLE WHIMSIES AND CAPRICES!
LET'S TALK, YOU AND I, *Hmm*?
SCRAM, YOU CRUMMY TRAITOR!
YOU ARE NOT **WELCOME** HERE.
"Thar She Brews!"
THAT'S NOT TRUE. E-**EVERYONE** IS WELCOME AT POP'S.*
SEE? WE CAN ALL GET ALONG.
*EXCEPT **CLOWNS!** SEE ISSUE #1 FOR MORE DETAILS.
COME ON, SIT. YOU'VE GOT MASHED POTATOES ON YOUR KNEES.
THEY'RE FOR LATER.
WHAT DO YOU **WANT,** VERONICA?

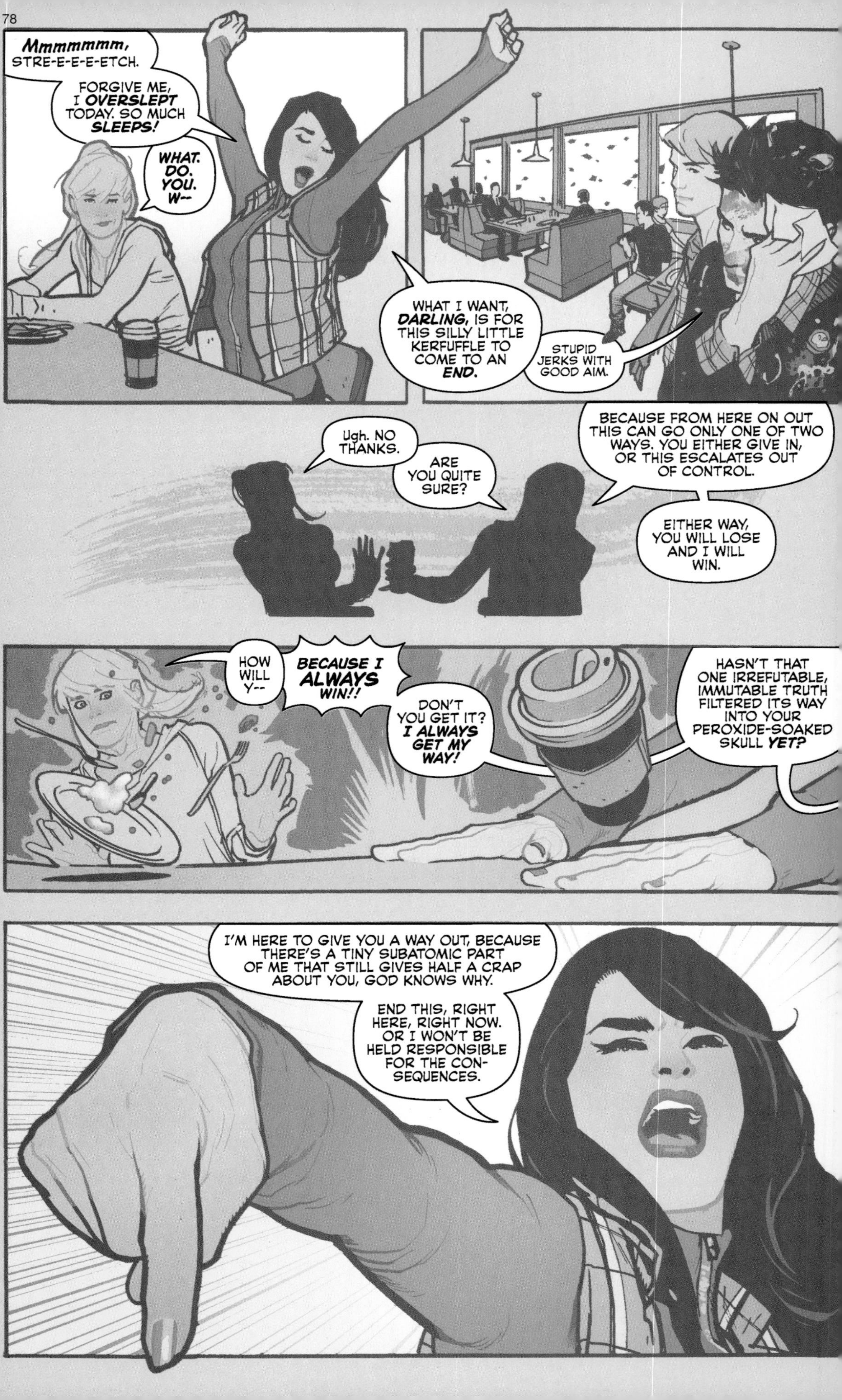
Mmmmmmm, STRE-E-E-E-ETCH.
FORGIVE ME, I OVERSLEPT TODAY. SO MUCH SLEEPS!
WHAT. DO. YOU. W--
WHAT I WANT, DARLING, IS FOR THIS SILLY LITTLE KERFUFFLE TO COME TO AN END.
STUPID JERKS WITH GOOD AIM.
BECAUSE FROM HERE ON OUT THIS CAN GO ONLY ONE OF TWO WAYS. YOU EITHER GIVE IN, OR THIS ESCALATES OUT OF CONTROL.
Ugh. NO THANKS.
ARE YOU QUITE SURE?
EITHER WAY, YOU WILL LOSE AND I WILL WIN.
HOW WILL Y--
BECAUSE I ALWAYS WIN!!
DON'T YOU GET IT? I ALWAYS GET MY WAY!
HASN'T THAT ONE IRREFUTABLE, IMMUTABLE TRUTH FILTERED ITS WAY INTO YOUR PEROXIDE-SOAKED SKULL YET?
I'M HERE TO GIVE YOU A WAY OUT, BECAUSE THERE'S A TINY SUBATOMIC PART OF ME THAT STILL GIVES HALF A CRAP ABOUT YOU, GOD KNOWS WHY.
END THIS, RIGHT HERE, RIGHT NOW. OR I WON'T BE HELD RESPONSIBLE FOR THE CON-SEQUENCES.

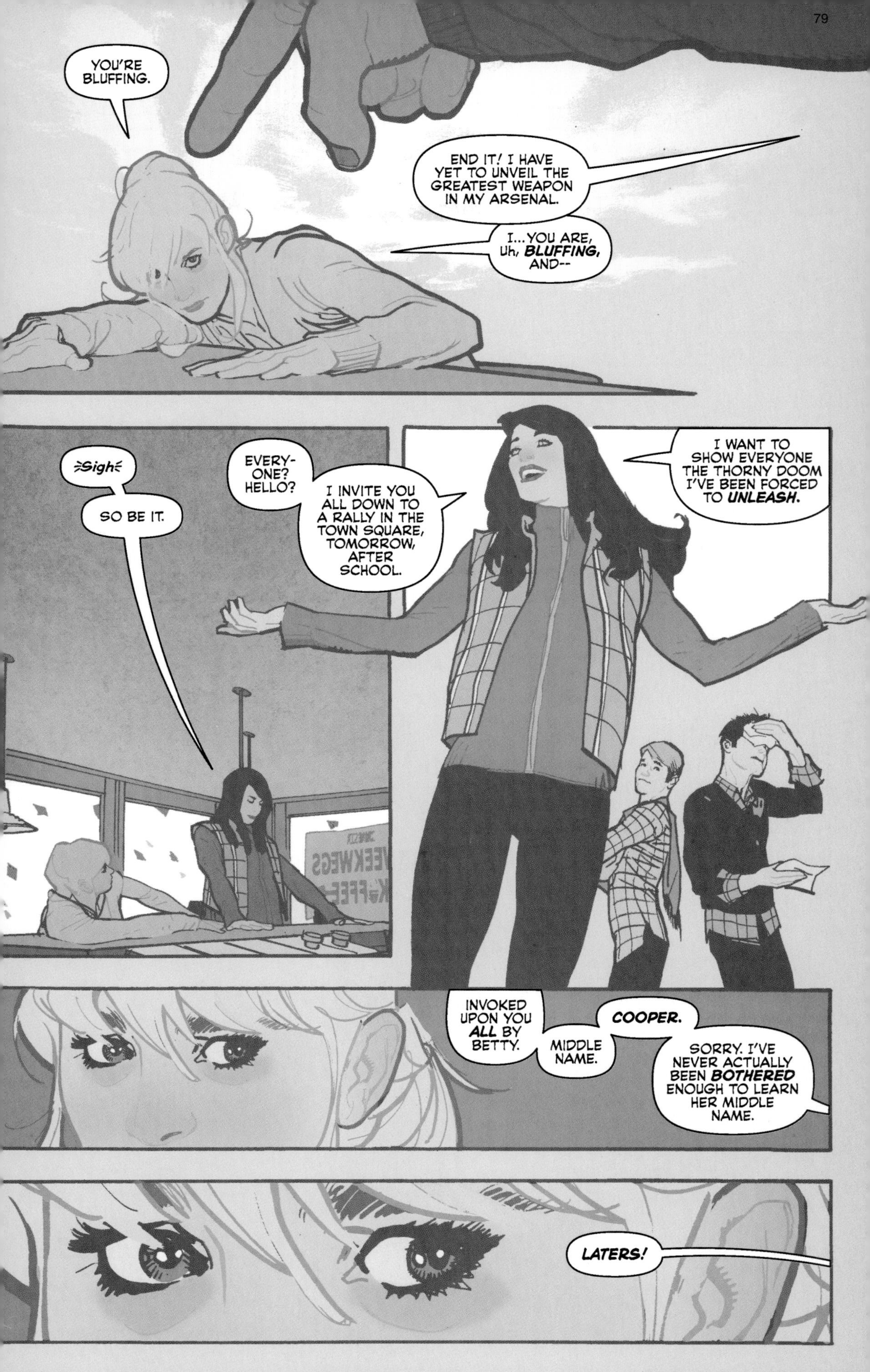
YOU'RE BLUFFING.
END IT! I HAVE YET TO UNVEIL THE GREATEST WEAPON IN MY ARSENAL.
I...YOU ARE, Uh, BLUFFING, AND--
EVERY-ONE? HELLO?
I INVITE YOU ALL DOWN TO A RALLY IN THE TOWN SQUARE, TOMORROW, AFTER SCHOOL.
I WANT TO SHOW EVERYONE THE THORNY DOOM I'VE BEEN FORCED TO UNLEASH.
Sigh
SO BE IT.
INVOKED UPON YOU ALL BY BETTY.
MIDDLE NAME.
COOPER.
SORRY. I'VE NEVER ACTUALLY BEEN BOTHERED ENOUGH TO LEARN HER MIDDLE NAME.
LATERS!

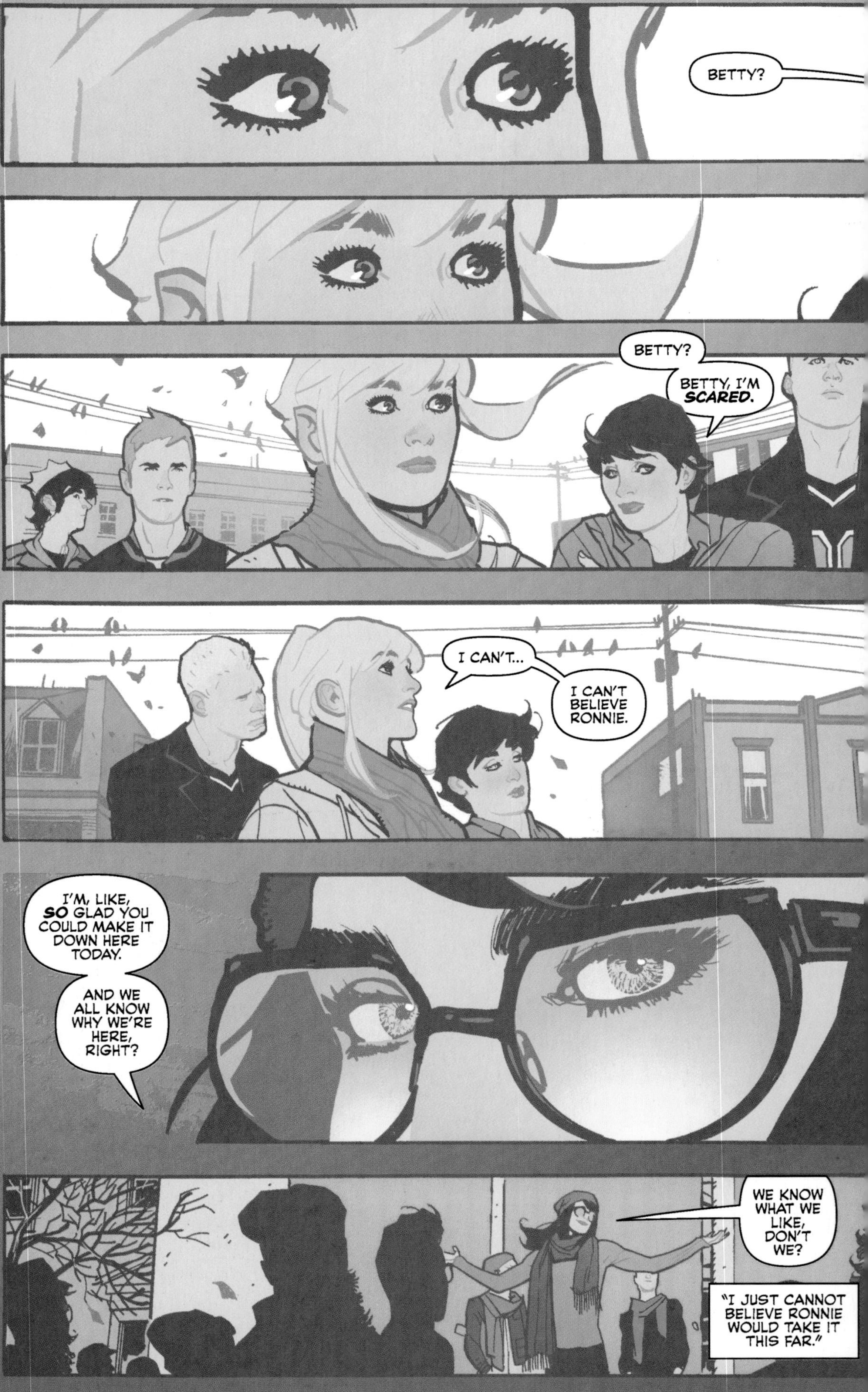
BETTY?
BETTY?
BETTY, I'M **SCARED.**
I CAN'T...
I CAN'T BELIEVE RONNIE.
I'M, LIKE, **SO** GLAD YOU COULD MAKE IT DOWN HERE TODAY.
AND WE ALL KNOW WHY WE'RE HERE, RIGHT?
WE KNOW WHAT WE LIKE, DON'T WE?
"I JUST CANNOT BELIEVE RONNIE WOULD TAKE IT THIS FAR."

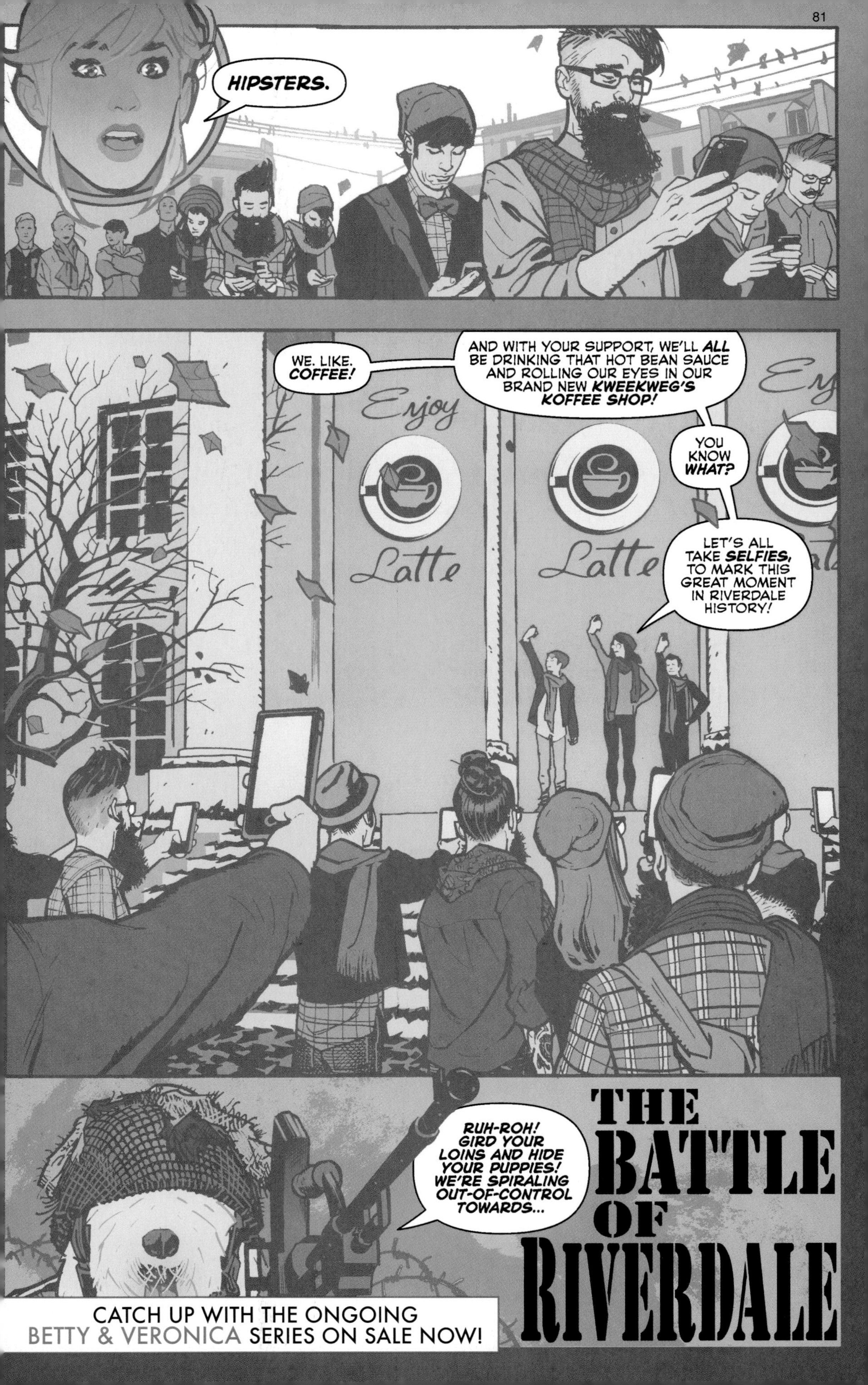
HIPSTERS.
WE. LIKE. COFFEE!
AND WITH YOUR SUPPORT, WE'LL ALL BE DRINKING THAT HOT BEAN SAUCE AND ROLLING OUR EYES IN OUR BRAND NEW KWEEKWEG'S KOFFEE SHOP!
Enjoy
Latte
YOU KNOW WHAT?
LET'S ALL TAKE SELFIES, TO MARK THIS GREAT MOMENT IN RIVERDALE HISTORY!
RUH-ROH! GIRD YOUR LOINS AND HIDE YOUR PUPPIES! WE'RE SPIRALING OUT-OF-CONTROL TOWARDS...
THE BATTLE OF RIVERDALE
CATCH UP WITH THE ONGOING BETTY & VERONICA SERIES ON SALE NOW!

Josie and the Pussycats®

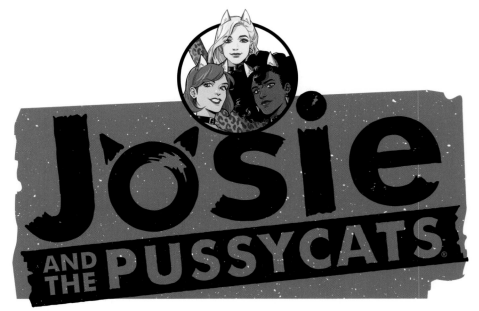

PREVIOUSLY IN THE TOWN OF RIVERDALE...

Josie McCoy wants to be a superstar singer, but she's not getting too far playing her local coffee shop. Fortunately the power of homeless animals has brought her a step closer to realizing her dreams.

With her roommate, Melody Valentine, on drums and her new friend, Valerie Brown—a veterinarian's assistant—on bass and vocals, the three girls formed a band and blew the audience away at a local animal charity show. Not only did the newly-named Josie and the Pussycats impress the audience, but they also caught the eye of a rich mogul named Alan M., who's promising them fame and riches beyond their wildest dreams.

Everything seems to be coming up Josie, unless her nemesis Alexandra Cabot has anything to say about it...

STORY BY
MARGUERITE BENNETT
& CAMERON DeORDIO

ART BY
AUDREY MOK

COLORING BY
KELLY FITZPATRICK

LETTERING BY
JACK MORELLI

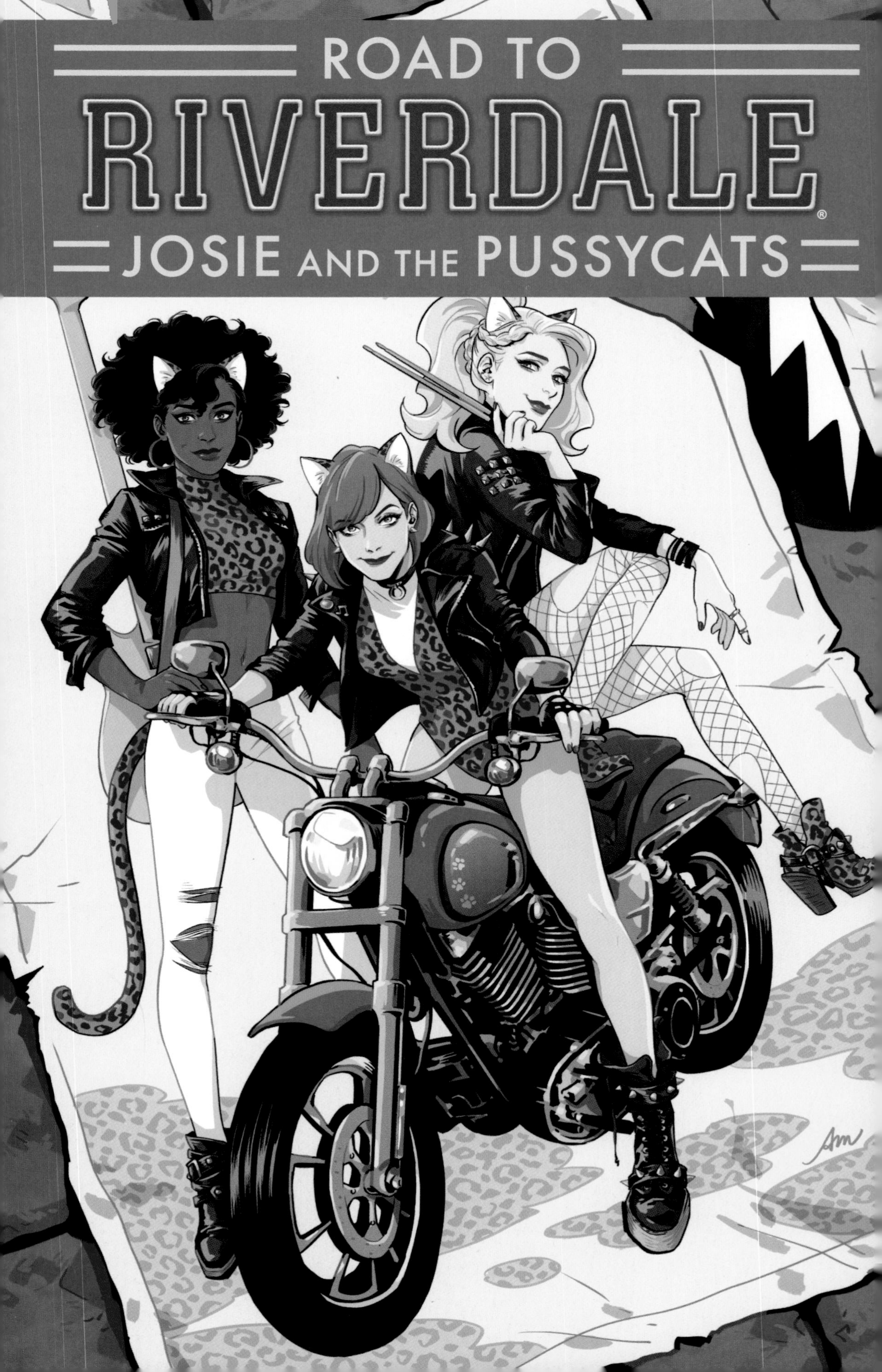
ROAD TO
RIVERDALE®
JOSIE AND THE PUSSYCATS

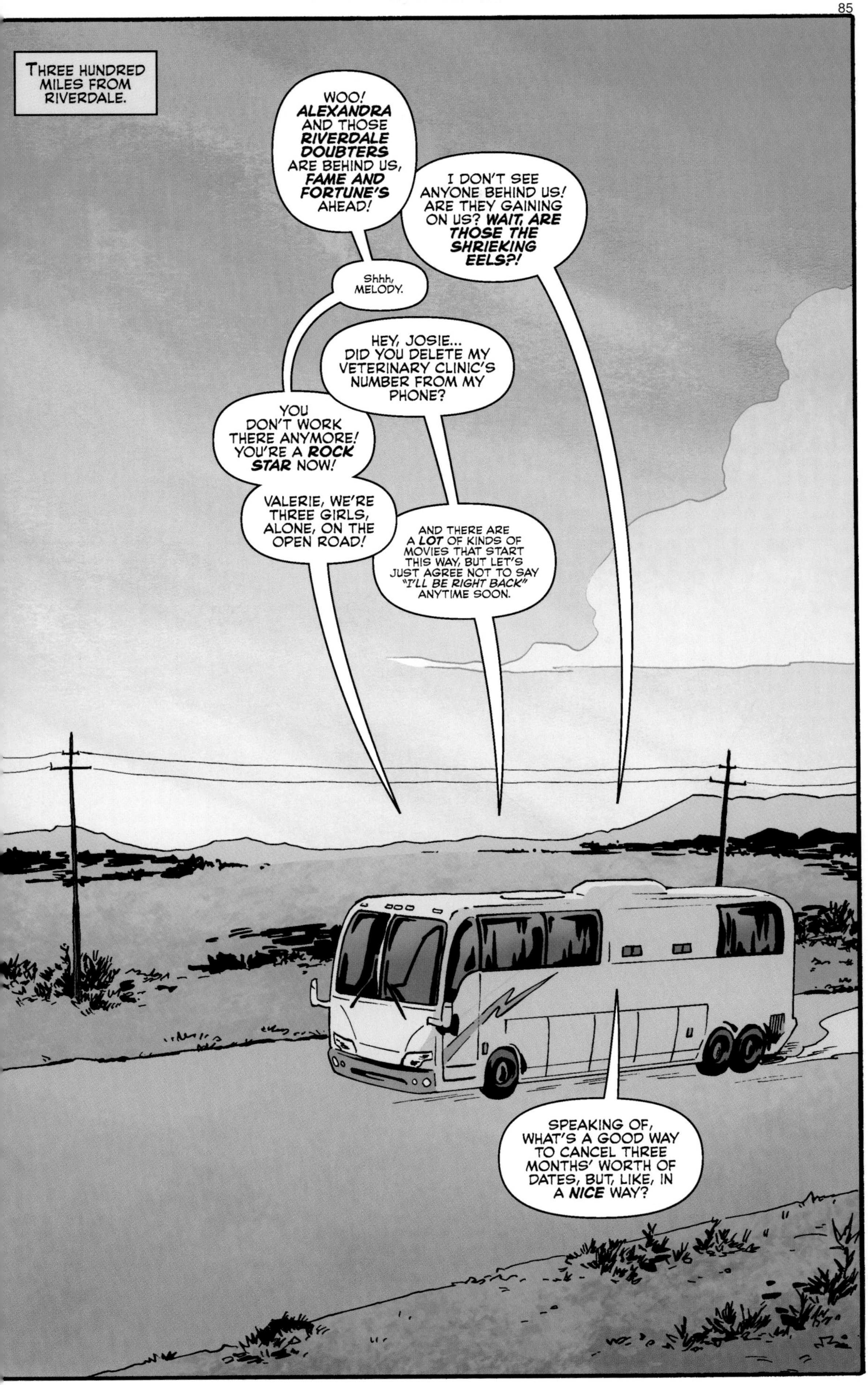
THREE HUNDRED MILES FROM RIVERDALE.
WOO! ALEXANDRA AND THOSE RIVERDALE DOUBTERS ARE BEHIND US, FAME AND FORTUNE'S AHEAD!
I DON'T SEE ANYONE BEHIND US! ARE THEY GAINING ON US? WAIT, ARE THOSE THE SHRIEKING EELS?!
Shhh, MELODY.
HEY, JOSIE... DID YOU DELETE MY VETERINARY CLINIC'S NUMBER FROM MY PHONE?
YOU DON'T WORK THERE ANYMORE! YOU'RE A ROCK STAR NOW!
VALERIE, WE'RE THREE GIRLS, ALONE, ON THE OPEN ROAD!
AND THERE ARE A LOT OF KINDS OF MOVIES THAT START THIS WAY, BUT LET'S JUST AGREE NOT TO SAY "I'LL BE RIGHT BACK" ANYTIME SOON.
SPEAKING OF, WHAT'S A GOOD WAY TO CANCEL THREE MONTHS' WORTH OF DATES, BUT, LIKE, IN A NICE WAY?

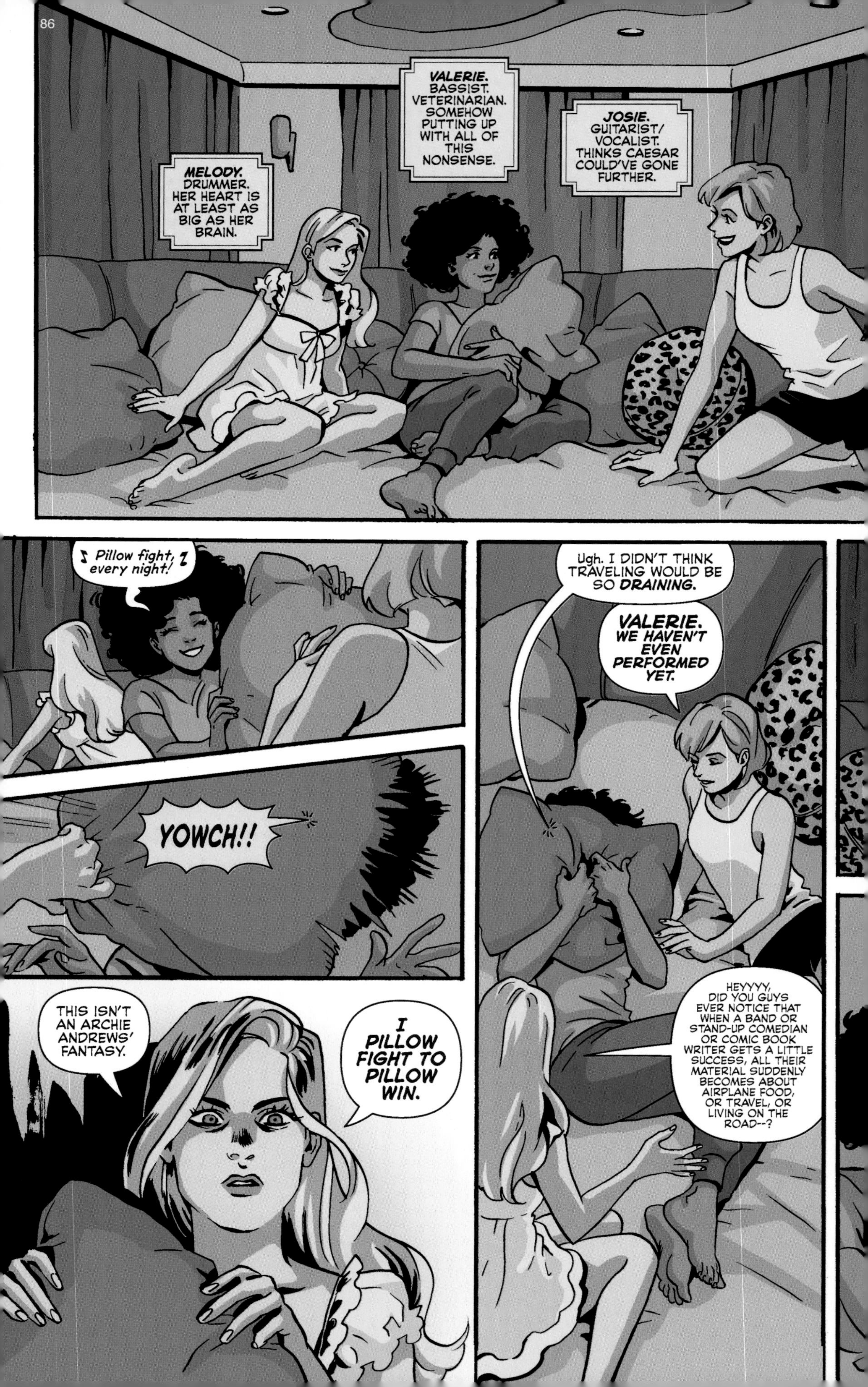
MELODY. DRUMMER. HER HEART IS AT LEAST AS BIG AS HER BRAIN.
VALERIE. BASSIST. VETERINARIAN. SOMEHOW PUTTING UP WITH ALL OF THIS NONSENSE.
JOSIE. GUITARIST/ VOCALIST. THINKS CAESAR COULD'VE GONE FURTHER.
Pillow fight, every night!
YOWCH!!
THIS ISN'T AN ARCHIE ANDREWS' FANTASY.
I PILLOW FIGHT TO PILLOW WIN.
Ugh. I DIDN'T THINK TRAVELING WOULD BE SO DRAINING.
VALERIE. WE HAVEN'T EVEN PERFORMED YET.
HEYYYY, DID YOU GUYS EVER NOTICE THAT WHEN A BAND OR STAND-UP COMEDIAN OR COMIC BOOK WRITER GETS A LITTLE SUCCESS, ALL THEIR MATERIAL SUDDENLY BECOMES ABOUT AIRPLANE FOOD, OR TRAVEL, OR LIVING ON THE ROAD--?

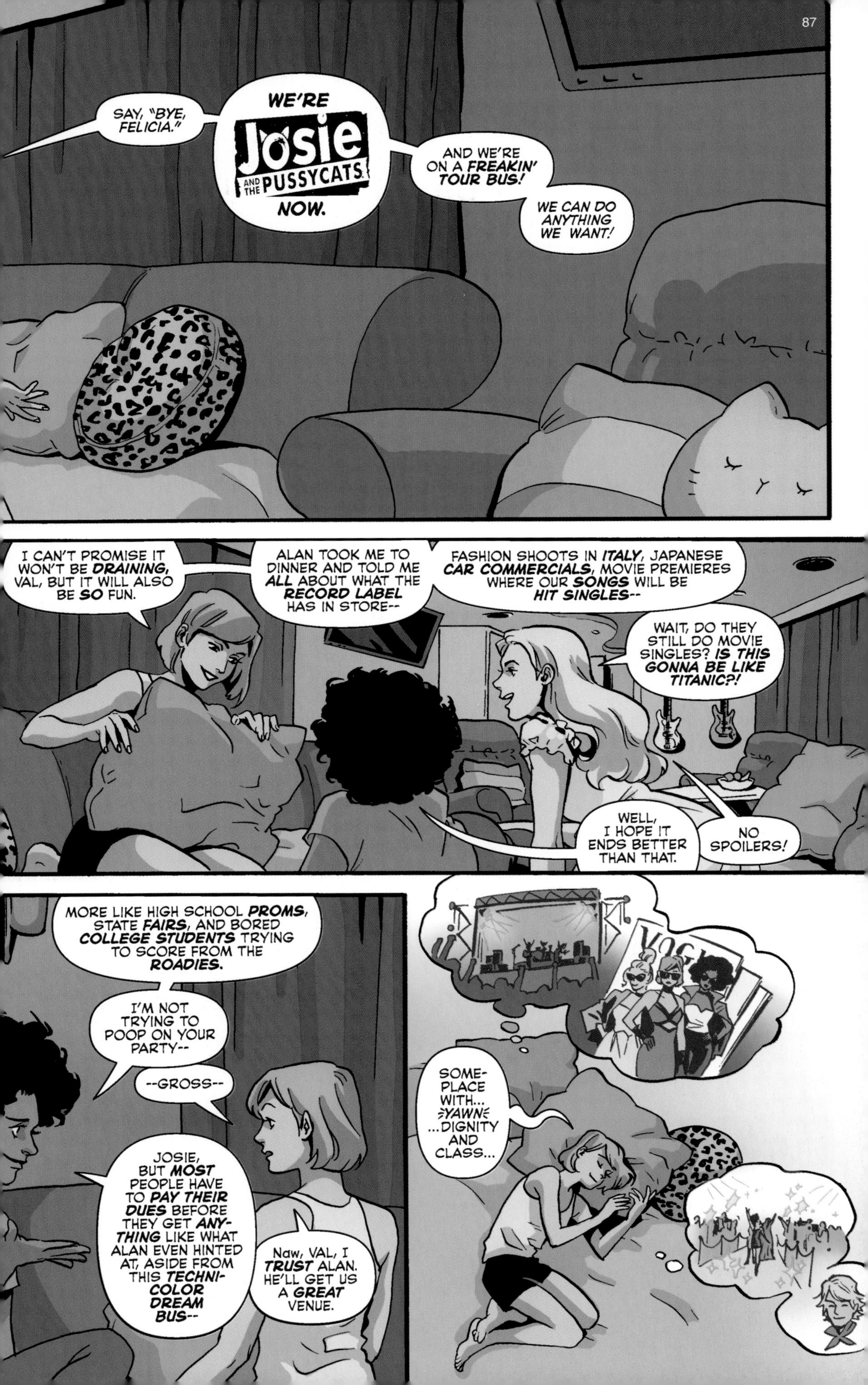
SAY, "BYE, FELICIA."
WE'RE JOSIE AND THE PUSSYCATS NOW.
AND WE'RE ON A FREAKIN' TOUR BUS!
WE CAN DO ANYTHING WE WANT!
I CAN'T PROMISE IT WON'T BE DRAINING, VAL, BUT IT WILL ALSO BE SO FUN.
ALAN TOOK ME TO DINNER AND TOLD ME ALL ABOUT WHAT THE RECORD LABEL HAS IN STORE--
FASHION SHOOTS IN ITALY, JAPANESE CAR COMMERCIALS, MOVIE PREMIERES WHERE OUR SONGS WILL BE HIT SINGLES--
WAIT, DO THEY STILL DO MOVIE SINGLES? IS THIS GONNA BE LIKE TITANIC?!
WELL, I HOPE IT ENDS BETTER THAN THAT.
NO SPOILERS!
MORE LIKE HIGH SCHOOL PROMS, STATE FAIRS, AND BORED COLLEGE STUDENTS TRYING TO SCORE FROM THE ROADIES.
I'M NOT TRYING TO POOP ON YOUR PARTY--
--GROSS--
JOSIE, BUT MOST PEOPLE HAVE TO PAY THEIR DUES BEFORE THEY GET ANYTHING LIKE WHAT ALAN EVEN HINTED AT, ASIDE FROM THIS TECHNICOLOR DREAM BUS--
Naw, VAL, I TRUST ALAN. HE'LL GET US A GREAT VENUE.
SOMEPLACE WITH... YAWN ...DIGNITY AND CLASS...

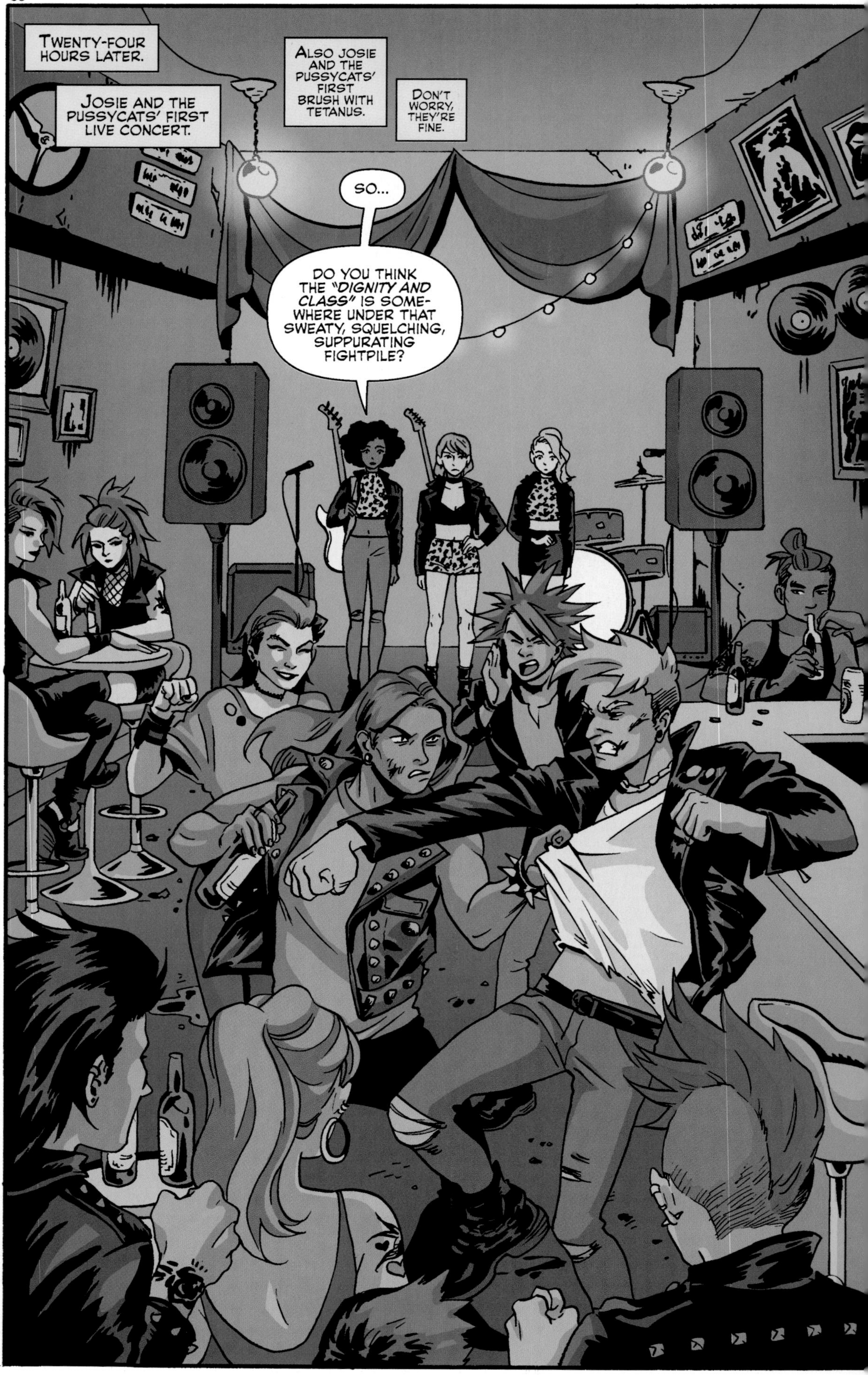
TWENTY-FOUR HOURS LATER.
JOSIE AND THE PUSSYCATS' FIRST LIVE CONCERT.
ALSO JOSIE AND THE PUSSYCATS' FIRST BRUSH WITH TETANUS.
DON'T WORRY, THEY'RE FINE.
SO...
DO YOU THINK THE "DIGNITY AND CLASS" IS SOMEWHERE UNDER THAT SWEATY, SQUELCHING, SUPPURATING FIGHTPILE?

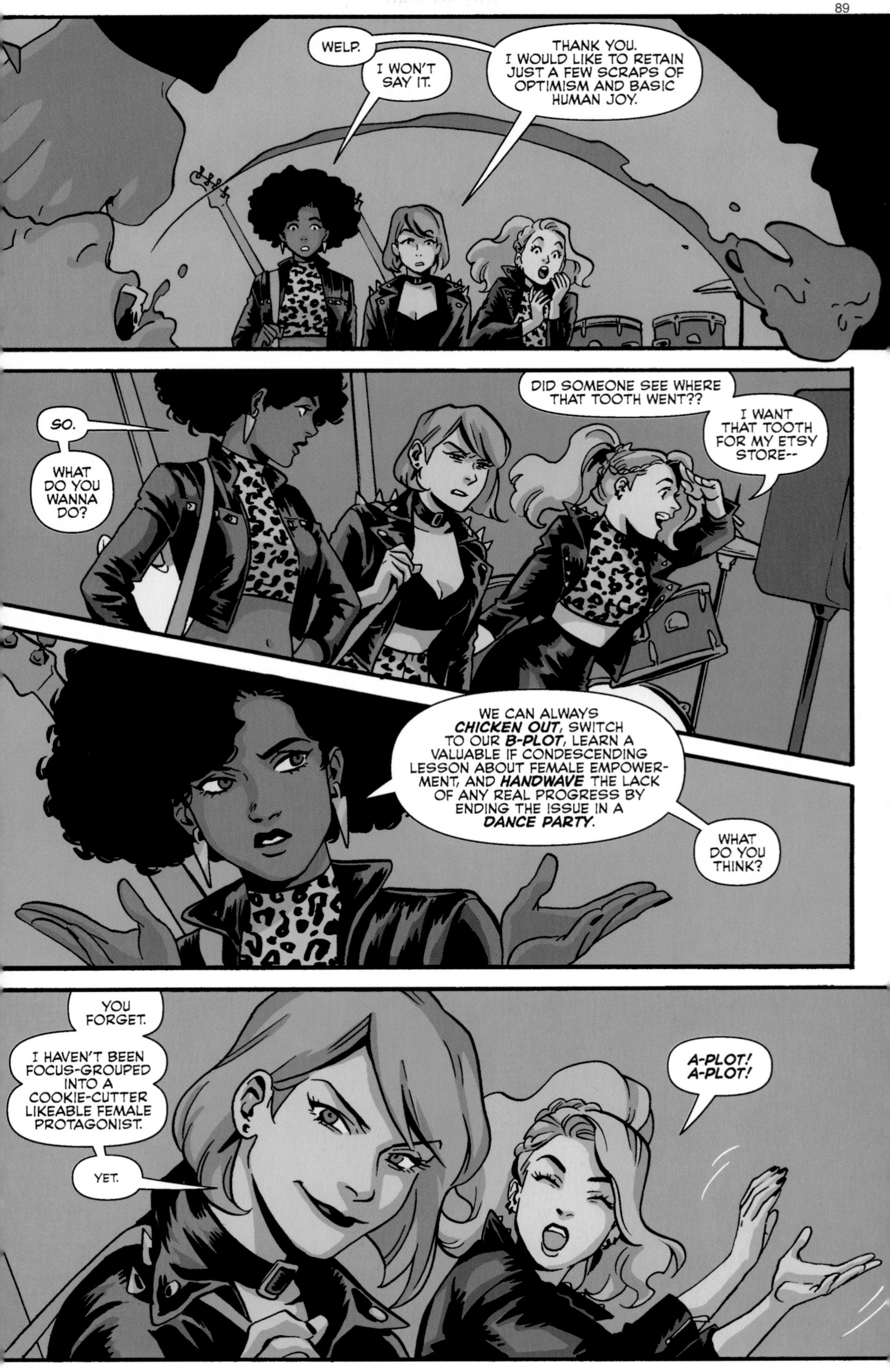
WELP.
I WON'T SAY IT.
THANK YOU. I WOULD LIKE TO RETAIN JUST A FEW SCRAPS OF OPTIMISM AND BASIC HUMAN JOY.
SO.
WHAT DO YOU WANNA DO?
DID SOMEONE SEE WHERE THAT TOOTH WENT??
I WANT THAT TOOTH FOR MY ETSY STORE--
WE CAN ALWAYS ***CHICKEN OUT***, SWITCH TO OUR ***B-PLOT***, LEARN A VALUABLE IF CONDESCENDING LESSON ABOUT FEMALE EMPOWER-MENT, AND ***HANDWAVE*** THE LACK OF ANY REAL PROGRESS BY ENDING THE ISSUE IN A ***DANCE PARTY***.
WHAT DO YOU THINK?
YOU FORGET.
I HAVEN'T BEEN FOCUS-GROUPED INTO A COOKIE-CUTTER LIKEABLE FEMALE PROTAGONIST.
YET.
A-PLOT! A-PLOT!

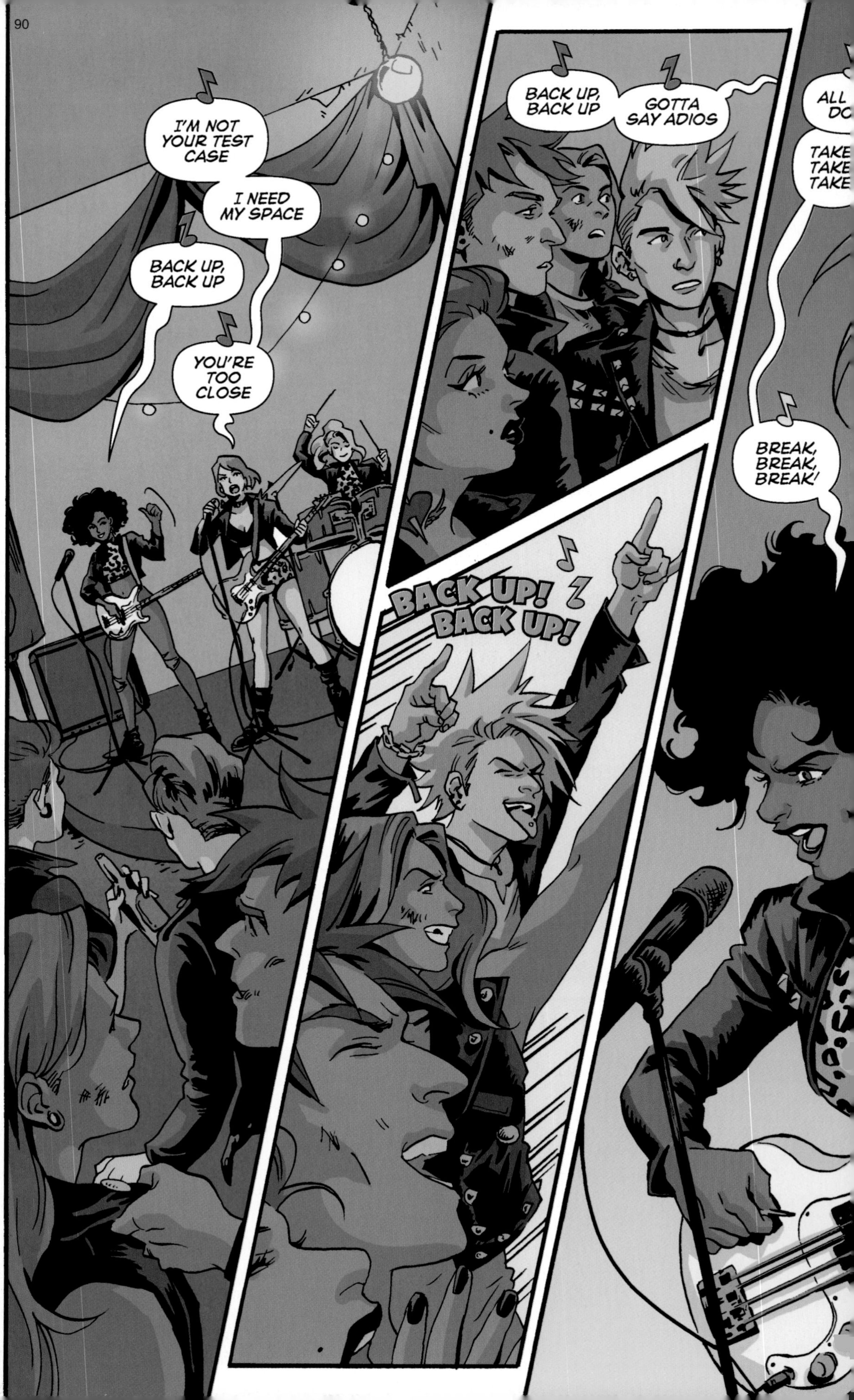
I'M NOT YOUR TEST CASE
I NEED MY SPACE
BACK UP, BACK UP
YOU'RE TOO CLOSE
BACK UP, BACK UP
GOTTA SAY ADIOS
BACK UP! BACK UP!
ALL
BREAK, BREAK, BREAK!

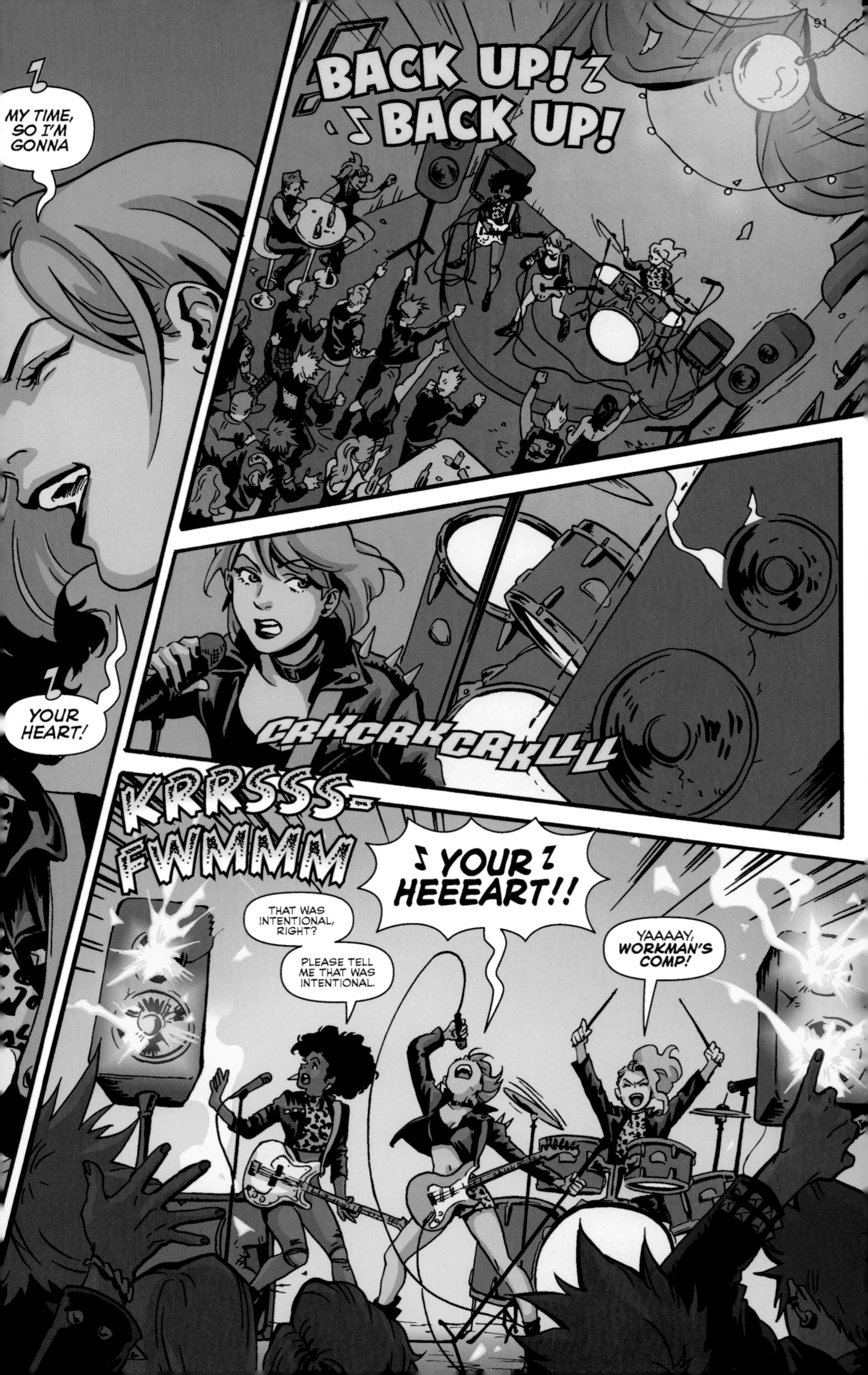
MY TIME, SO I'M GONNA
BACK UP! BACK UP!
YOUR HEART!
CRKCRKCRKLLL
KRRSSS-FWMMM
YOUR HEEEART!!
THAT WAS INTENTIONAL, RIGHT?
PLEASE TELL ME THAT WAS INTENTIONAL.
YAAAAY, WORKMAN'S COMP!

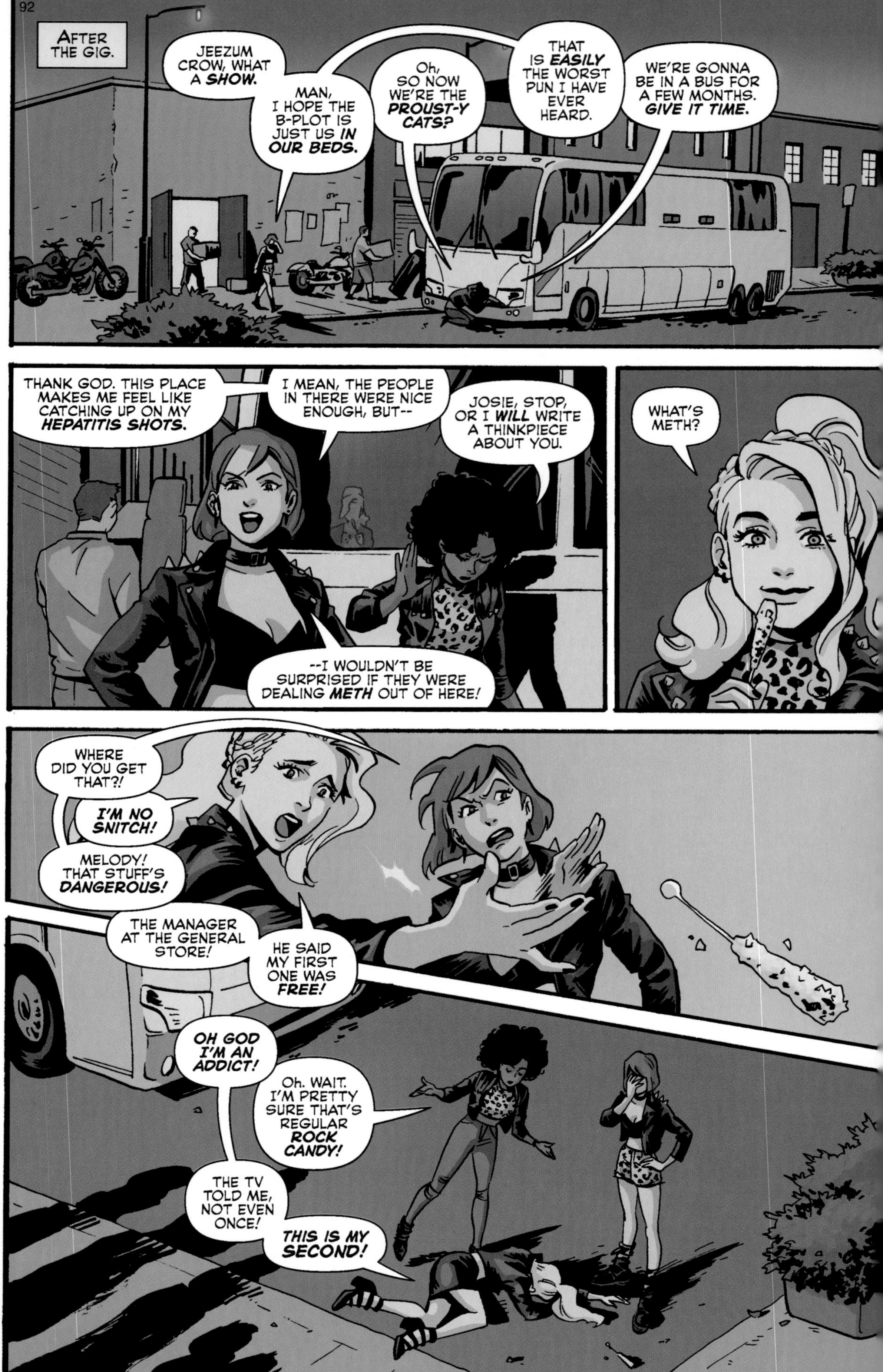
AFTER THE GIG.
JEEZUM CROW, WHAT A SHOW.
MAN, I HOPE THE B-PLOT IS JUST US IN OUR BEDS.
Oh, SO NOW WE'RE THE PROUST-Y CATS?
THAT IS EASILY THE WORST PUN I HAVE EVER HEARD.
WE'RE GONNA BE IN A BUS FOR A FEW MONTHS. GIVE IT TIME.
THANK GOD. THIS PLACE MAKES ME FEEL LIKE CATCHING UP ON MY HEPATITIS SHOTS.
I MEAN, THE PEOPLE IN THERE WERE NICE ENOUGH, BUT--
JOSIE, STOP, OR I WILL WRITE A THINKPIECE ABOUT YOU.
--I WOULDN'T BE SURPRISED IF THEY WERE DEALING METH OUT OF HERE!
WHAT'S METH?
WHERE DID YOU GET THAT?!
I'M NO SNITCH!
MELODY! THAT STUFF'S DANGEROUS!
THE MANAGER AT THE GENERAL STORE!
HE SAID MY FIRST ONE WAS FREE!
OH GOD I'M AN ADDICT!
Oh. WAIT. I'M PRETTY SURE THAT'S REGULAR ROCK CANDY!
THE TV TOLD ME, NOT EVEN ONCE!
THIS IS MY SECOND!

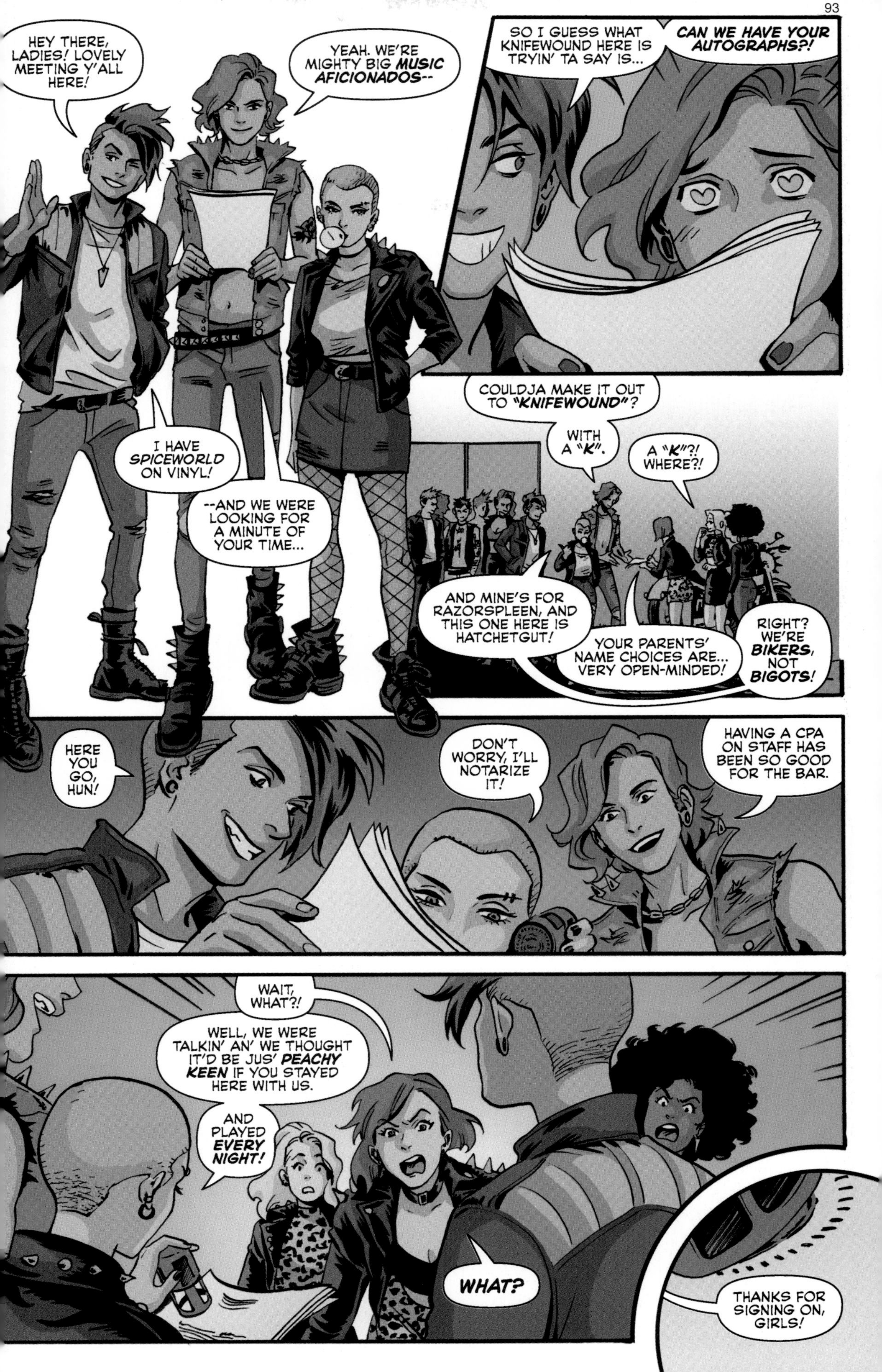
HEY THERE, LADIES! LOVELY MEETING Y'ALL HERE!
YEAH. WE'RE MIGHTY BIG MUSIC AFICIONADOS--
I HAVE SPICEWORLD ON VINYL!
--AND WE WERE LOOKING FOR A MINUTE OF YOUR TIME...
SO I GUESS WHAT KNIFEWOUND HERE IS TRYIN' TA SAY IS...
CAN WE HAVE YOUR AUTOGRAPHS?!
COULDJA MAKE IT OUT TO "KNIFEWOUND"?
WITH A "K".
A "K"?! WHERE?!
AND MINE'S FOR RAZORSPLEEN, AND THIS ONE HERE IS HATCHETGUT!
YOUR PARENTS' NAME CHOICES ARE... VERY OPEN-MINDED!
RIGHT? WE'RE BIKERS, NOT BIGOTS!
HERE YOU GO, HUN!
DON'T WORRY, I'LL NOTARIZE IT!
HAVING A CPA ON STAFF HAS BEEN SO GOOD FOR THE BAR.
WAIT, WHAT?!
WELL, WE WERE TALKIN' AN' WE THOUGHT IT'D BE JUS' PEACHY KEEN IF YOU STAYED HERE WITH US.
AND PLAYED EVERY NIGHT!
WHAT?
THANKS FOR SIGNING ON, GIRLS!

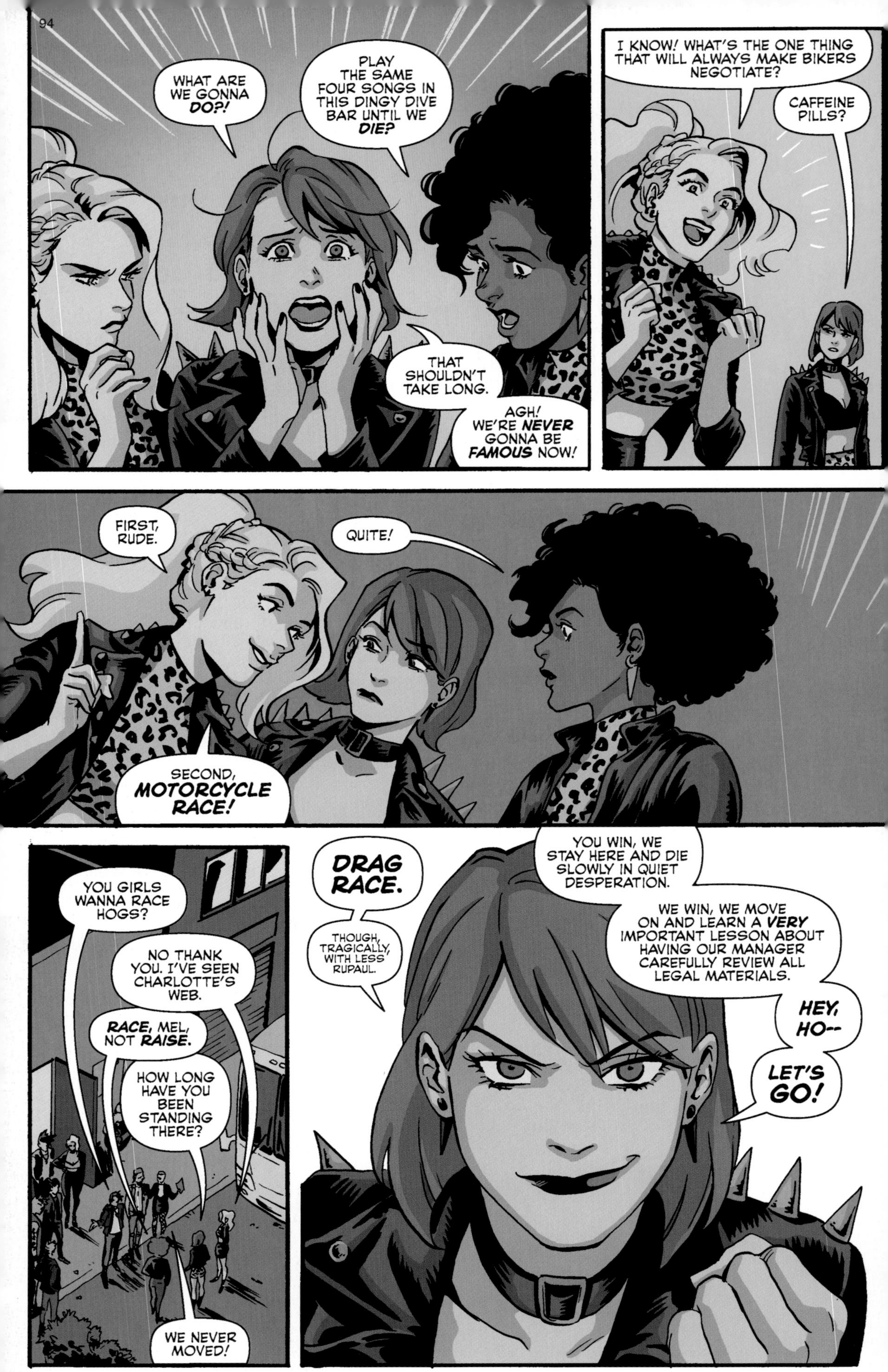
WHAT ARE WE GONNA DO?!
PLAY THE SAME FOUR SONGS IN THIS DINGY DIVE BAR UNTIL WE DIE?
THAT SHOULDN'T TAKE LONG.
AGH! WE'RE NEVER GONNA BE FAMOUS NOW!
I KNOW! WHAT'S THE ONE THING THAT WILL ALWAYS MAKE BIKERS NEGOTIATE?
CAFFEINE PILLS?
FIRST, RUDE.
QUITE!
SECOND, MOTORCYCLE RACE!
YOU GIRLS WANNA RACE HOGS?
NO THANK YOU. I'VE SEEN CHARLOTTE'S WEB.
RACE, MEL, NOT RAISE.
HOW LONG HAVE YOU BEEN STANDING THERE?
WE NEVER MOVED!
DRAG RACE.
THOUGH, TRAGICALLY, WITH LESS RUPAUL.
YOU WIN, WE STAY HERE AND DIE SLOWLY IN QUIET DESPERATION.
WE WIN, WE MOVE ON AND LEARN A VERY IMPORTANT LESSON ABOUT HAVING OUR MANAGER CAREFULLY REVIEW ALL LEGAL MATERIALS.
HEY, HO--
LET'S GO!

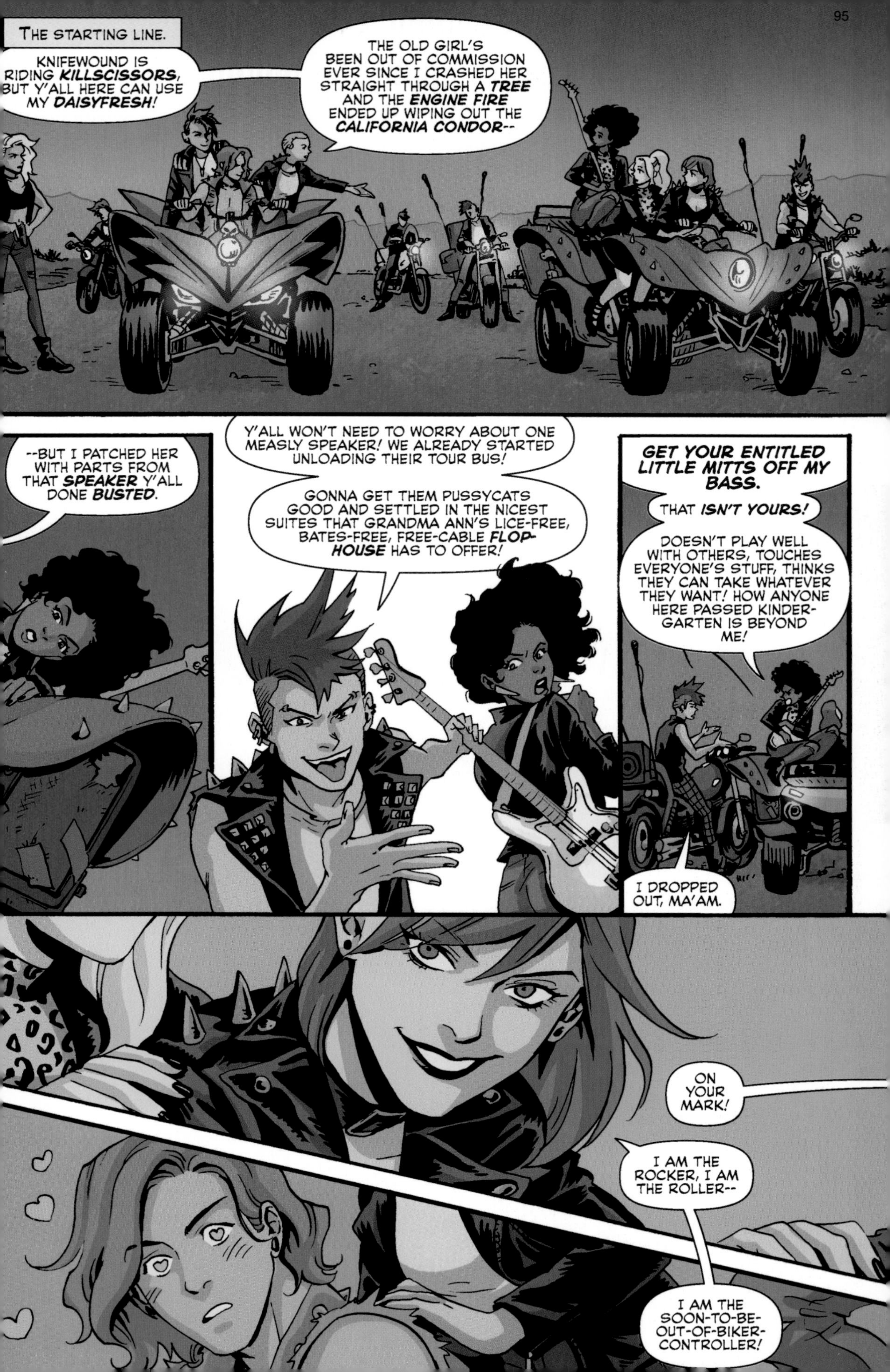
THE STARTING LINE.
KNIFEWOUND IS RIDING KILLSCISSORS, BUT Y'ALL HERE CAN USE MY DAISYFRESH!
THE OLD GIRL'S BEEN OUT OF COMMISSION EVER SINCE I CRASHED HER STRAIGHT THROUGH A TREE AND THE ENGINE FIRE ENDED UP WIPING OUT THE CALIFORNIA CONDOR--
--BUT I PATCHED HER WITH PARTS FROM THAT SPEAKER Y'ALL DONE BUSTED.
Y'ALL WON'T NEED TO WORRY ABOUT ONE MEASLY SPEAKER! WE ALREADY STARTED UNLOADING THEIR TOUR BUS!
GONNA GET THEM PUSSYCATS GOOD AND SETTLED IN THE NICEST SUITES THAT GRANDMA ANN'S LICE-FREE, BATES-FREE, FREE-CABLE FLOP-HOUSE HAS TO OFFER!
GET YOUR ENTITLED LITTLE MITTS OFF MY BASS.
THAT ISN'T YOURS!
DOESN'T PLAY WELL WITH OTHERS, TOUCHES EVERYONE'S STUFF, THINKS THEY CAN TAKE WHATEVER THEY WANT! HOW ANYONE HERE PASSED KINDER-GARTEN IS BEYOND ME!
I DROPPED OUT, MA'AM.
ON YOUR MARK!
I AM THE ROCKER, I AM THE ROLLER--
I AM THE SOON-TO-BE-OUT-OF-BIKER-CONTROLLER!

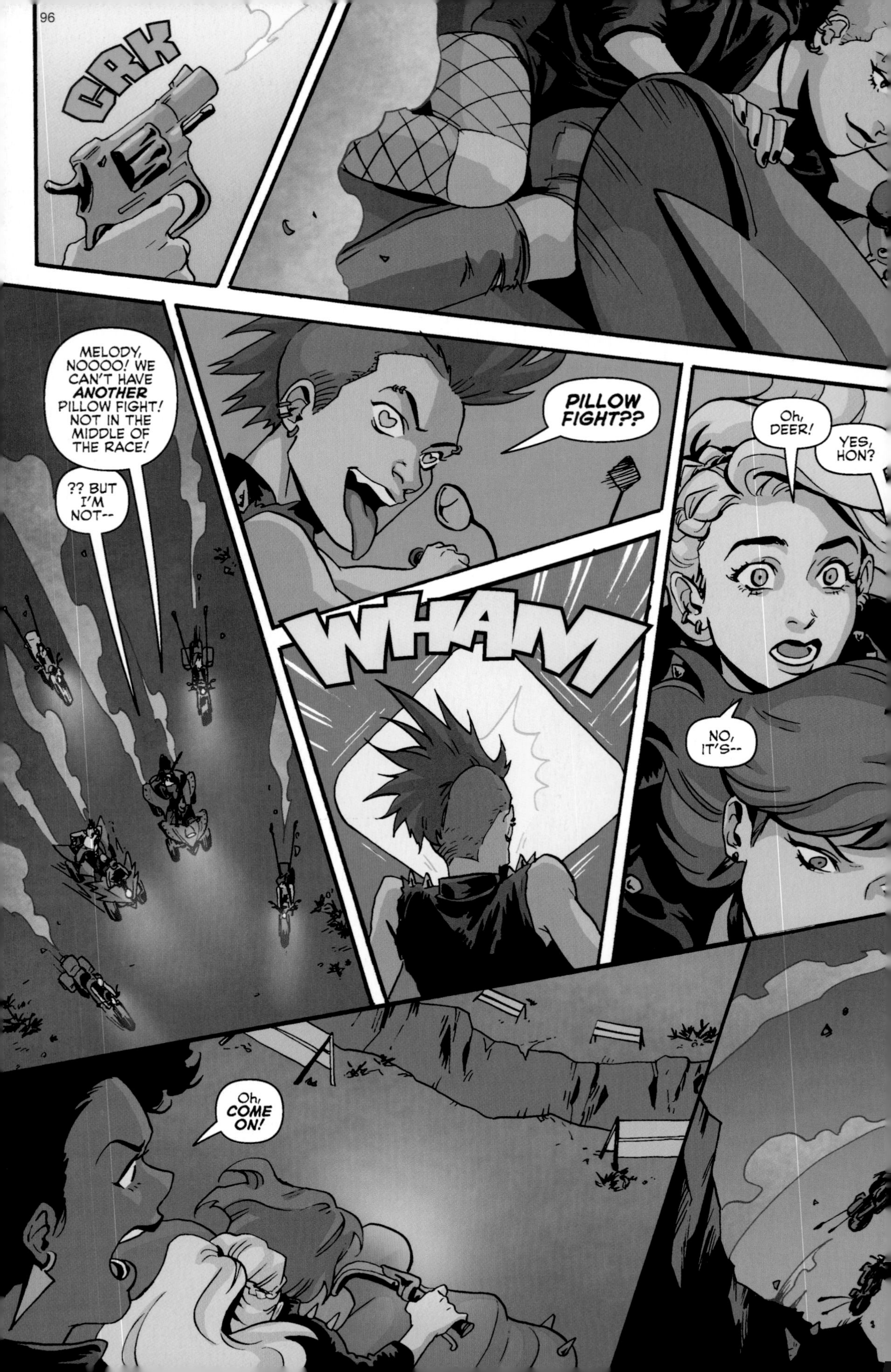
CRK
MELODY, NOOOO! WE CAN'T HAVE ANOTHER PILLOW FIGHT! NOT IN THE MIDDLE OF THE RACE!
?? BUT I'M NOT--
PILLOW FIGHT??
WHAM
Oh, DEER!
YES, HON?
NO, IT'S--
Oh, COME ON!

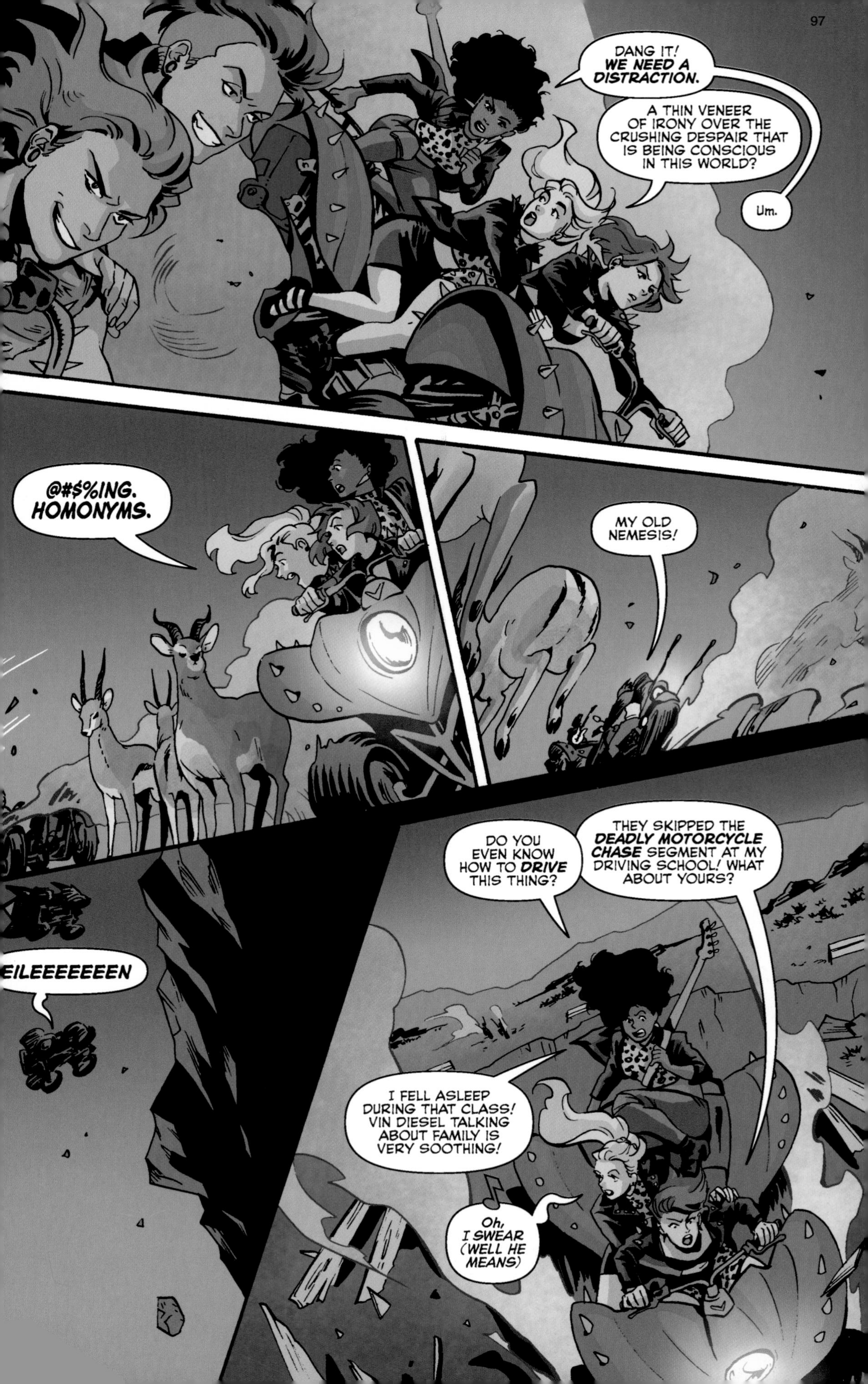
DANG IT! WE NEED A DISTRACTION.
A THIN VENEER OF IRONY OVER THE CRUSHING DESPAIR THAT IS BEING CONSCIOUS IN THIS WORLD?
Um.
@#$%ING. HOMONYMS.
MY OLD NEMESIS!
EILEEEEEEEN
DO YOU EVEN KNOW HOW TO DRIVE THIS THING?
THEY SKIPPED THE DEADLY MOTORCYCLE CHASE SEGMENT AT MY DRIVING SCHOOL! WHAT ABOUT YOURS?
I FELL ASLEEP DURING THAT CLASS! VIN DIESEL TALKING ABOUT FAMILY IS VERY SOOTHING!
Oh, I SWEAR (WELL HE MEANS)

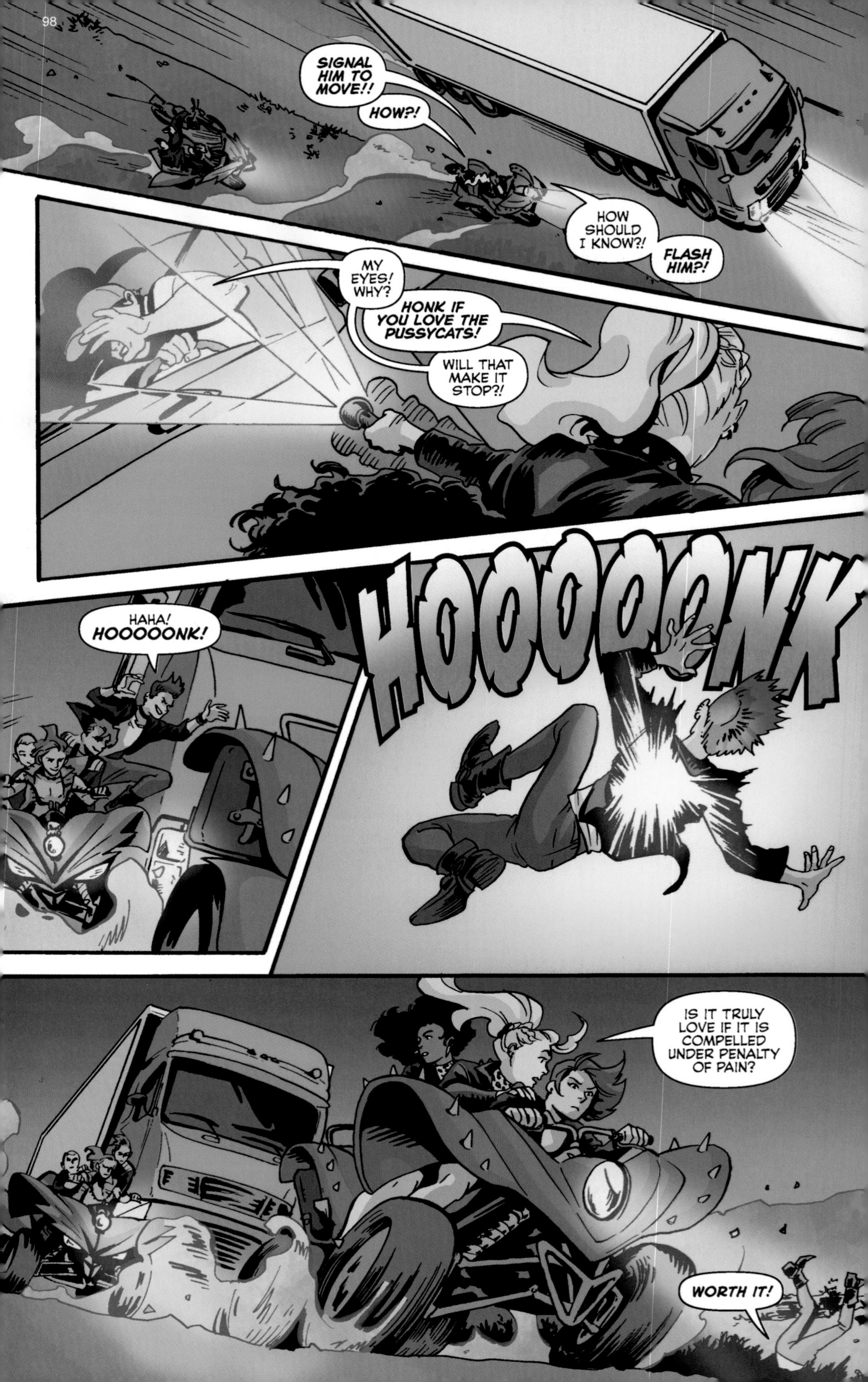
SIGNAL HIM TO MOVE!!
HOW?!
HOW SHOULD I KNOW?!
FLASH HIM?!
MY EYES! WHY?
HONK IF YOU LOVE THE PUSSYCATS!
WILL THAT MAKE IT STOP?!
HOOOOONK
HAHA! HOOOOONK!
IS IT TRULY LOVE IF IT IS COMPELLED UNDER PENALTY OF PAIN?
WORTH IT!

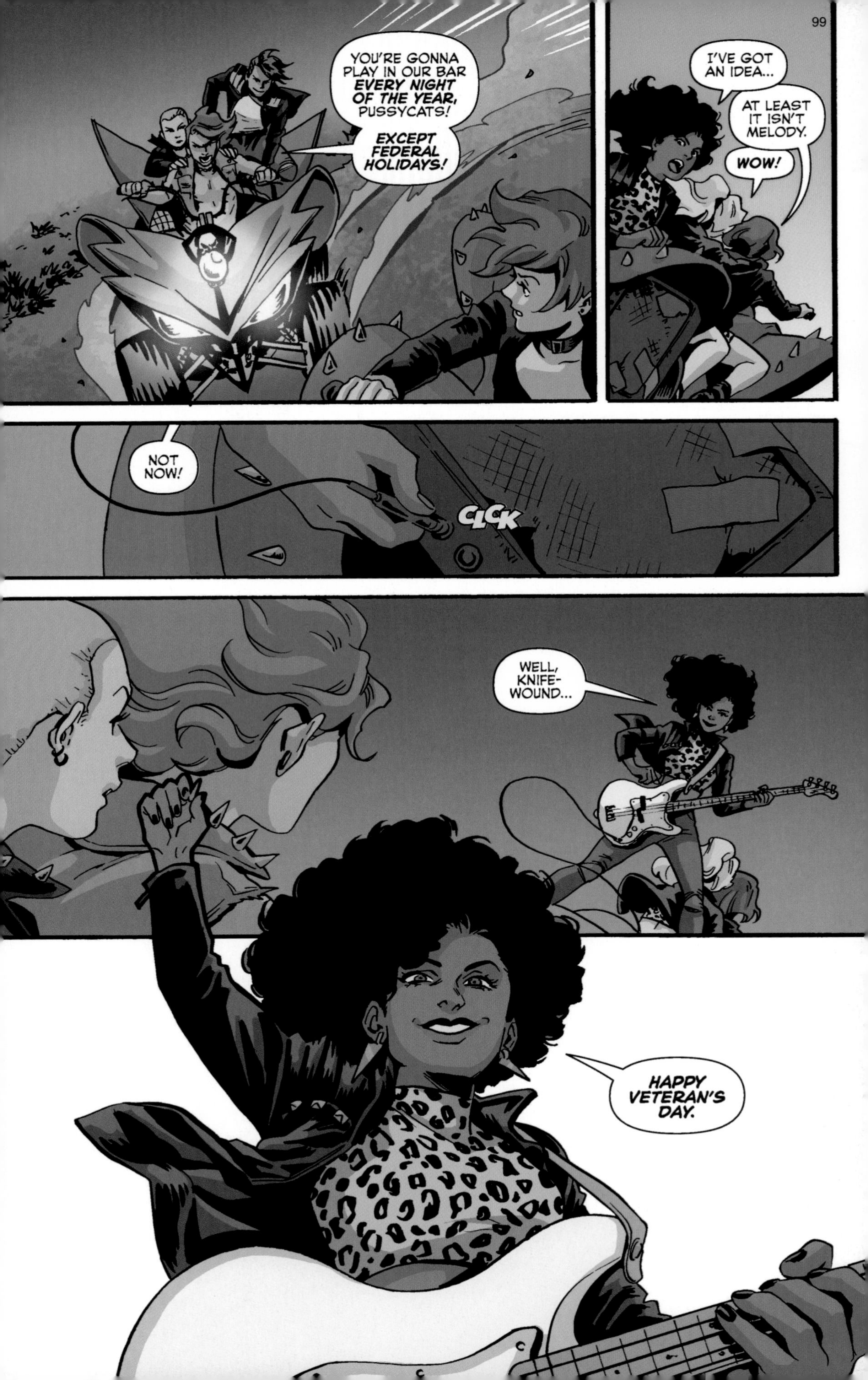
YOU'RE GONNA PLAY IN OUR BAR EVERY NIGHT OF THE YEAR, PUSSYCATS!
EXCEPT FEDERAL HOLIDAYS!
I'VE GOT AN IDEA...
AT LEAST IT ISN'T MELODY.
WOW!
NOT NOW!
CLCK
WELL, KNIFE-WOUND...
HAPPY VETERAN'S DAY.

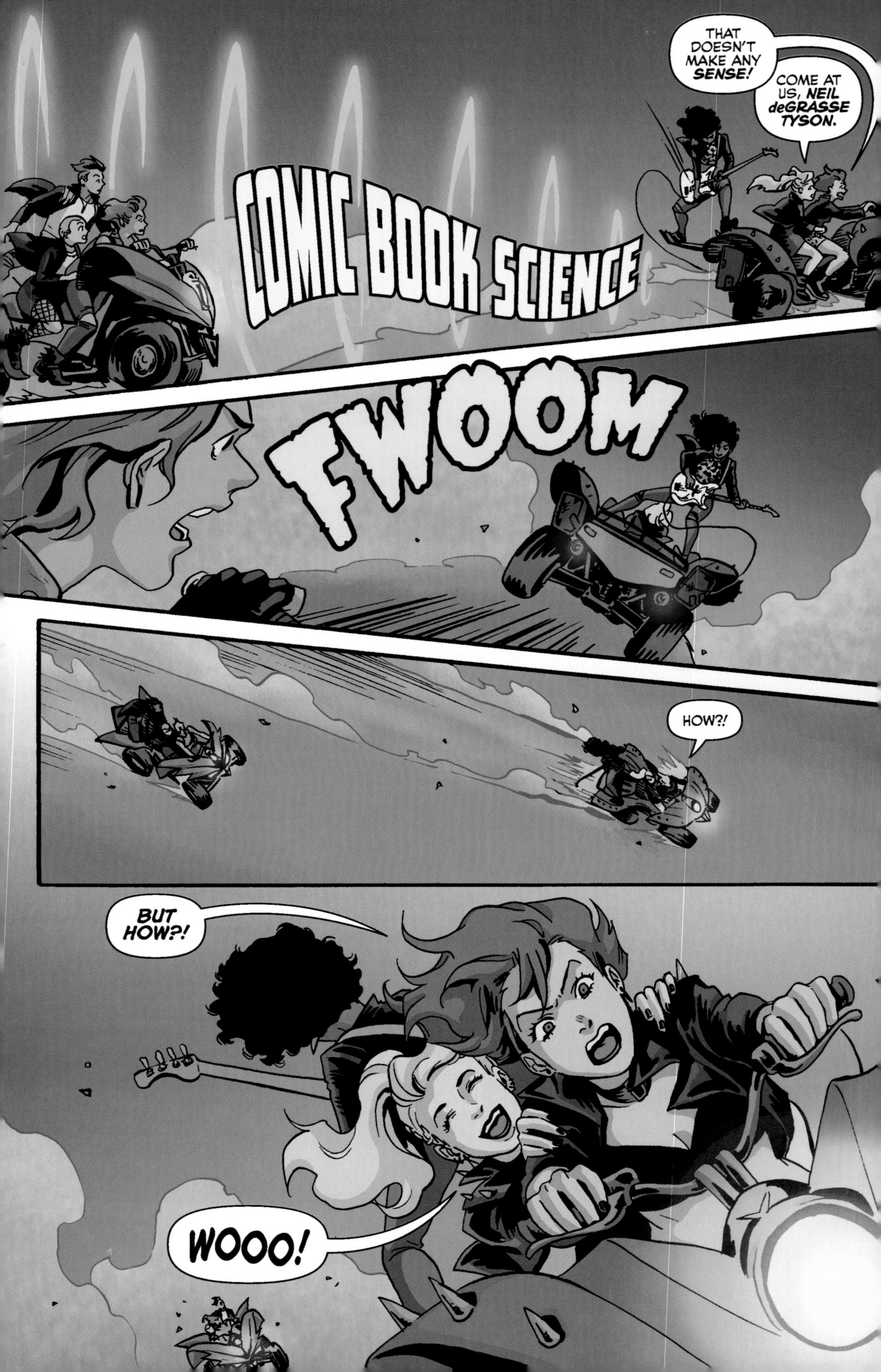
THAT DOESN'T MAKE ANY SENSE!
COME AT US, NEIL deGRASSE TYSON.
COMIC BOOK SCIENCE
FWOOM
HOW?!
BUT HOW?!
WOOO!

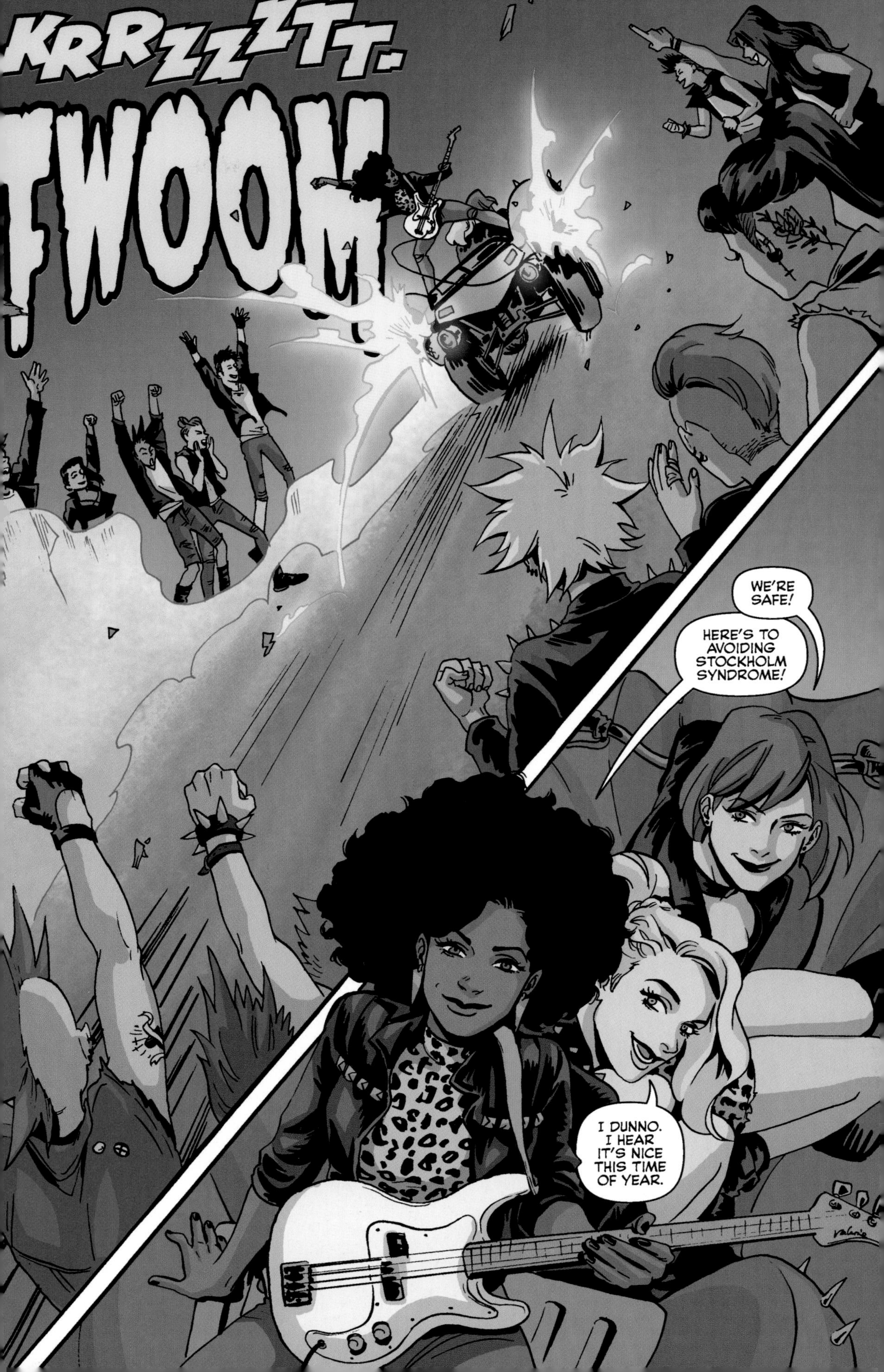
KRRZZZTT.
TWOOM
WE'RE SAFE!
HERE'S TO AVOIDING STOCKHOLM SYNDROME!
I DUNNO. I HEAR IT'S NICE THIS TIME OF YEAR.

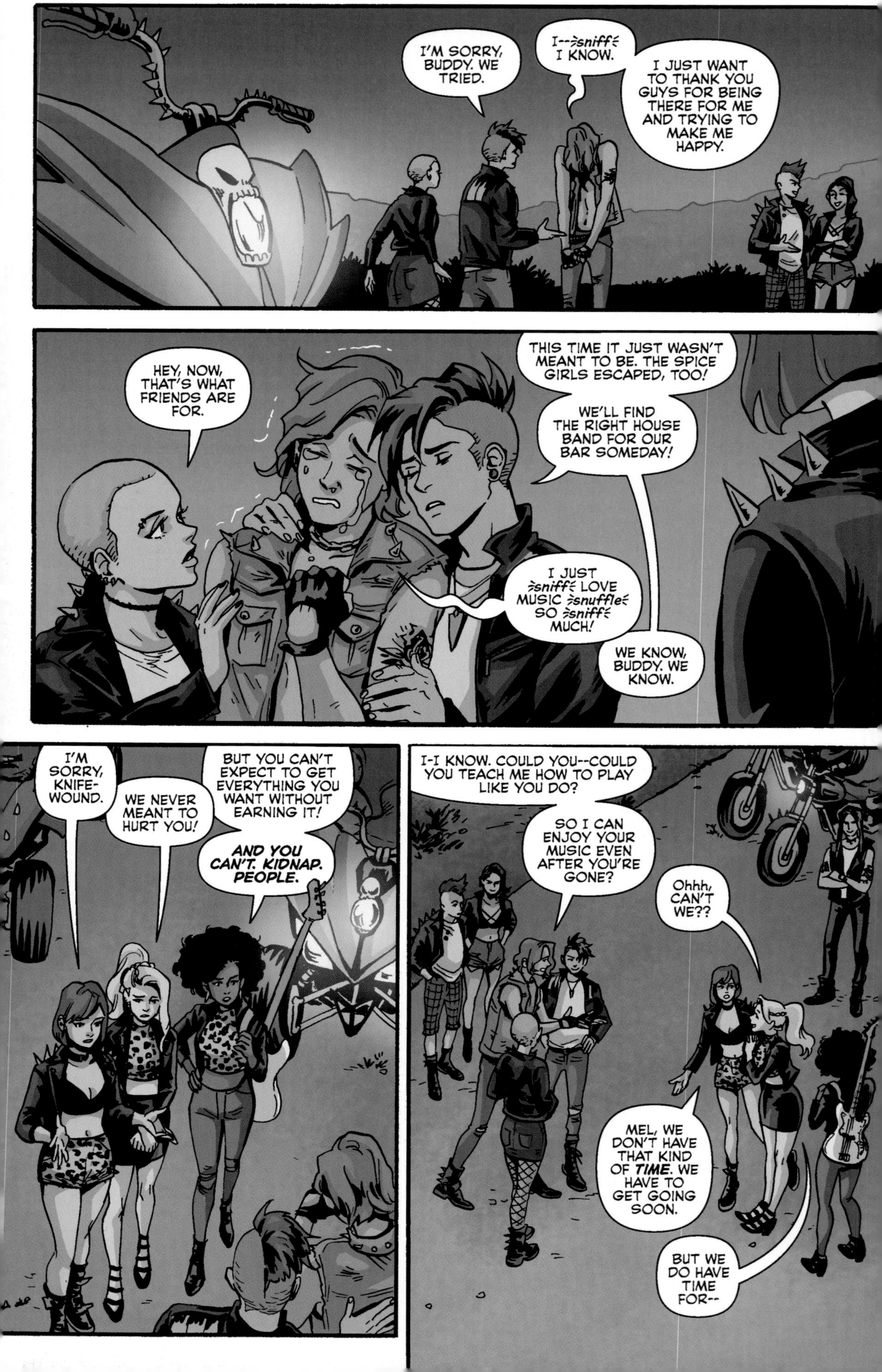

I'M SORRY, BUDDY. WE TRIED.
I--*sniff* I KNOW.
I JUST WANT TO THANK YOU GUYS FOR BEING THERE FOR ME AND TRYING TO MAKE ME HAPPY.
HEY, NOW, THAT'S WHAT FRIENDS ARE FOR.
THIS TIME IT JUST WASN'T MEANT TO BE. THE SPICE GIRLS ESCAPED, TOO!
WE'LL FIND THE RIGHT HOUSE BAND FOR OUR BAR SOMEDAY!
I JUST *sniff* LOVE MUSIC *snuffle* SO *sniff* MUCH!
WE KNOW, BUDDY. WE KNOW.
I'M SORRY, KNIFE-WOUND.
WE NEVER MEANT TO HURT YOU!
BUT YOU CAN'T EXPECT TO GET EVERYTHING YOU WANT WITHOUT EARNING IT!
AND YOU CAN'T. KIDNAP. PEOPLE.
I-I KNOW. COULD YOU--COULD YOU TEACH ME HOW TO PLAY LIKE YOU DO?
SO I CAN ENJOY YOUR MUSIC EVEN AFTER YOU'RE GONE?
Ohhh, CAN'T WE??
MEL, WE DON'T HAVE THAT KIND OF *TIME*. WE HAVE TO GET GOING SOON.
BUT WE DO HAVE TIME FOR--

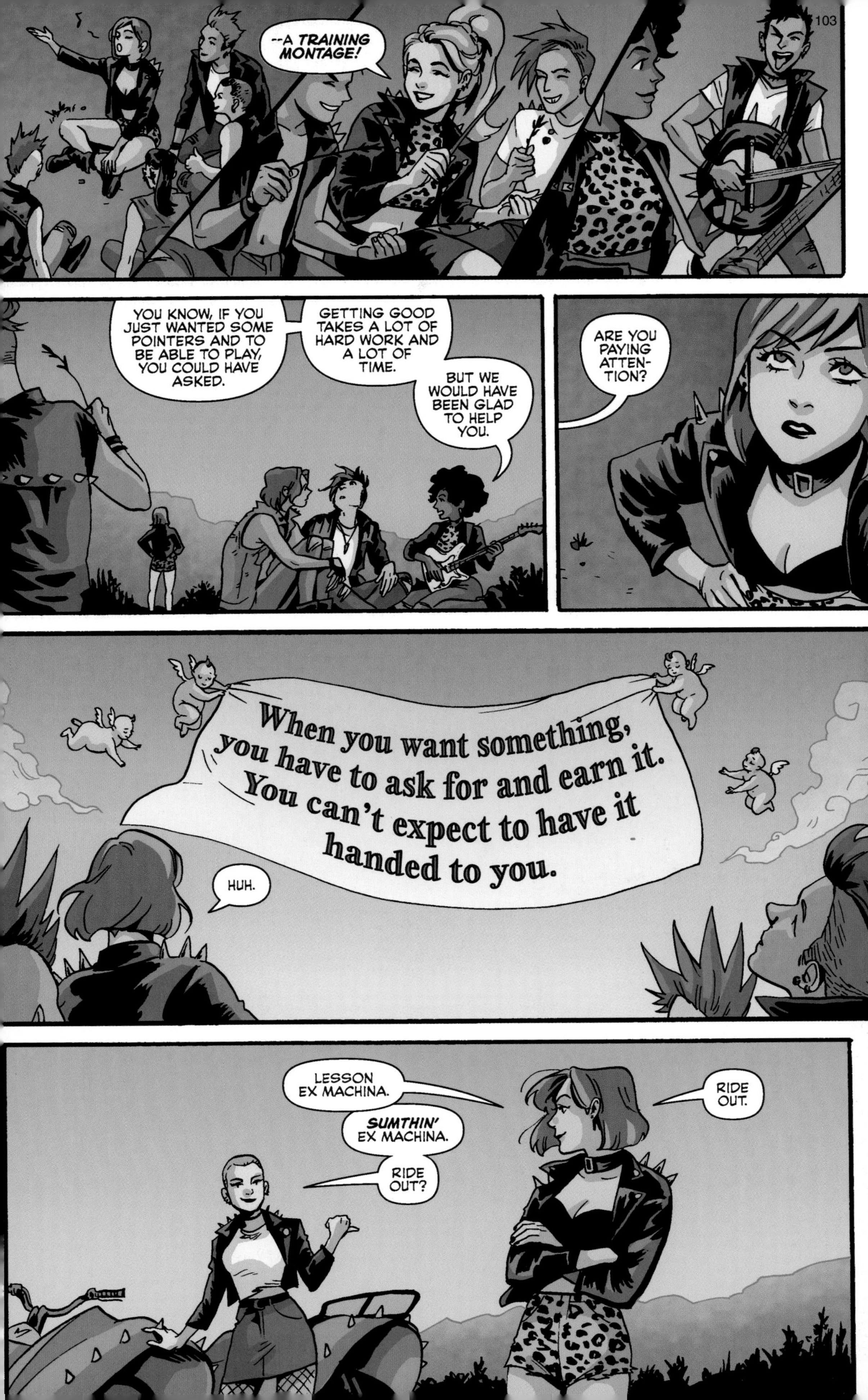
--A TRAINING MONTAGE!
YOU KNOW, IF YOU JUST WANTED SOME POINTERS AND TO BE ABLE TO PLAY, YOU COULD HAVE ASKED.
GETTING GOOD TAKES A LOT OF HARD WORK AND A LOT OF TIME.
BUT WE WOULD HAVE BEEN GLAD TO HELP YOU.
ARE YOU PAYING ATTEN-TION?
When you want something, you have to ask for and earn it. You can't expect to have it handed to you.
HUH.
LESSON EX MACHINA.
SUMTHIN' EX MACHINA.
RIDE OUT?
RIDE OUT.

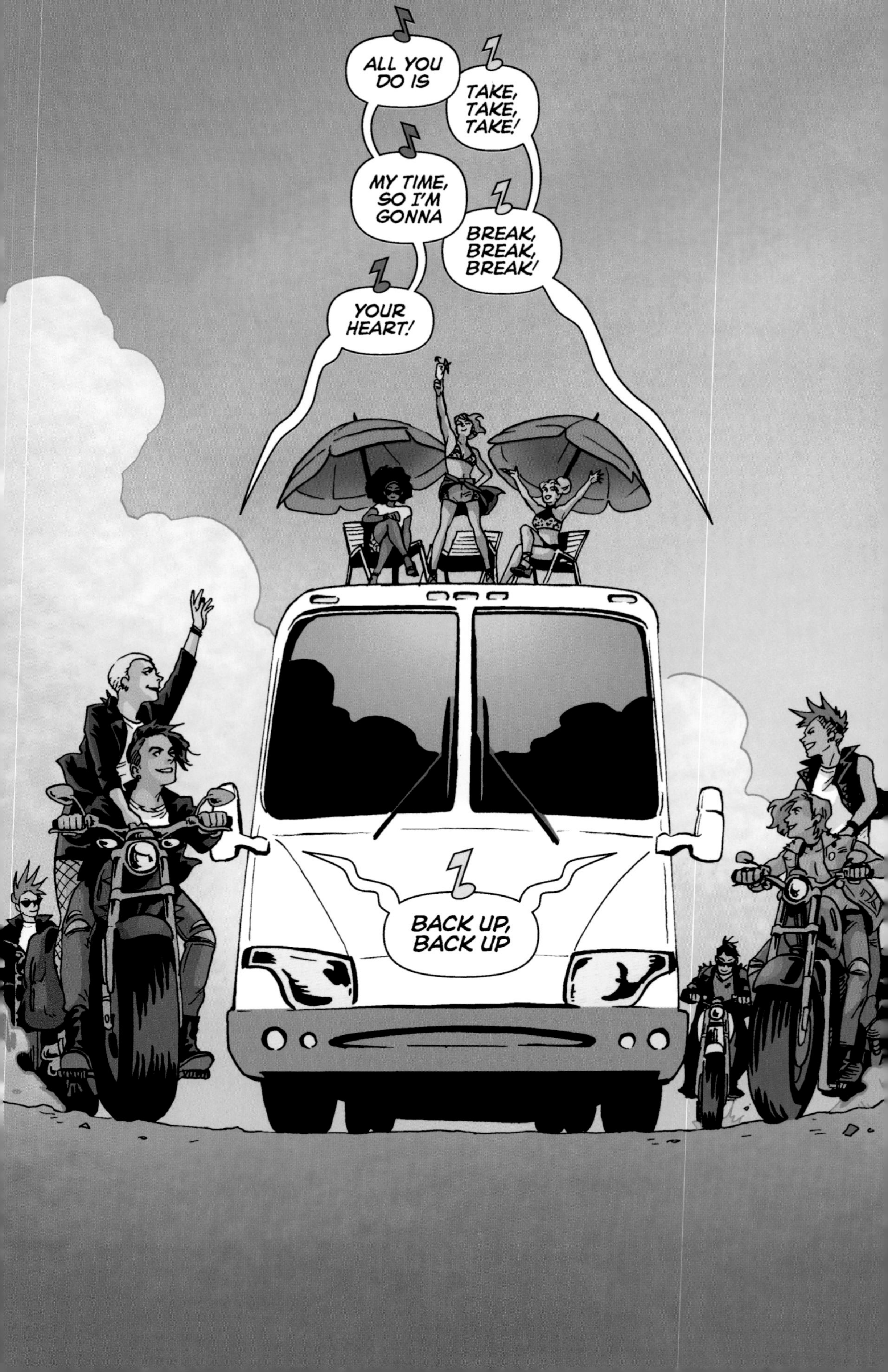
ALL YOU DO IS
TAKE, TAKE, TAKE!
MY TIME, SO I'M GONNA
BREAK, BREAK, BREAK!
YOUR HEART!
BACK UP, BACK UP

CATCH UP WITH THE ONGOING
JOSIE AND THE
PUSSYCATS
ON SALE NOW!

PREVIOUSLY IN THE TOWN OF RIVERDALE...

Reggie Mantle is the crowned prince of Riverdale High. He's well liked by everyone, he's got loads of friends, he throws the BEST parties around and he's got an awesome sidekick—his dog, Vader. And if ANYONE challenges to disrupt his status quo, they're going to pay for it.

Archie Andrews and Veronica Lodge have done just that when they decided to throw a party the same night as one of Reggie's infamous shindigs, causing everyone to bail on him and go to their party instead.

Now Reggie's got to make everyone who ditched him pay for their mistakes, with Archie Andrews landing himself at the top of Reggie's hit list!

STORY BY
TOM DeFALCO

ART BY
SANDY JARRELL

COLORING BY
KELLY FITZPATRICK

LETTERING BY
JACK MORELLI

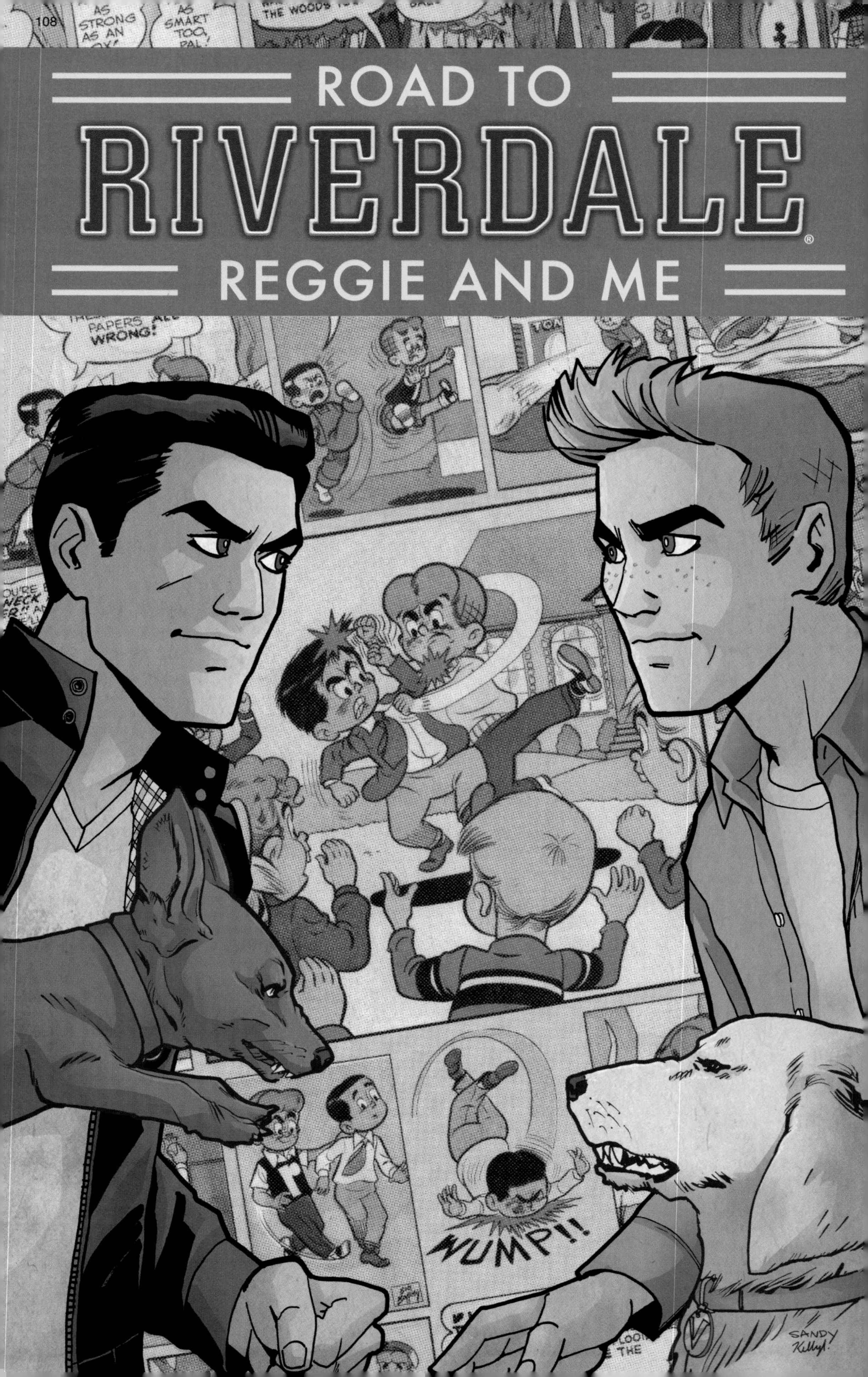
ROAD TO
RIVERDALE®
REGGIE AND ME
WUMP!!
SANDY Kelly!

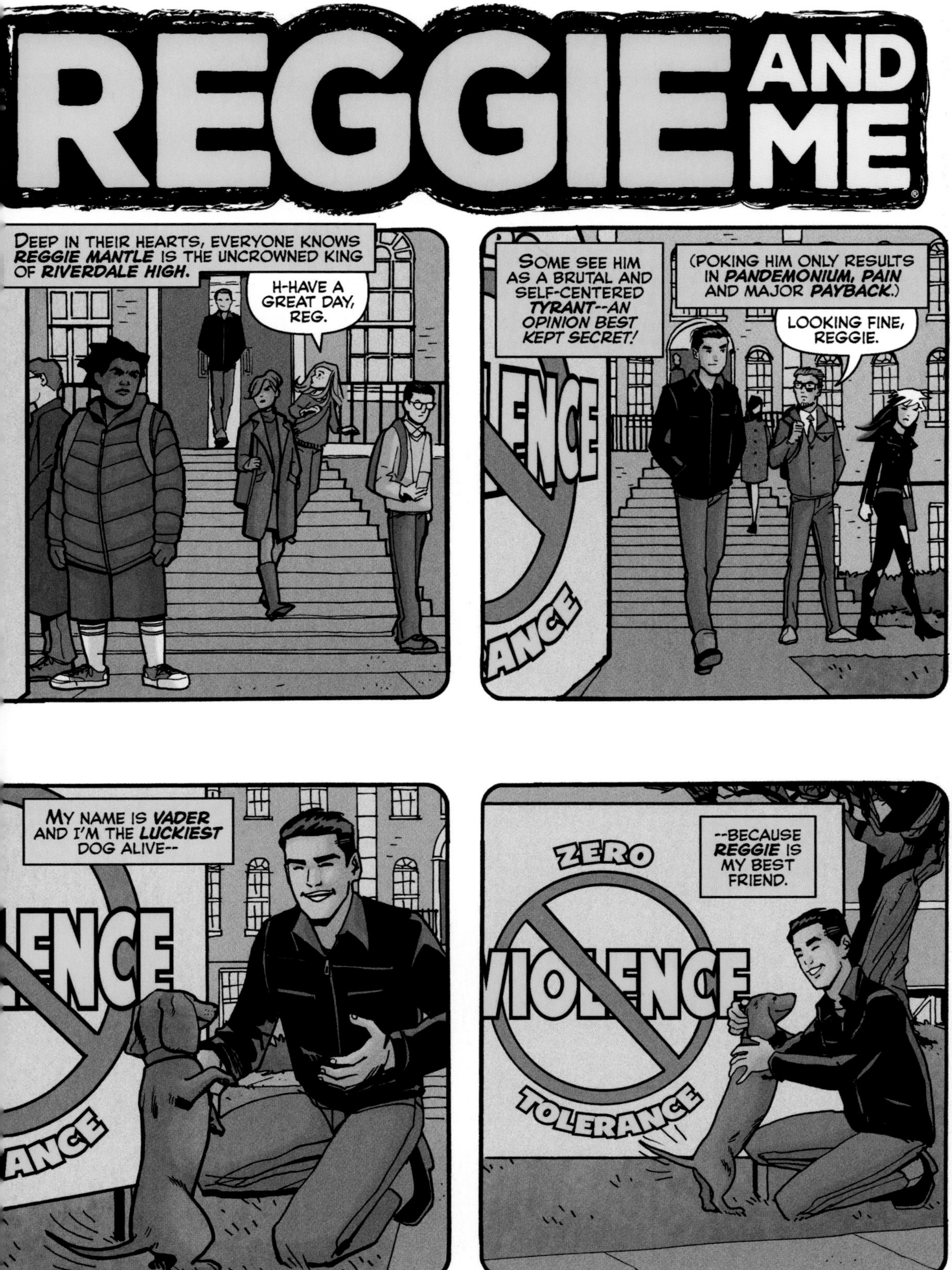
REGGIE AND ME
DEEP IN THEIR HEARTS, EVERYONE KNOWS REGGIE MANTLE IS THE UNCROWNED KING OF RIVERDALE HIGH.
H-HAVE A GREAT DAY, REG.
SOME SEE HIM AS A BRUTAL AND SELF-CENTERED TYRANT--AN OPINION BEST KEPT SECRET!
(POKING HIM ONLY RESULTS IN PANDEMONIUM, PAIN AND MAJOR PAYBACK.)
LOOKING FINE, REGGIE.
MY NAME IS VADER AND I'M THE LUCKIEST DOG ALIVE--
--BECAUSE REGGIE IS MY BEST FRIEND.
ZERO
VIOLENCE
TOLERANCE

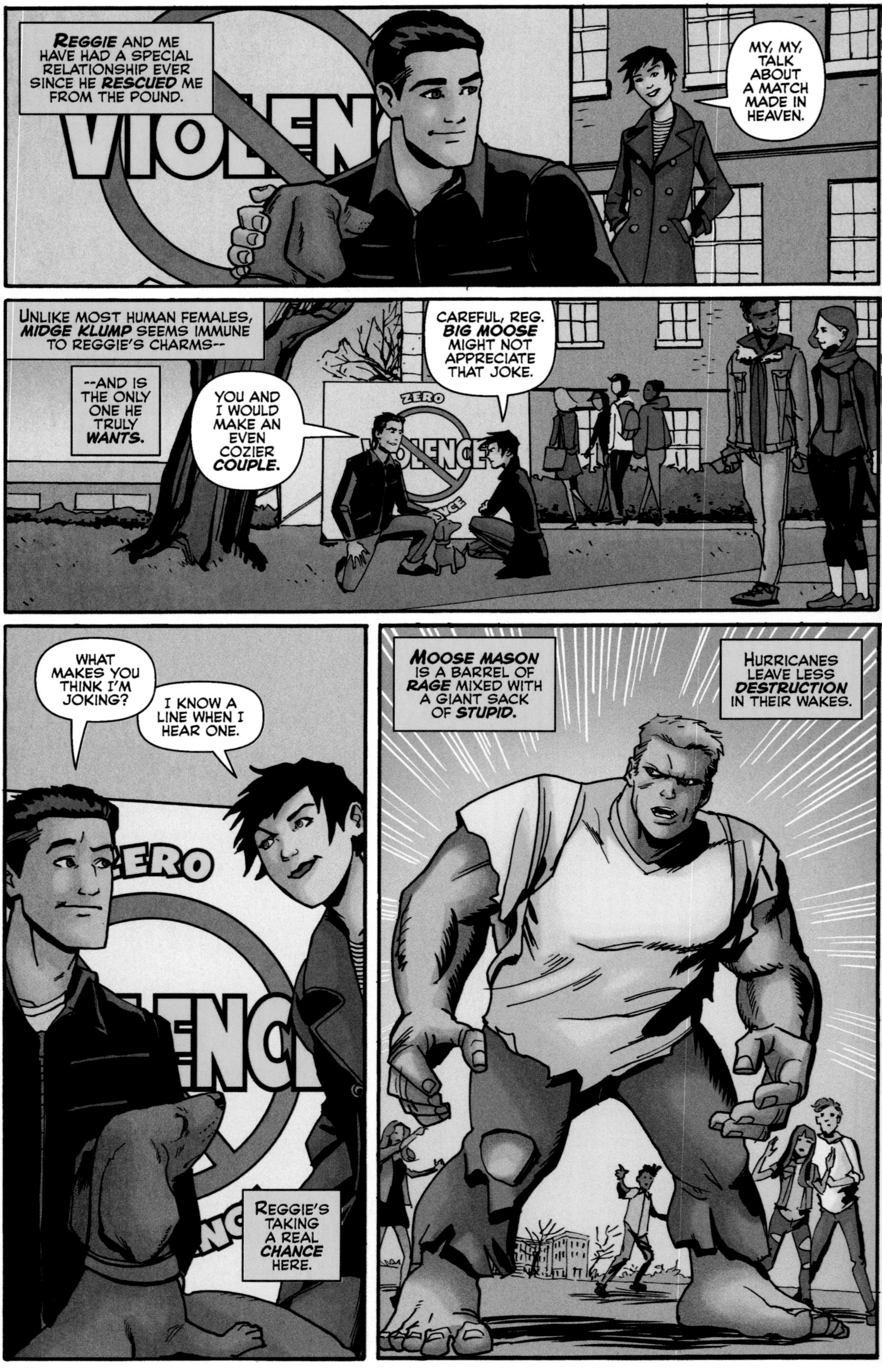
REGGIE AND ME HAVE HAD A SPECIAL RELATIONSHIP EVER SINCE HE RESCUED ME FROM THE POUND.
MY, MY, TALK ABOUT A MATCH MADE IN HEAVEN.
VIOLENC
UNLIKE MOST HUMAN FEMALES, MIDGE KLUMP SEEMS IMMUNE TO REGGIE'S CHARMS--
--AND IS THE ONLY ONE HE TRULY WANTS.
YOU AND I WOULD MAKE AN EVEN COZIER COUPLE.
CAREFUL, REG. BIG MOOSE MIGHT NOT APPRECIATE THAT JOKE.
ZERO
VIOLENCE
WHAT MAKES YOU THINK I'M JOKING?
I KNOW A LINE WHEN I HEAR ONE.
ZERO
LENC
REGGIE'S TAKING A REAL CHANCE HERE.
MOOSE MASON IS A BARREL OF RAGE MIXED WITH A GIANT SACK OF STUPID.
HURRICANES LEAVE LESS DESTRUCTION IN THEIR WAKES.

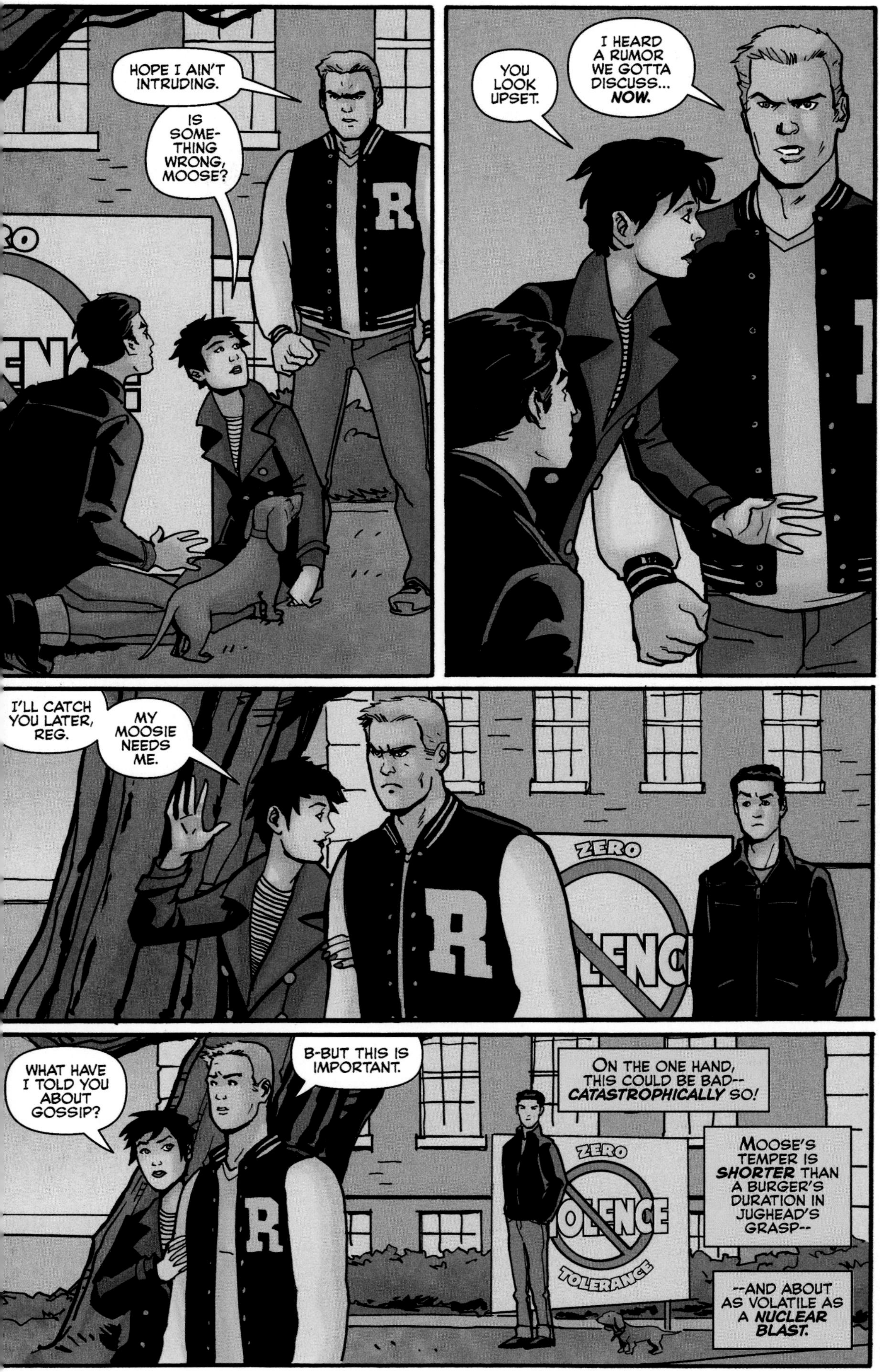
HOPE I AIN'T INTRUDING.
IS SOMETHING WRONG, MOOSE?
YOU LOOK UPSET.
I HEARD A RUMOR WE GOTTA DISCUSS... **NOW.**
I'LL CATCH YOU LATER, REG.
MY MOOSIE NEEDS ME.
ZERO
WHAT HAVE I TOLD YOU ABOUT GOSSIP?
B-BUT THIS IS IMPORTANT.
ON THE ONE HAND, THIS COULD BE BAD-- ***CATASTROPHICALLY*** SO!
ZERO
TOLERANCE
MOOSE'S TEMPER IS ***SHORTER*** THAN A BURGER'S DURATION IN JUGHEAD'S GRASP--
--AND ABOUT AS VOLATILE AS A ***NUCLEAR BLAST.***

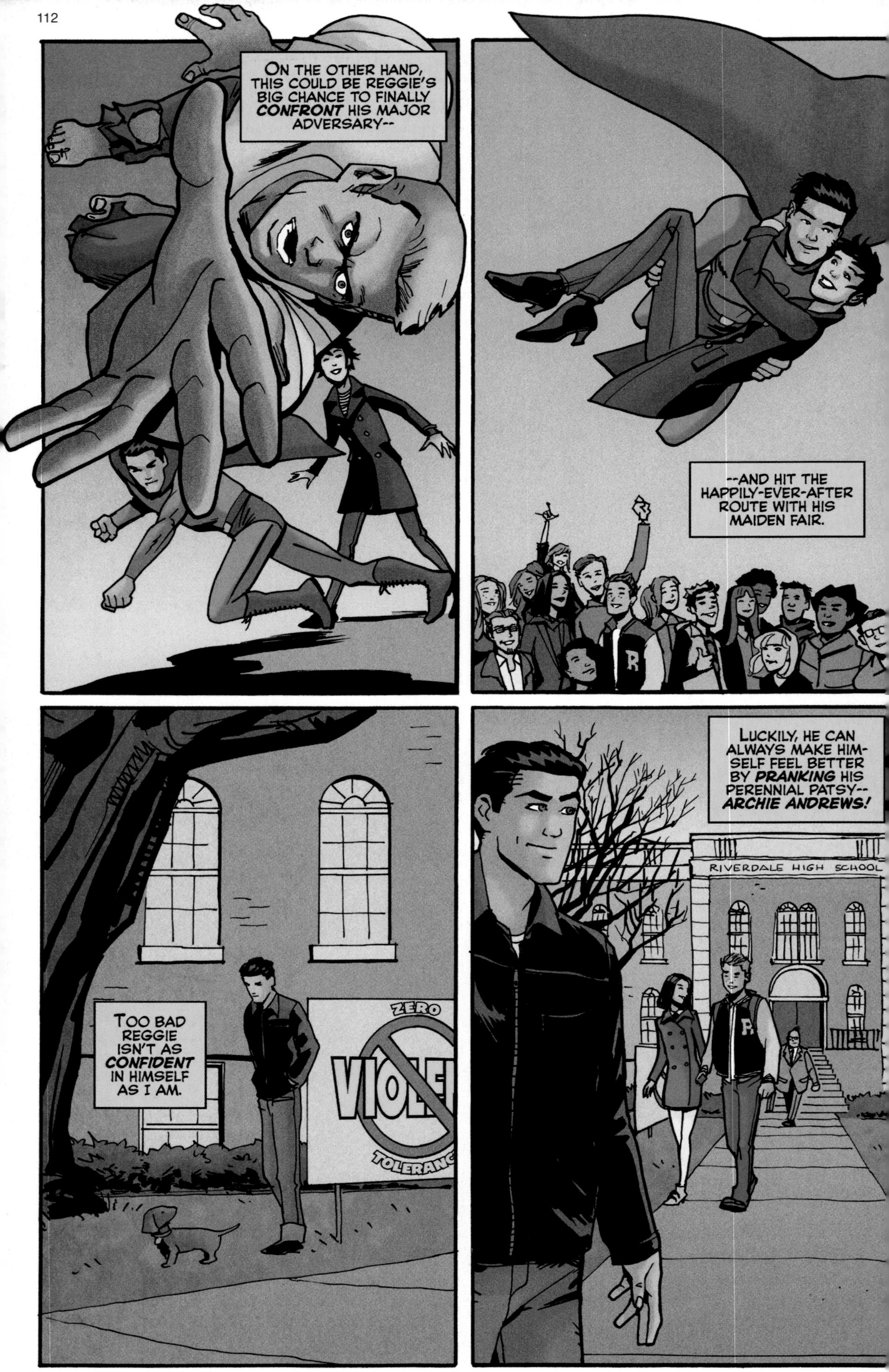
ON THE OTHER HAND, THIS COULD BE REGGIE'S BIG CHANCE TO FINALLY *CONFRONT* HIS MAJOR ADVERSARY--
--AND HIT THE HAPPILY-EVER-AFTER ROUTE WITH HIS MAIDEN FAIR.
TOO BAD REGGIE ISN'T AS *CONFIDENT* IN HIMSELF AS I AM.
ZERO
VIOLE
TOLERANC
LUCKILY, HE CAN ALWAYS MAKE HIMSELF FEEL BETTER BY *PRANKING* HIS PERENNIAL PATSY-- *ARCHIE ANDREWS!*
RIVERDALE HIGH SCHOOL

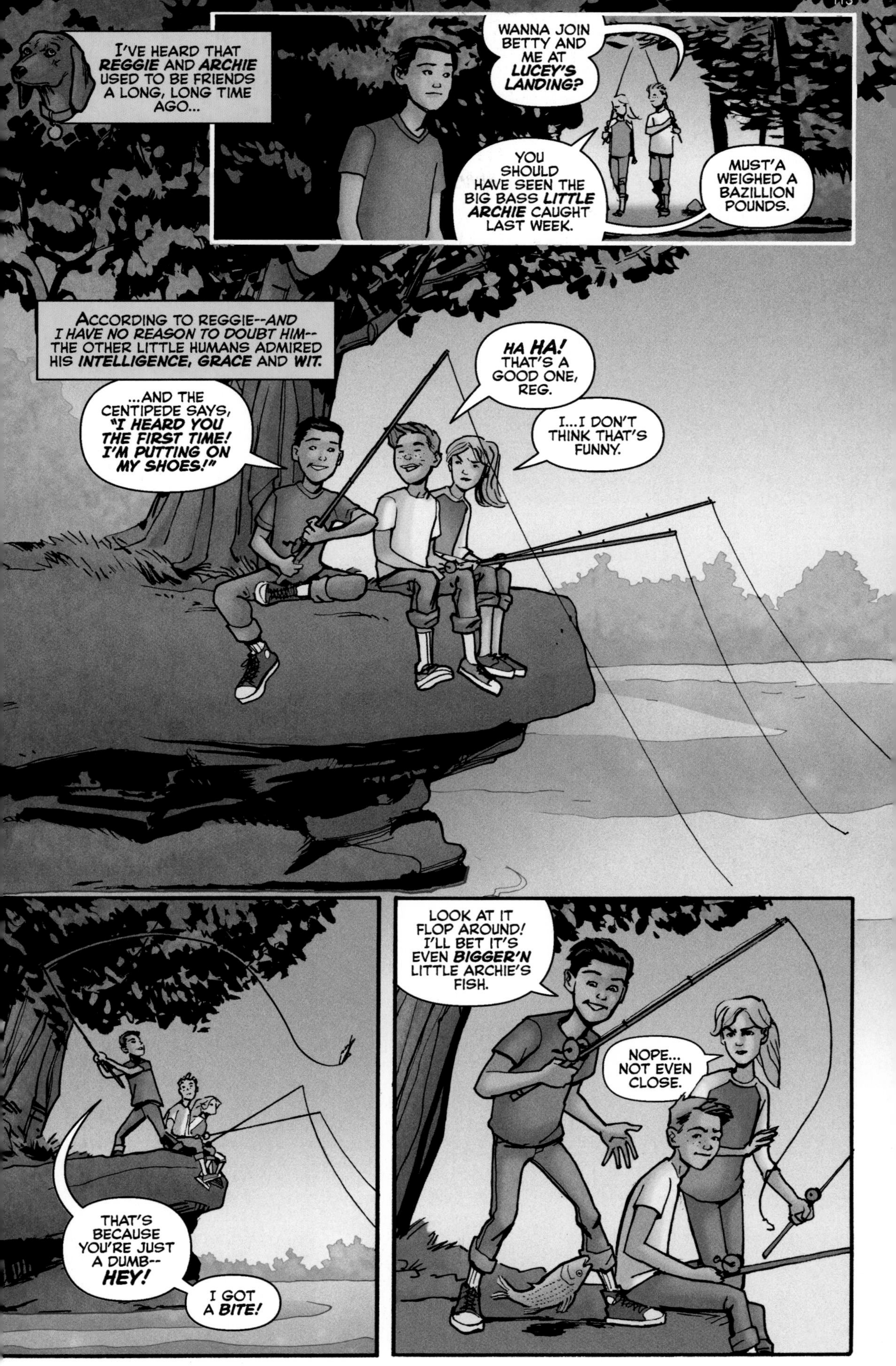
I'VE HEARD THAT REGGIE AND ARCHIE USED TO BE FRIENDS A LONG, LONG TIME AGO...
WANNA JOIN BETTY AND ME AT LUCEY'S LANDING?
YOU SHOULD HAVE SEEN THE BIG BASS LITTLE ARCHIE CAUGHT LAST WEEK.
MUST'A WEIGHED A BAZILLION POUNDS.
ACCORDING TO REGGIE--AND I HAVE NO REASON TO DOUBT HIM--THE OTHER LITTLE HUMANS ADMIRED HIS INTELLIGENCE, GRACE AND WIT.
...AND THE CENTIPEDE SAYS, "I HEARD YOU THE FIRST TIME! I'M PUTTING ON MY SHOES!"
HA HA! THAT'S A GOOD ONE, REG.
I...I DON'T THINK THAT'S FUNNY.
THAT'S BECAUSE YOU'RE JUST A DUMB-- HEY!
I GOT A BITE!
LOOK AT IT FLOP AROUND! I'LL BET IT'S EVEN BIGGER'N LITTLE ARCHIE'S FISH.
NOPE... NOT EVEN CLOSE.

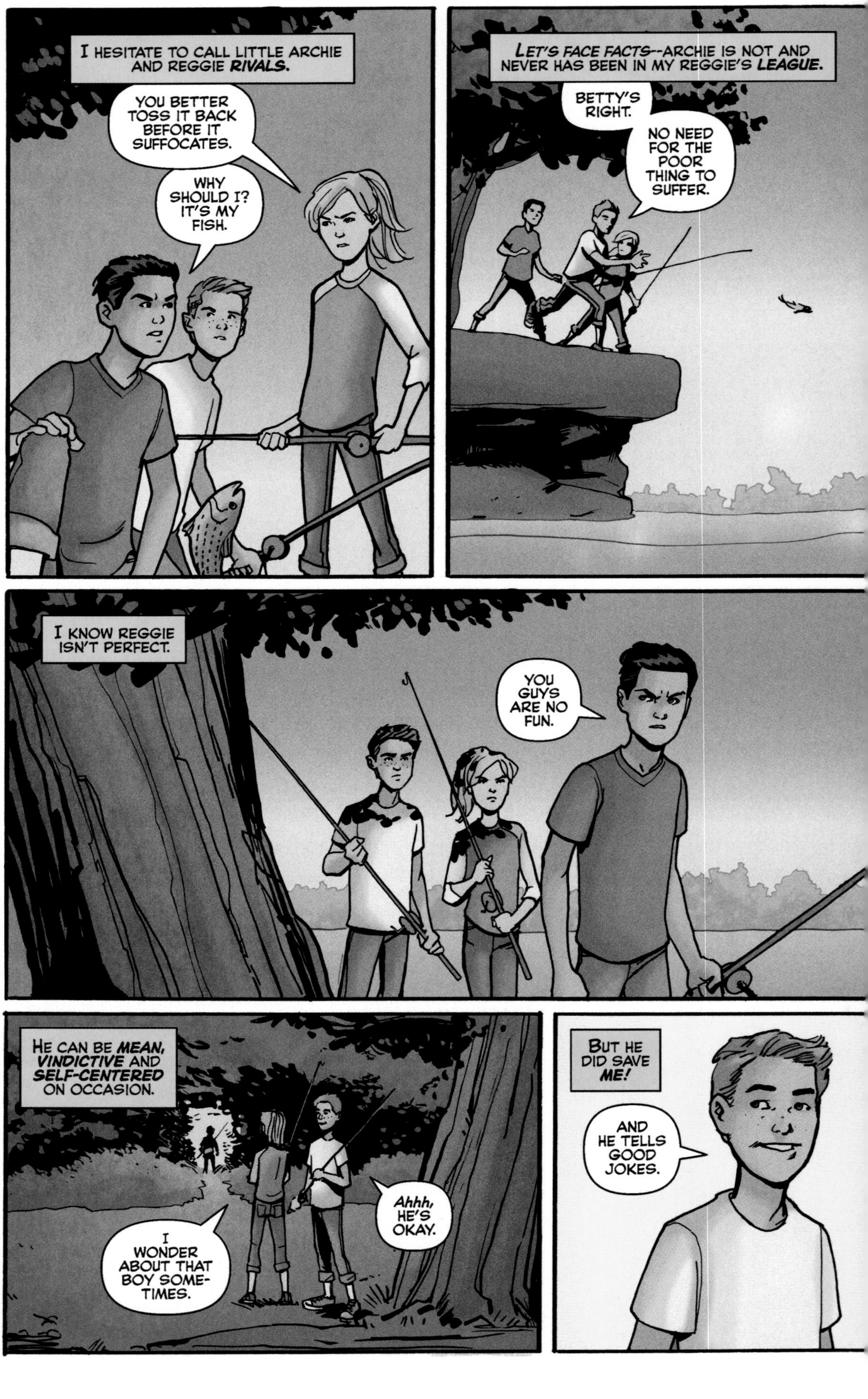

I HESITATE TO CALL LITTLE ARCHIE AND REGGIE *RIVALS.*
YOU BETTER TOSS IT BACK BEFORE IT SUFFOCATES.
WHY SHOULD I? IT'S MY FISH.
LET'S FACE FACTS--ARCHIE IS NOT AND NEVER HAS BEEN IN MY REGGIE'S *LEAGUE.*
BETTY'S RIGHT.
NO NEED FOR THE POOR THING TO SUFFER.
I KNOW REGGIE ISN'T PERFECT.
YOU GUYS ARE NO FUN.
HE CAN BE *MEAN, VINDICTIVE* AND *SELF-CENTERED* ON OCCASION.
I WONDER ABOUT THAT BOY SOME-TIMES.
Ahhh, HE'S OKAY.
BUT HE DID SAVE *ME!*
AND HE TELLS GOOD JOKES.

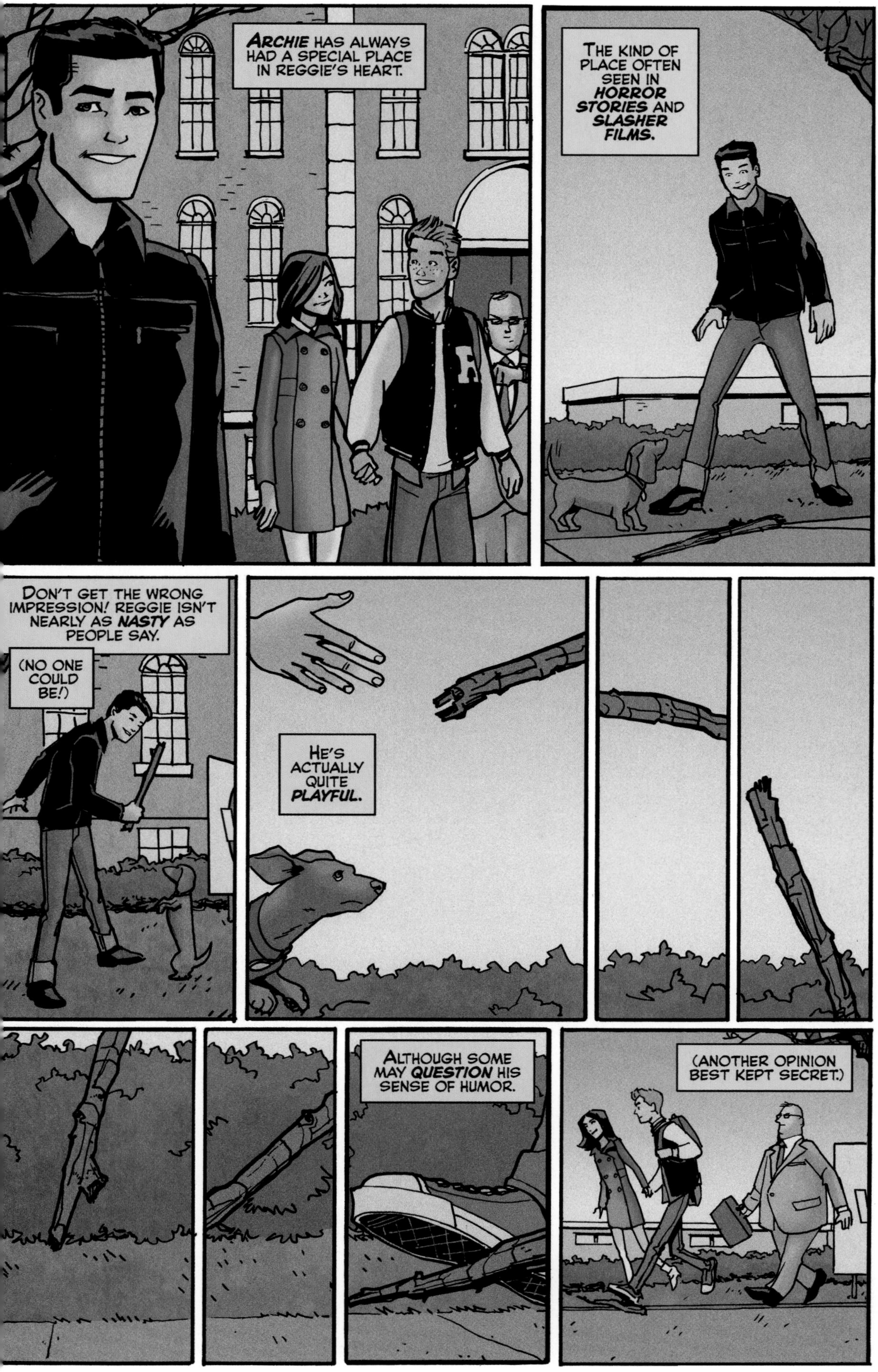
ARCHIE HAS ALWAYS HAD A SPECIAL PLACE IN REGGIE'S HEART.
THE KIND OF PLACE OFTEN SEEN IN HORROR STORIES AND SLASHER FILMS.
DON'T GET THE WRONG IMPRESSION! REGGIE ISN'T NEARLY AS NASTY AS PEOPLE SAY.
(NO ONE COULD BE!)
HE'S ACTUALLY QUITE PLAYFUL.
ALTHOUGH SOME MAY QUESTION HIS SENSE OF HUMOR.
(ANOTHER OPINION BEST KEPT SECRET.)

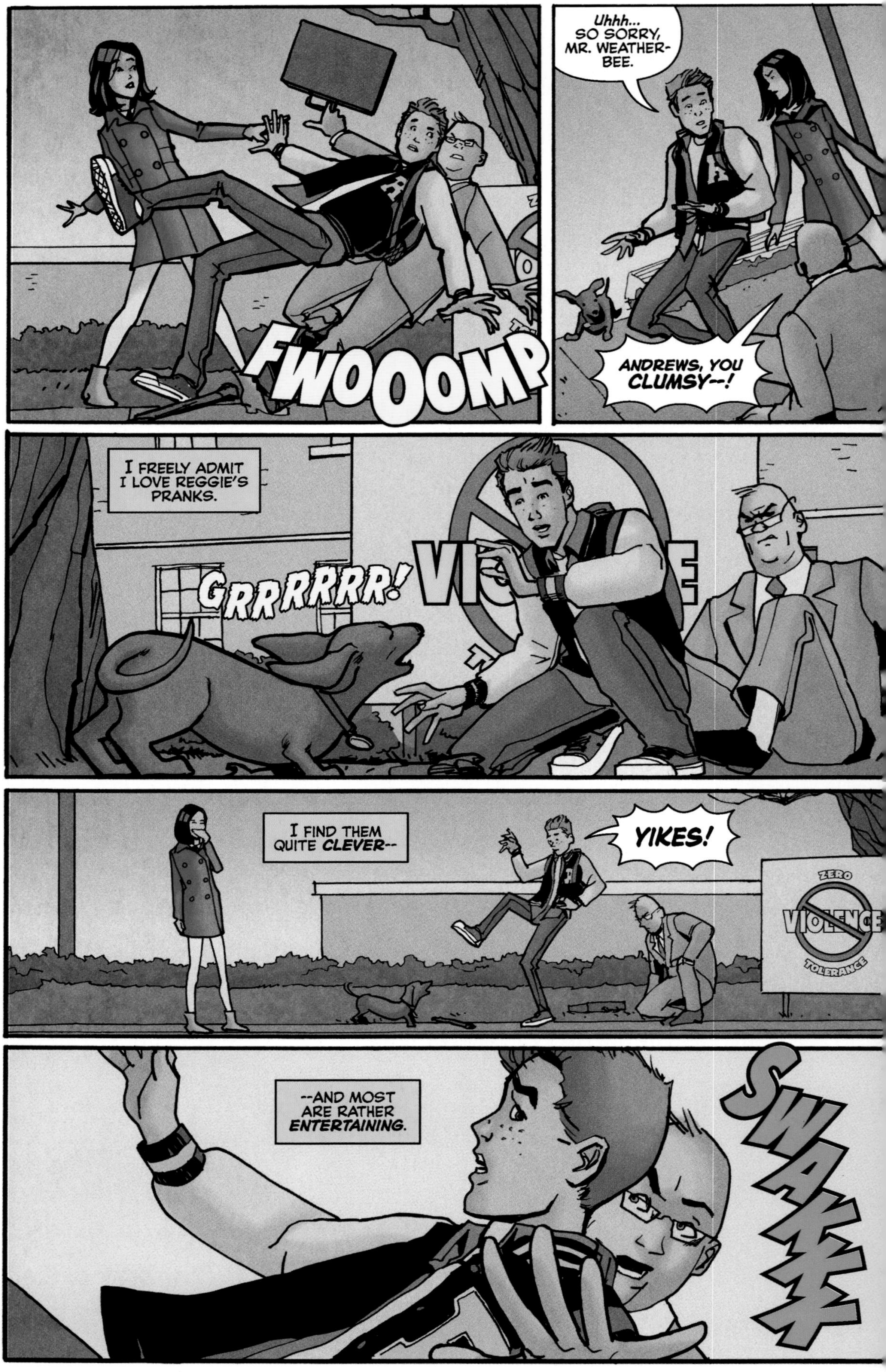
FWOOOMP
Uhhh... SO SORRY, MR. WEATHER-BEE.
ANDREWS, YOU CLUMSY--!
I FREELY ADMIT I LOVE REGGIE'S PRANKS.
GRRRRRR!
I FIND THEM QUITE CLEVER--
YIKES!
ZERO
VIOLENCE
TOLERANCE
--AND MOST ARE RATHER ENTERTAINING.
SWAKK

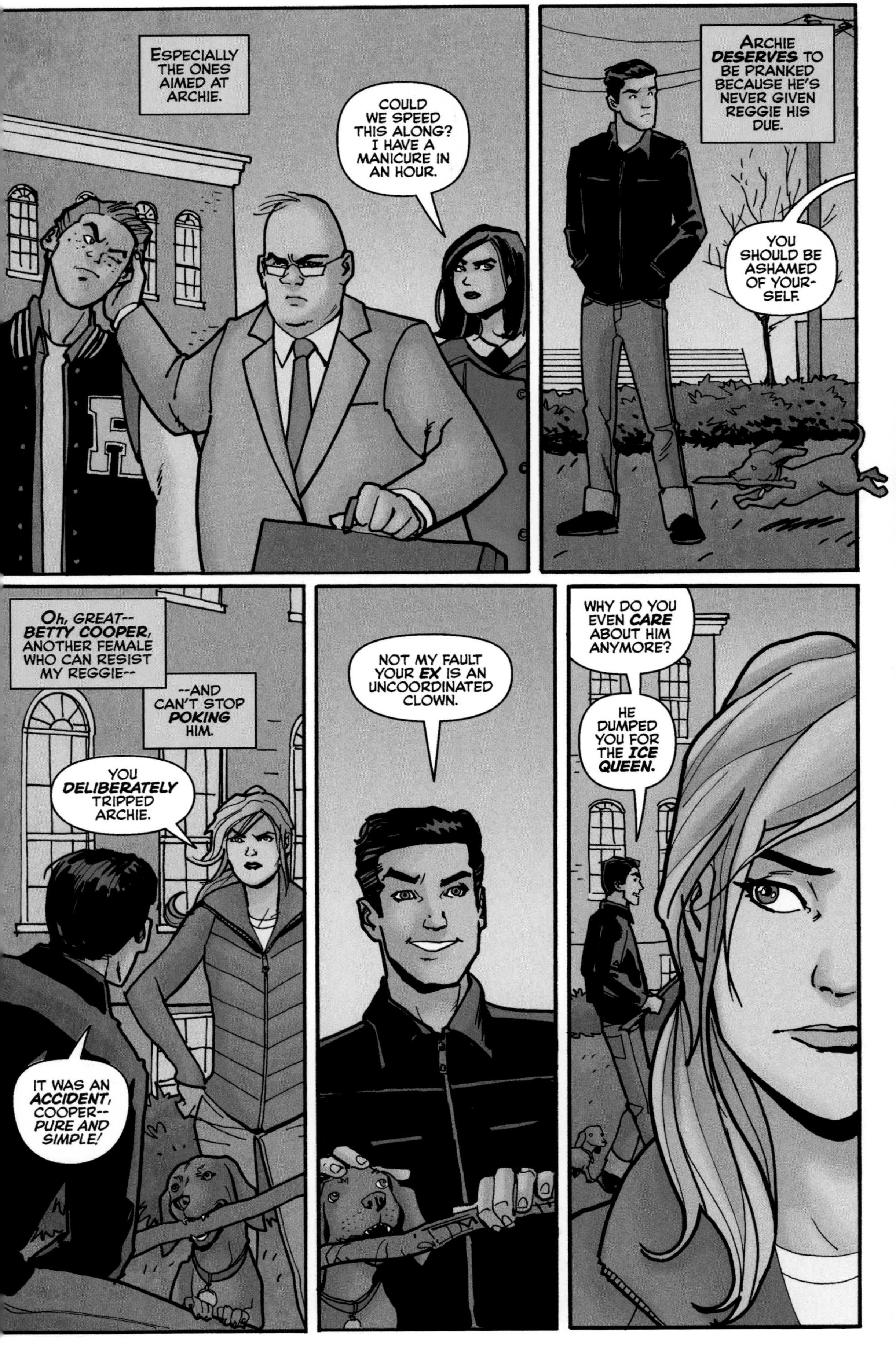
ESPECIALLY THE ONES AIMED AT ARCHIE.
COULD WE SPEED THIS ALONG? I HAVE A MANICURE IN AN HOUR.
ARCHIE DESERVES TO BE PRANKED BECAUSE HE'S NEVER GIVEN REGGIE HIS DUE.
YOU SHOULD BE ASHAMED OF YOURSELF.
Oh, GREAT-- BETTY COOPER, ANOTHER FEMALE WHO CAN RESIST MY REGGIE--
--AND CAN'T STOP POKING HIM.
YOU DELIBERATELY TRIPPED ARCHIE.
IT WAS AN ACCIDENT, COOPER-- PURE AND SIMPLE!
NOT MY FAULT YOUR EX IS AN UNCOORDINATED CLOWN.
WHY DO YOU EVEN CARE ABOUT HIM ANYMORE?
HE DUMPED YOU FOR THE ICE QUEEN.

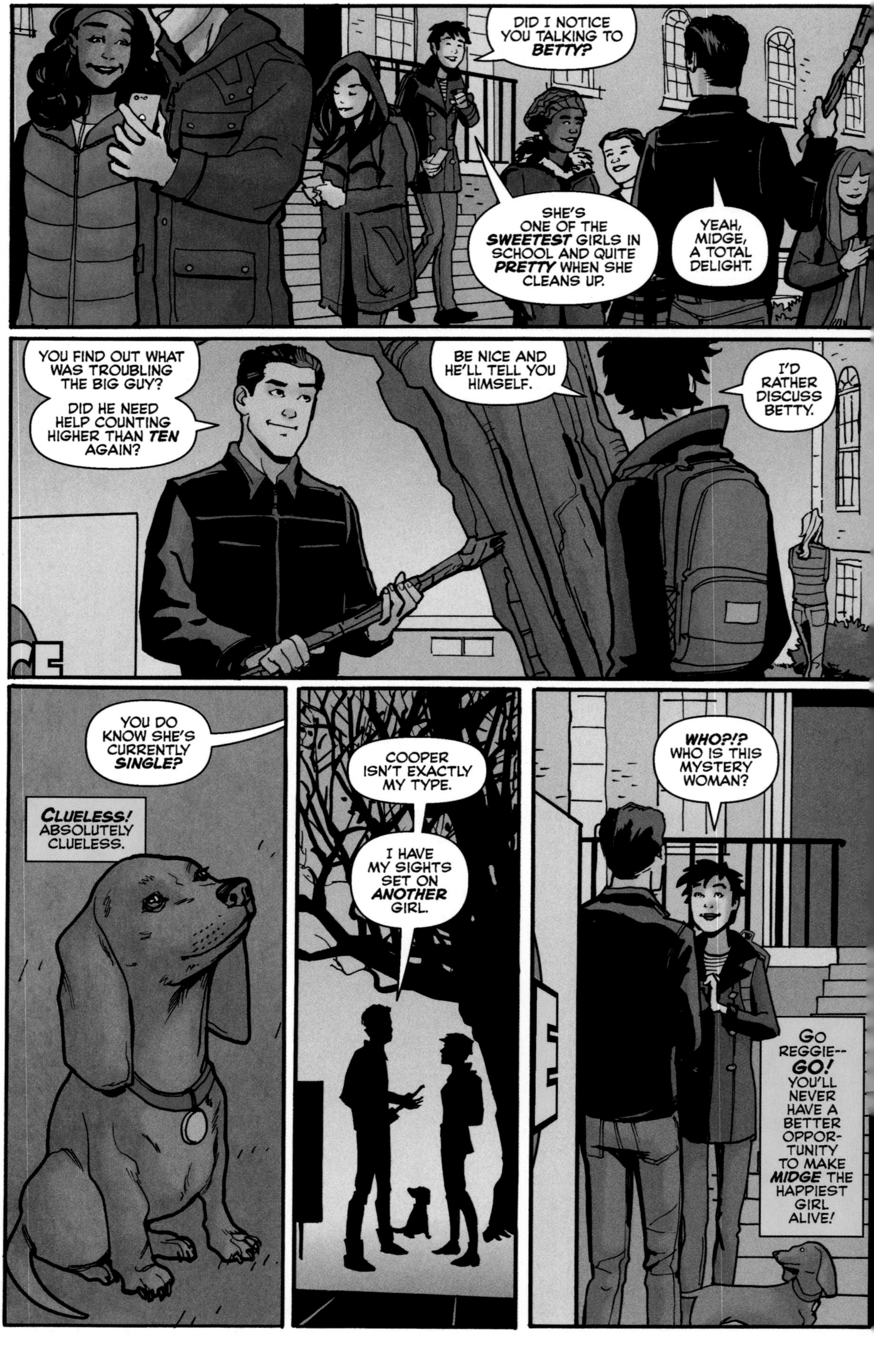
DID I NOTICE YOU TALKING TO BETTY?
SHE'S ONE OF THE SWEETEST GIRLS IN SCHOOL AND QUITE PRETTY WHEN SHE CLEANS UP.
YEAH, MIDGE, A TOTAL DELIGHT.
YOU FIND OUT WHAT WAS TROUBLING THE BIG GUY?
DID HE NEED HELP COUNTING HIGHER THAN TEN AGAIN?
BE NICE AND HE'LL TELL YOU HIMSELF.
I'D RATHER DISCUSS BETTY.
YOU DO KNOW SHE'S CURRENTLY SINGLE?
CLUELESS! ABSOLUTELY CLUELESS.
COOPER ISN'T EXACTLY MY TYPE.
I HAVE MY SIGHTS SET ON ANOTHER GIRL.
WHO?!? WHO IS THIS MYSTERY WOMAN?
GO REGGIE-- GO! YOU'LL NEVER HAVE A BETTER OPPOR-TUNITY TO MAKE MIDGE THE HAPPIEST GIRL ALIVE!

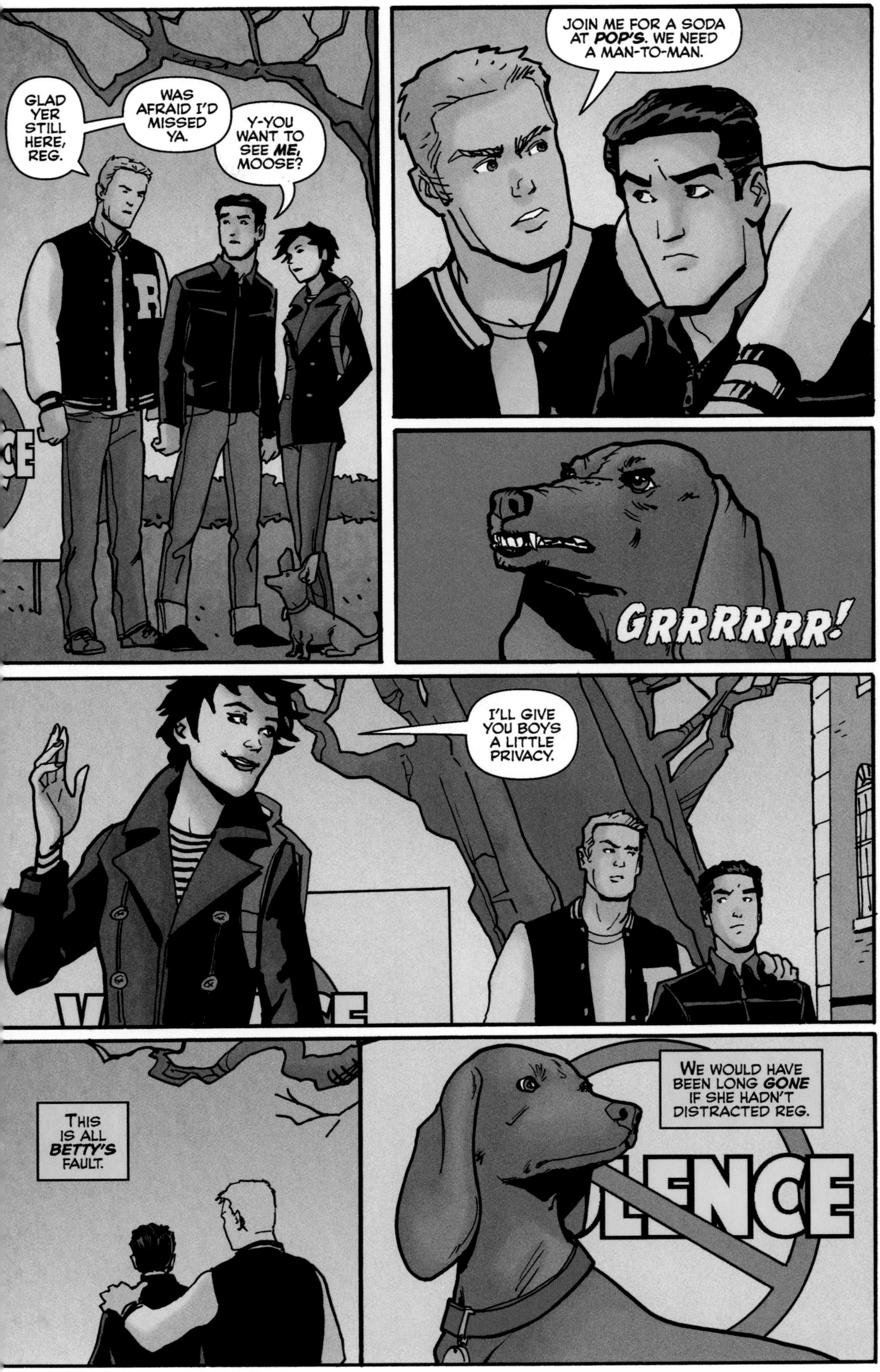
GLAD YER STILL HERE, REG.
WAS AFRAID I'D MISSED YA.
Y-YOU WANT TO SEE ME, MOOSE?
JOIN ME FOR A SODA AT POP'S. WE NEED A MAN-TO-MAN.
GRRRRRRR!
I'LL GIVE YOU BOYS A LITTLE PRIVACY.
THIS IS ALL BETTY'S FAULT.
WE WOULD HAVE BEEN LONG GONE IF SHE HADN'T DISTRACTED REG.
LENCE

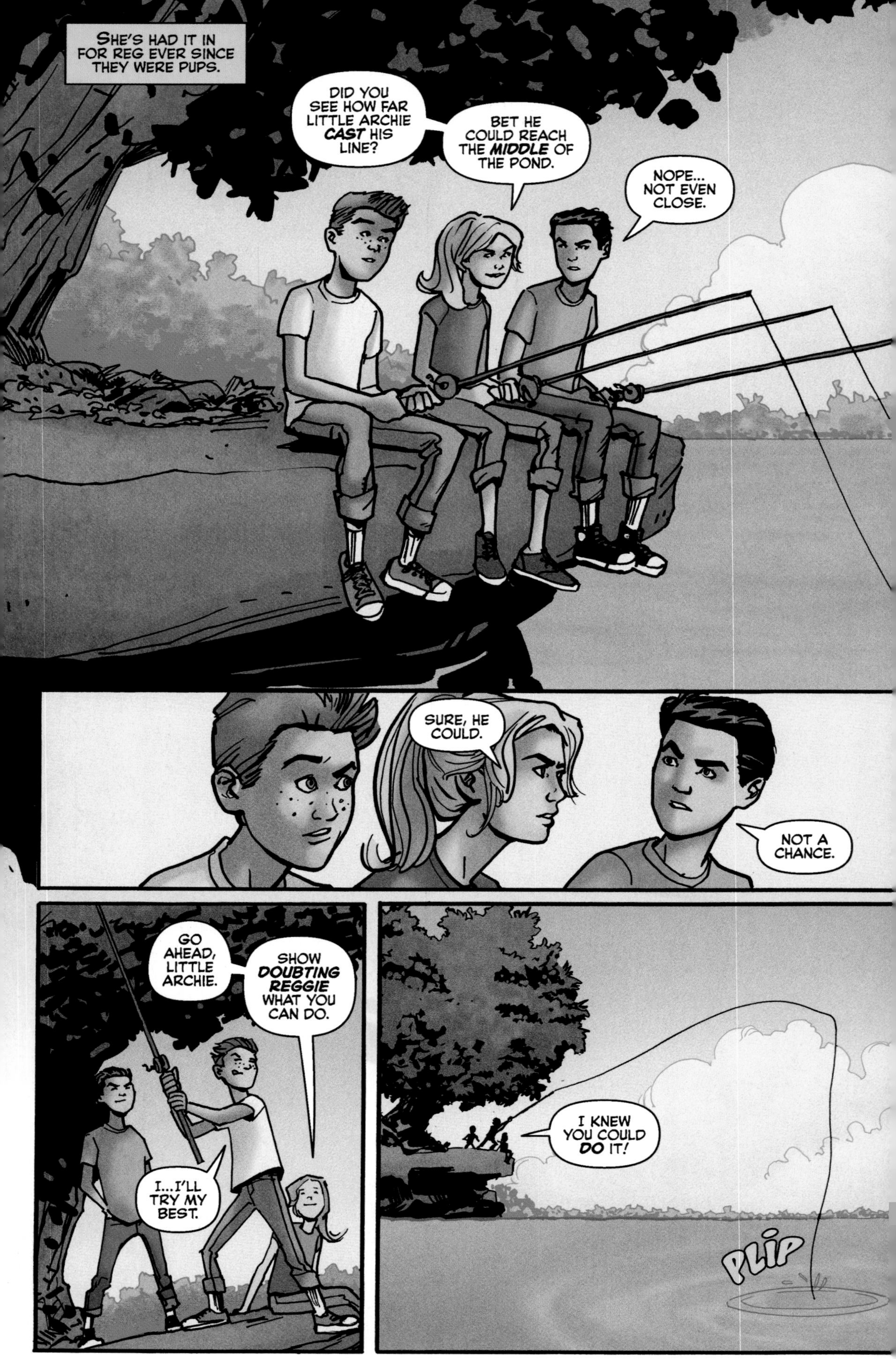
SHE'S HAD IT IN FOR REG EVER SINCE THEY WERE PUPS.
DID YOU SEE HOW FAR LITTLE ARCHIE CAST HIS LINE?
BET HE COULD REACH THE MIDDLE OF THE POND.
NOPE... NOT EVEN CLOSE.
SURE, HE COULD.
NOT A CHANCE.
GO AHEAD, LITTLE ARCHIE.
SHOW DOUBTING REGGIE WHAT YOU CAN DO.
I...I'LL TRY MY BEST.
I KNEW YOU COULD DO IT!
PLIP

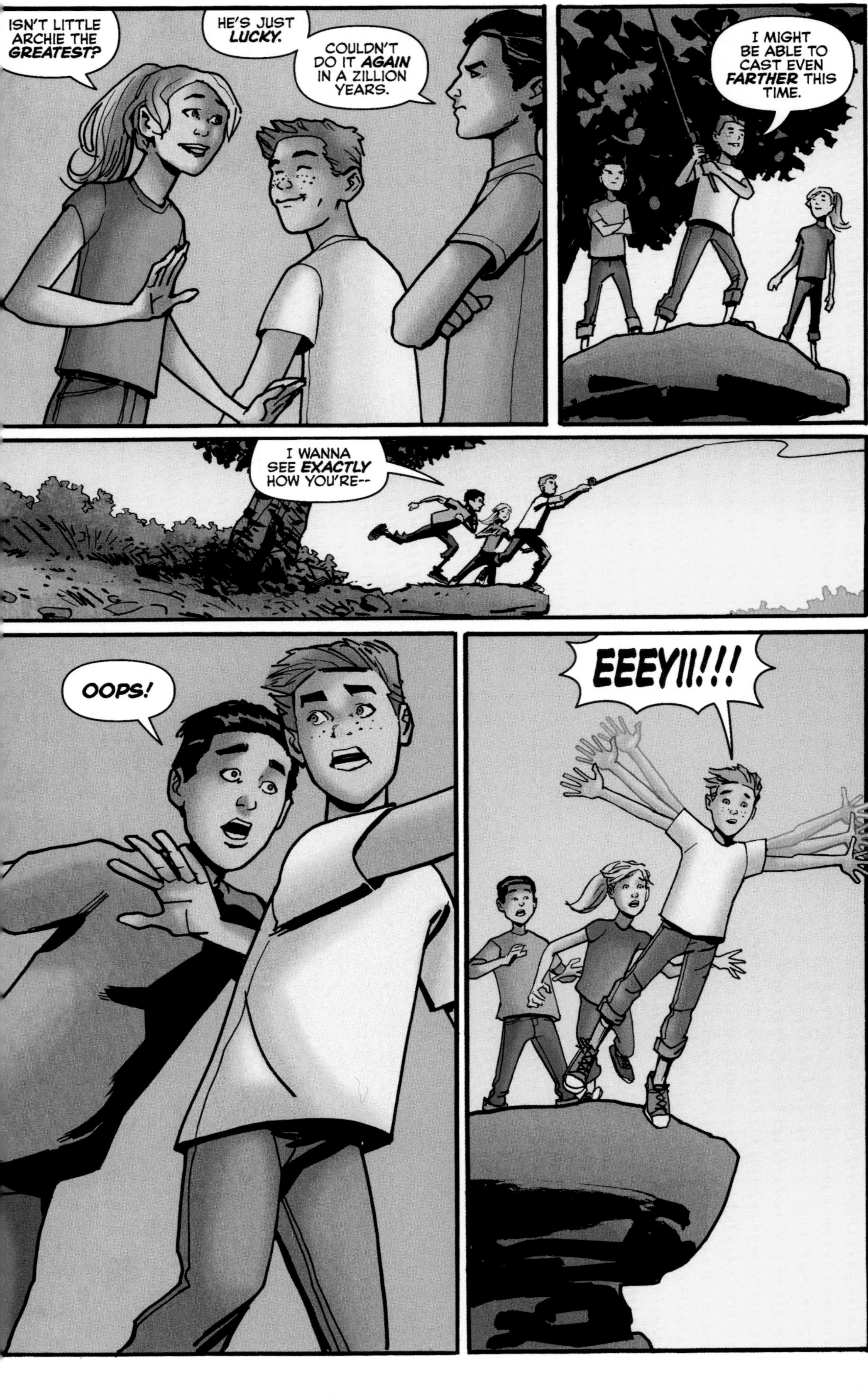
ISN'T LITTLE ARCHIE THE GREATEST?
HE'S JUST LUCKY.
COULDN'T DO IT AGAIN IN A ZILLION YEARS.
I MIGHT BE ABLE TO CAST EVEN FARTHER THIS TIME.
I WANNA SEE EXACTLY HOW YOU'RE--
OOPS!
EEEYII!!!

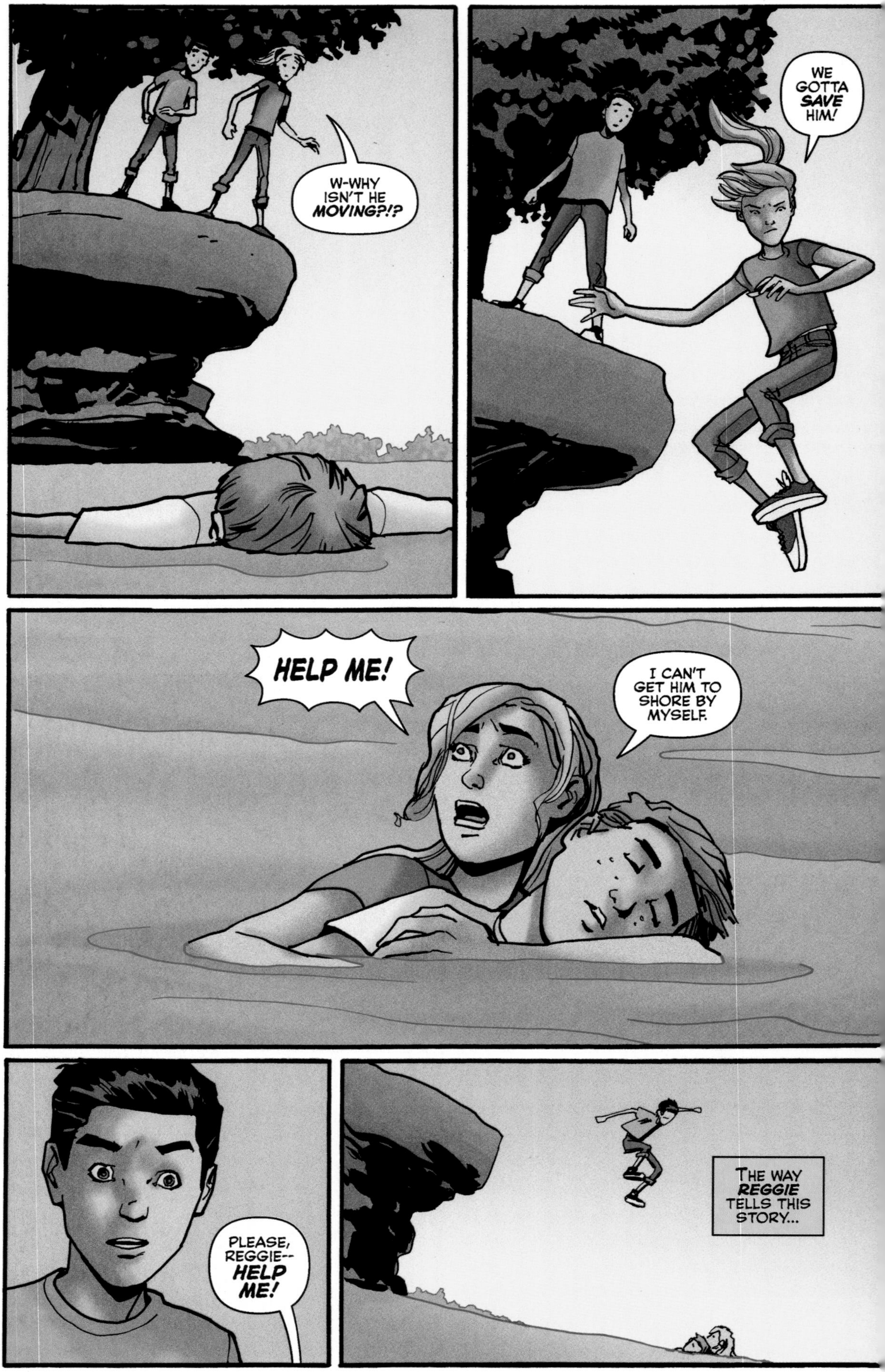
W-WHY ISN'T HE MOVING?!?
WE GOTTA SAVE HIM!
HELP ME!
I CAN'T GET HIM TO SHORE BY MYSELF.
PLEASE, REGGIE-- HELP ME!
THE WAY REGGIE TELLS THIS STORY...

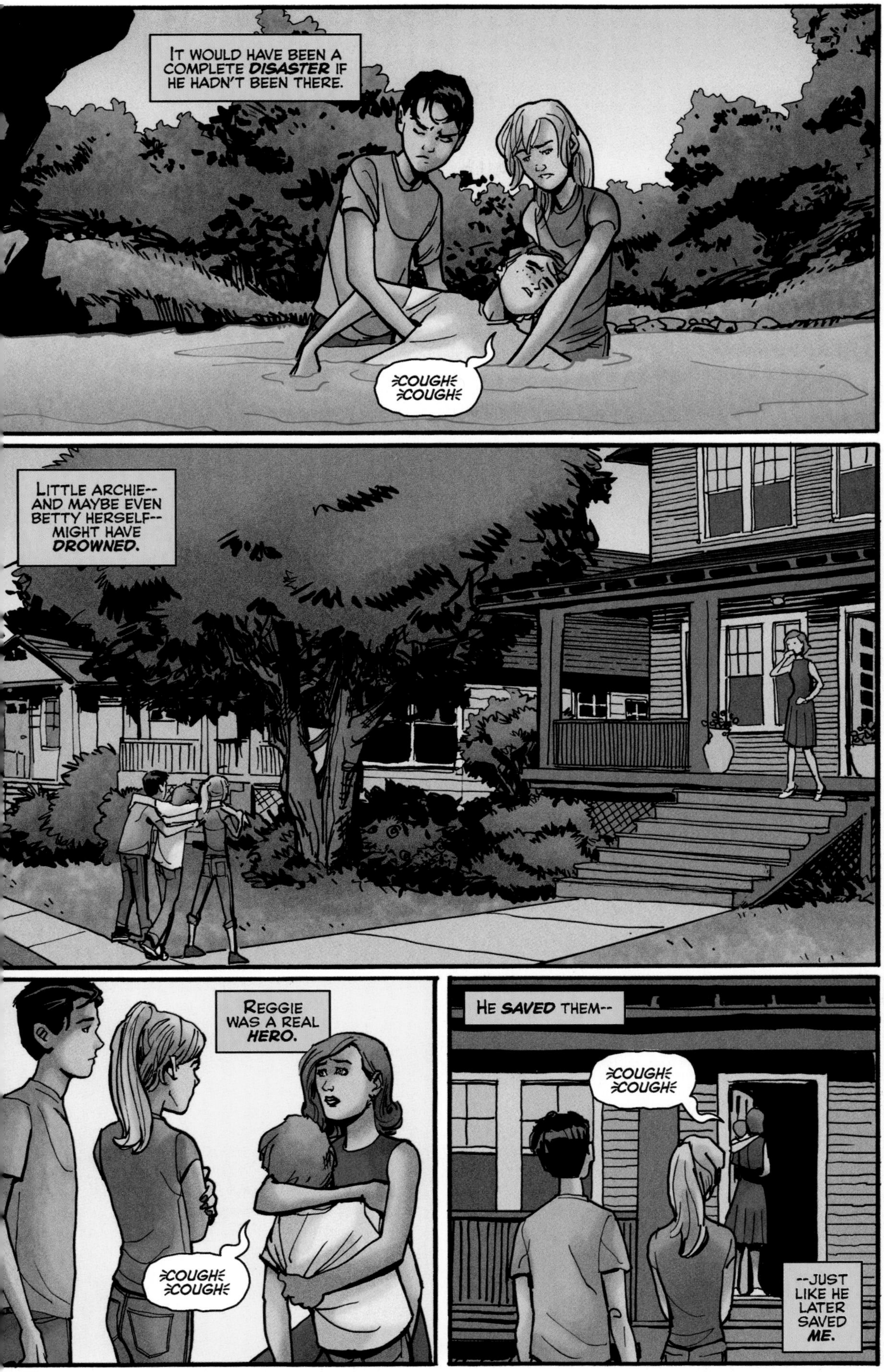
IT WOULD HAVE BEEN A COMPLETE DISASTER IF HE HADN'T BEEN THERE.
≽COUGH≼ ≽COUGH≼
LITTLE ARCHIE-- AND MAYBE EVEN BETTY HERSELF-- MIGHT HAVE DROWNED.
REGGIE WAS A REAL HERO.
≽COUGH≼ ≽COUGH≼
HE SAVED THEM--
≽COUGH≼ ≽COUGH≼
--JUST LIKE HE LATER SAVED ME.

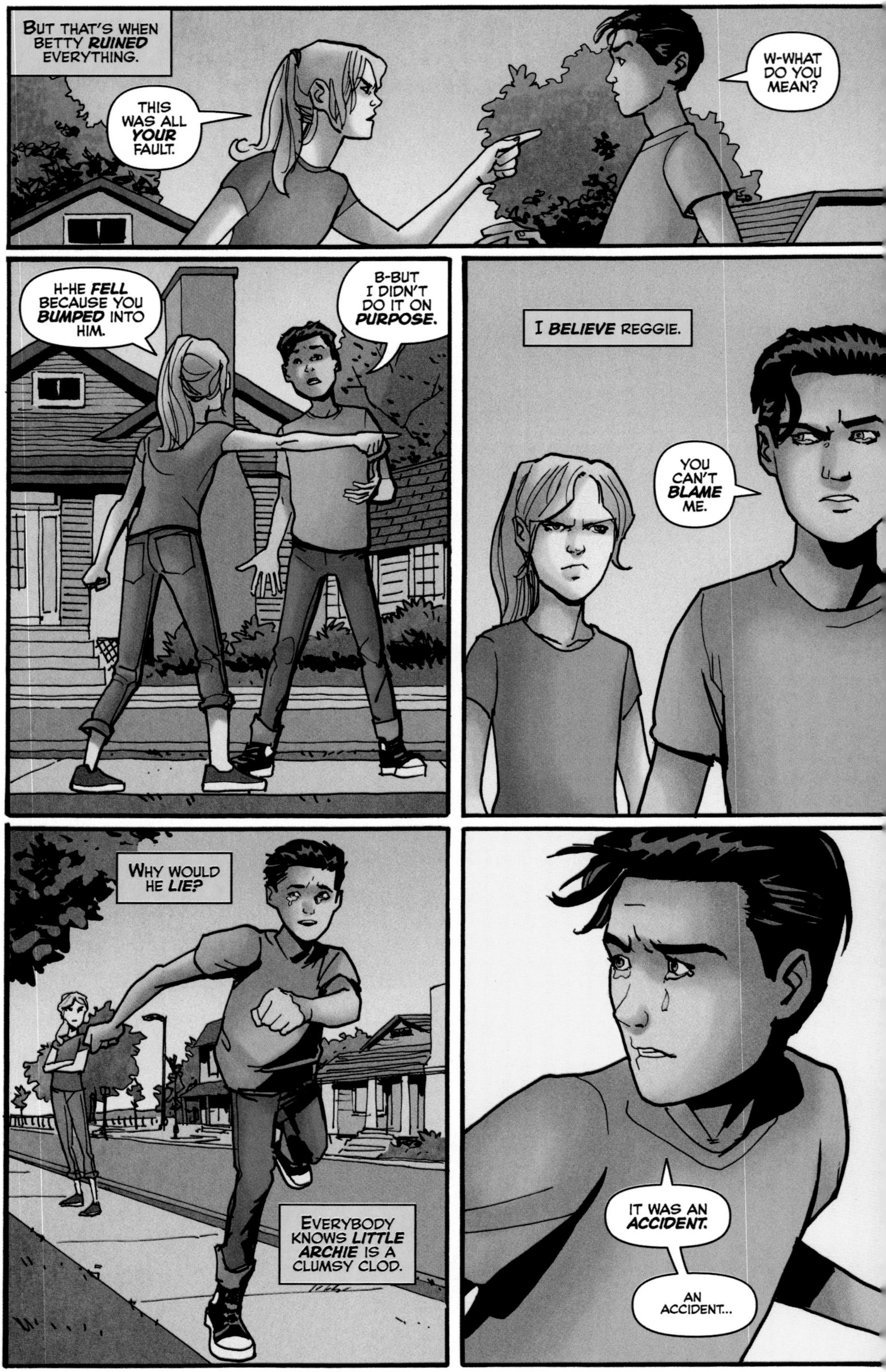
BUT THAT'S WHEN BETTY RUINED EVERYTHING.
THIS WAS ALL YOUR FAULT.
W-WHAT DO YOU MEAN?
H-HE FELL BECAUSE YOU BUMPED INTO HIM.
B-BUT I DIDN'T DO IT ON PURPOSE.
I BELIEVE REGGIE.
YOU CAN'T BLAME ME.
WHY WOULD HE LIE?
EVERYBODY KNOWS LITTLE ARCHIE IS A CLUMSY CLOD.
IT WAS AN ACCIDENT.
AN ACCIDENT...

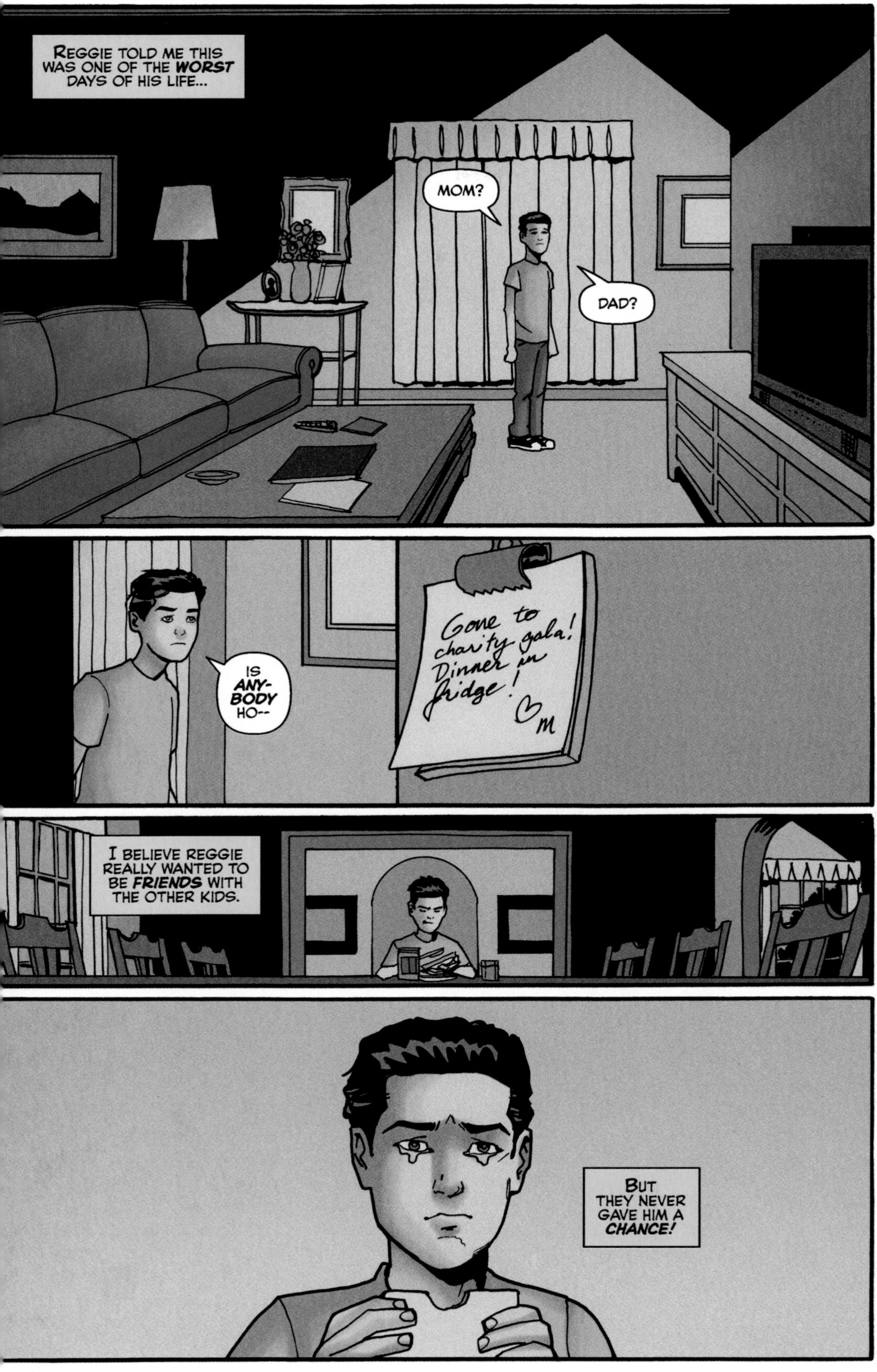
REGGIE TOLD ME THIS WAS ONE OF THE WORST DAYS OF HIS LIFE...
MOM?
DAD?
IS ANY-BODY HO--
Gone to charity gala! Dinner in fridge! M
I BELIEVE REGGIE REALLY WANTED TO BE FRIENDS WITH THE OTHER KIDS.
BUT THEY NEVER GAVE HIM A CHANCE!

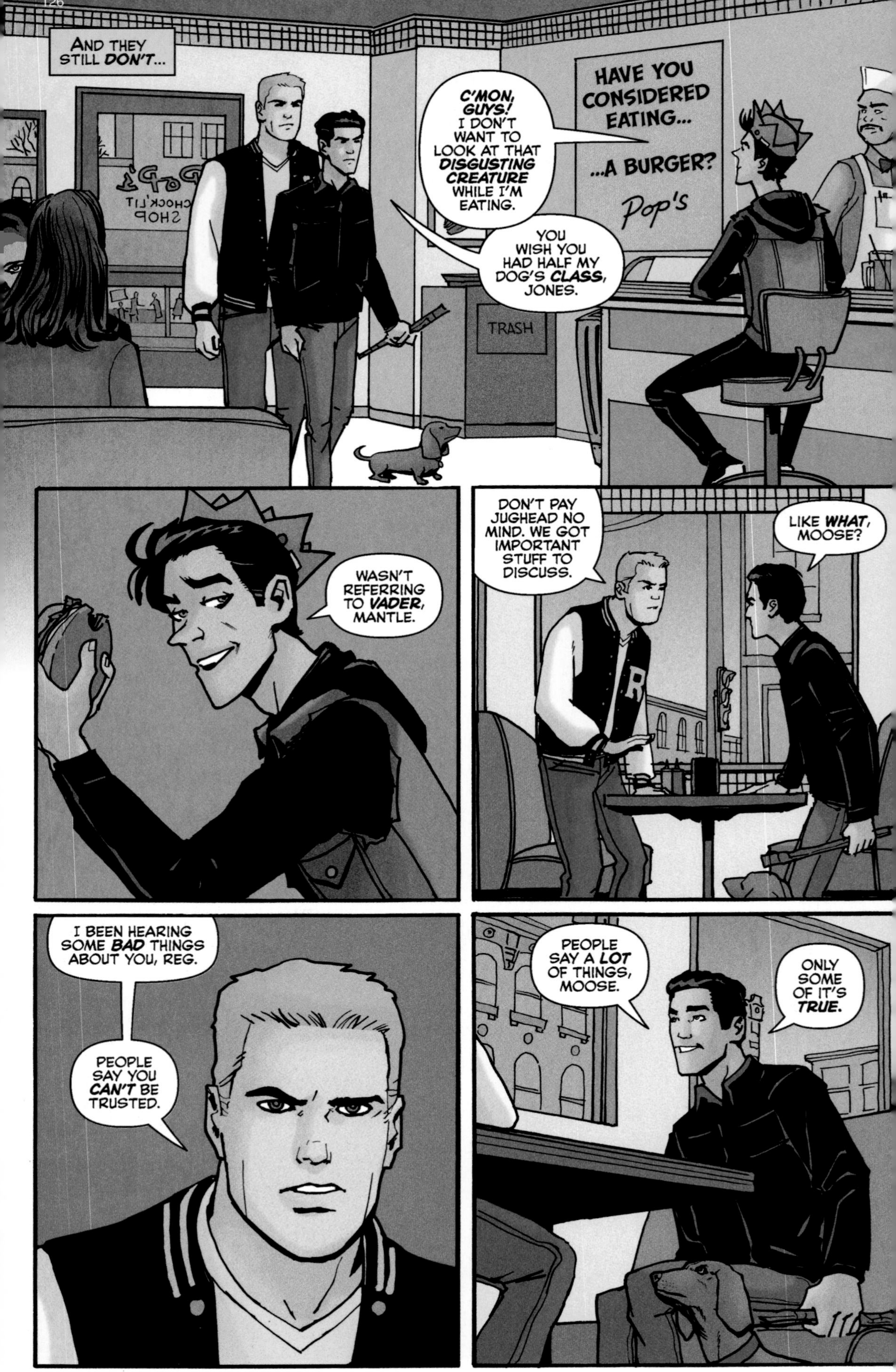
AND THEY STILL DON'T...
HAVE YOU CONSIDERED EATING... ...A BURGER? Pop's
C'MON, GUYS! I DON'T WANT TO LOOK AT THAT DISGUSTING CREATURE WHILE I'M EATING.
YOU WISH YOU HAD HALF MY DOG'S CLASS, JONES.
Pop's CHOCK'LIT SHOP
TRASH
WASN'T REFERRING TO VADER, MANTLE.
DON'T PAY JUGHEAD NO MIND. WE GOT IMPORTANT STUFF TO DISCUSS.
LIKE WHAT, MOOSE?
I BEEN HEARING SOME BAD THINGS ABOUT YOU, REG.
PEOPLE SAY YOU CAN'T BE TRUSTED.
PEOPLE SAY A LOT OF THINGS, MOOSE.
ONLY SOME OF IT'S TRUE.

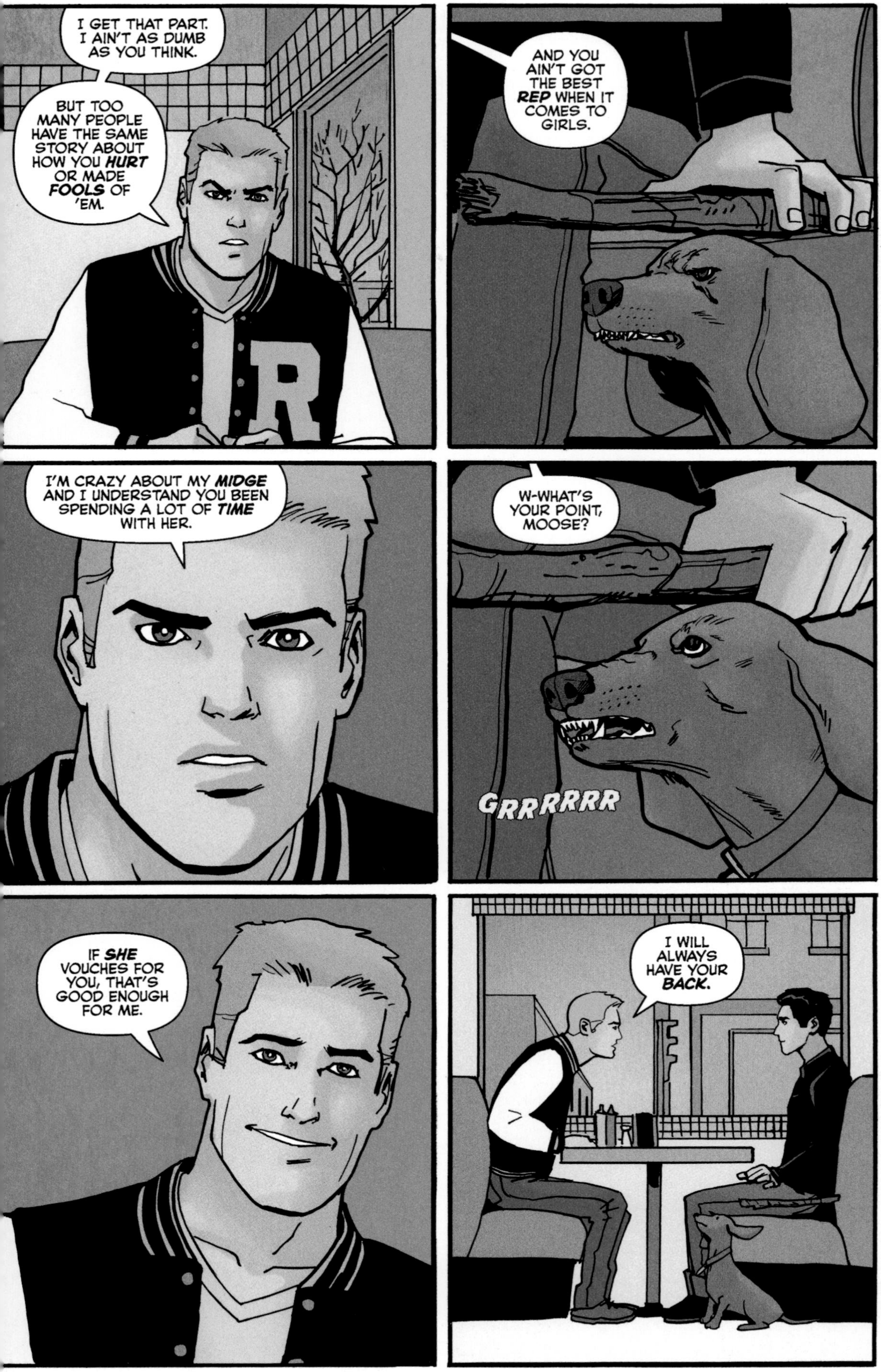
I GET THAT PART. I AIN'T AS DUMB AS YOU THINK.
BUT TOO MANY PEOPLE HAVE THE SAME STORY ABOUT HOW YOU HURT OR MADE FOOLS OF 'EM.
AND YOU AIN'T GOT THE BEST REP WHEN IT COMES TO GIRLS.
I'M CRAZY ABOUT MY MIDGE AND I UNDERSTAND YOU BEEN SPENDING A LOT OF TIME WITH HER.
W-WHAT'S YOUR POINT, MOOSE?
GRRRRRR
IF SHE VOUCHES FOR YOU, THAT'S GOOD ENOUGH FOR ME.
I WILL ALWAYS HAVE YOUR BACK.

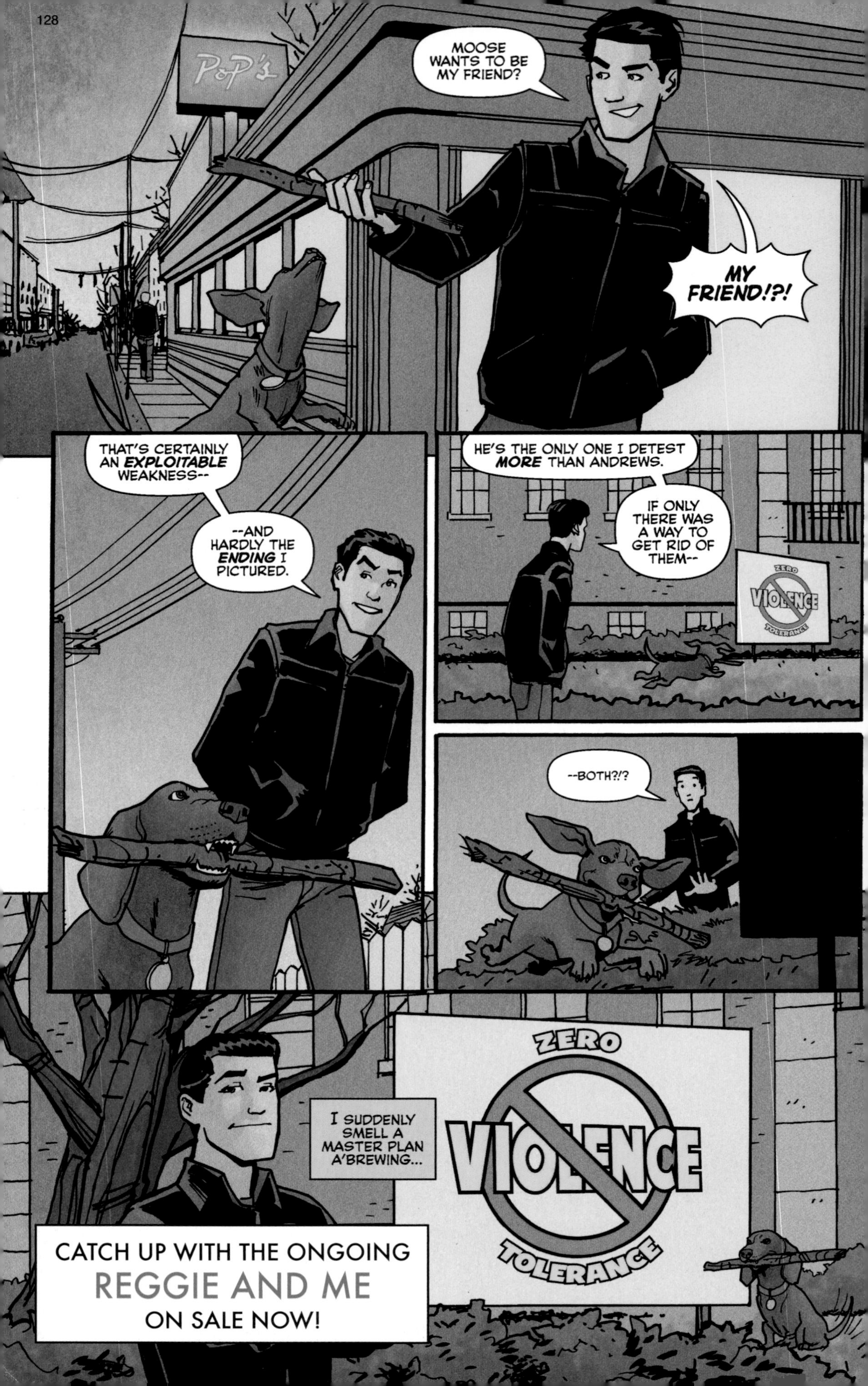
POP'S
MOOSE WANTS TO BE MY FRIEND?
MY FRIEND!?!
THAT'S CERTAINLY AN EXPLOITABLE WEAKNESS--
--AND HARDLY THE ENDING I PICTURED.
HE'S THE ONLY ONE I DETEST MORE THAN ANDREWS.
IF ONLY THERE WAS A WAY TO GET RID OF THEM--
--BOTH?!?
I SUDDENLY SMELL A MASTER PLAN A'BREWING...
ZERO VIOLENCE TOLERANCE
CATCH UP WITH THE ONGOING
REGGIE AND ME
ON SALE NOW!

ROAD TO RIVERDALE® SPECIAL FEATURES

To serve as a comic primer for The CW *Riverdale* TV show, we launched a special 48-page one-shot with four ALL-NEW individual stories by Roberto Aguirre-Sacasa and The CW writers room focusing on the main players of the series. The next few pages feature a story from the one-shot that puts the spotlight on Jughead.

Look for the ongoing *Riverdale* comic also available now!

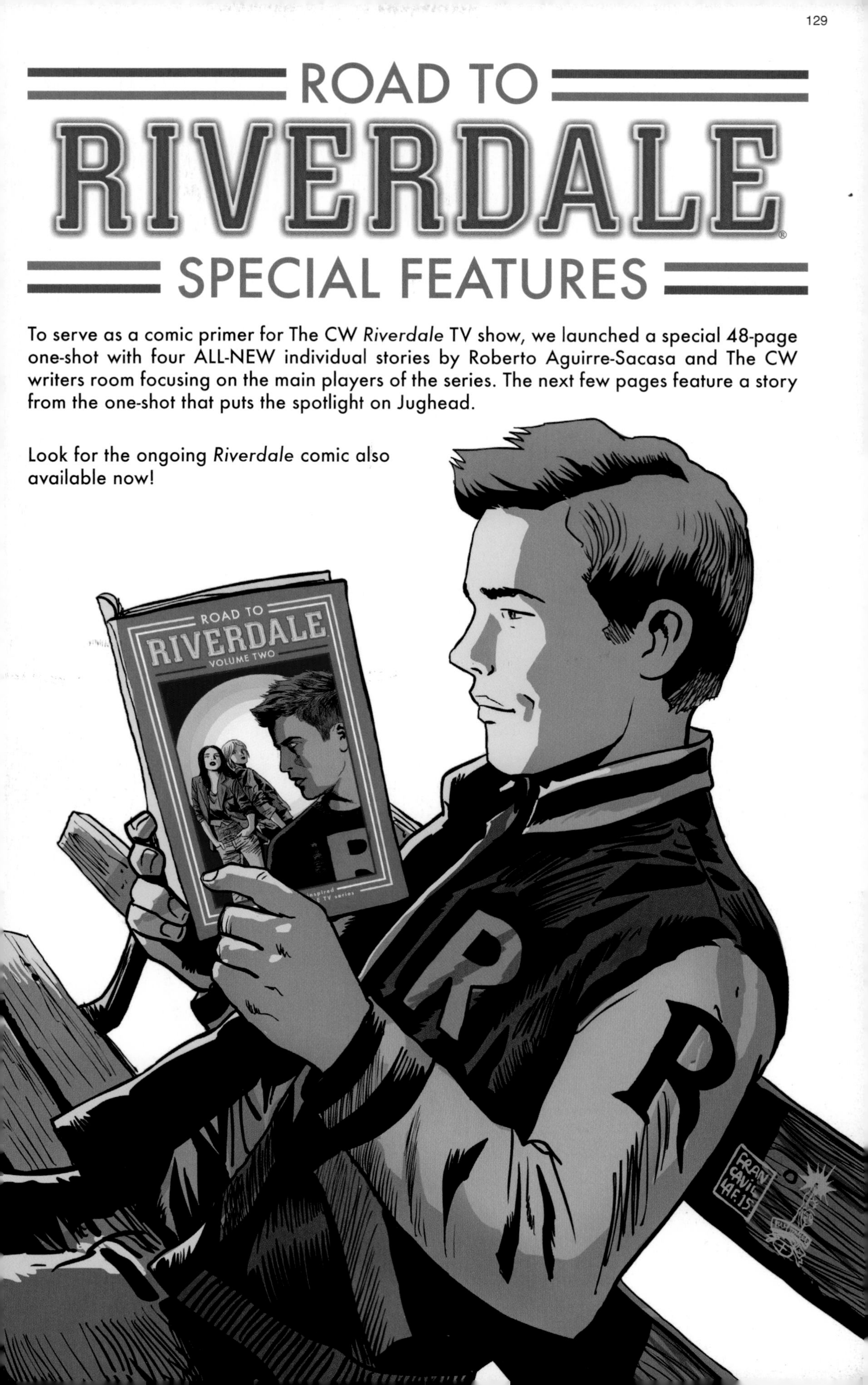
ROAD TO
RIVERDALE
VOLUME TWO

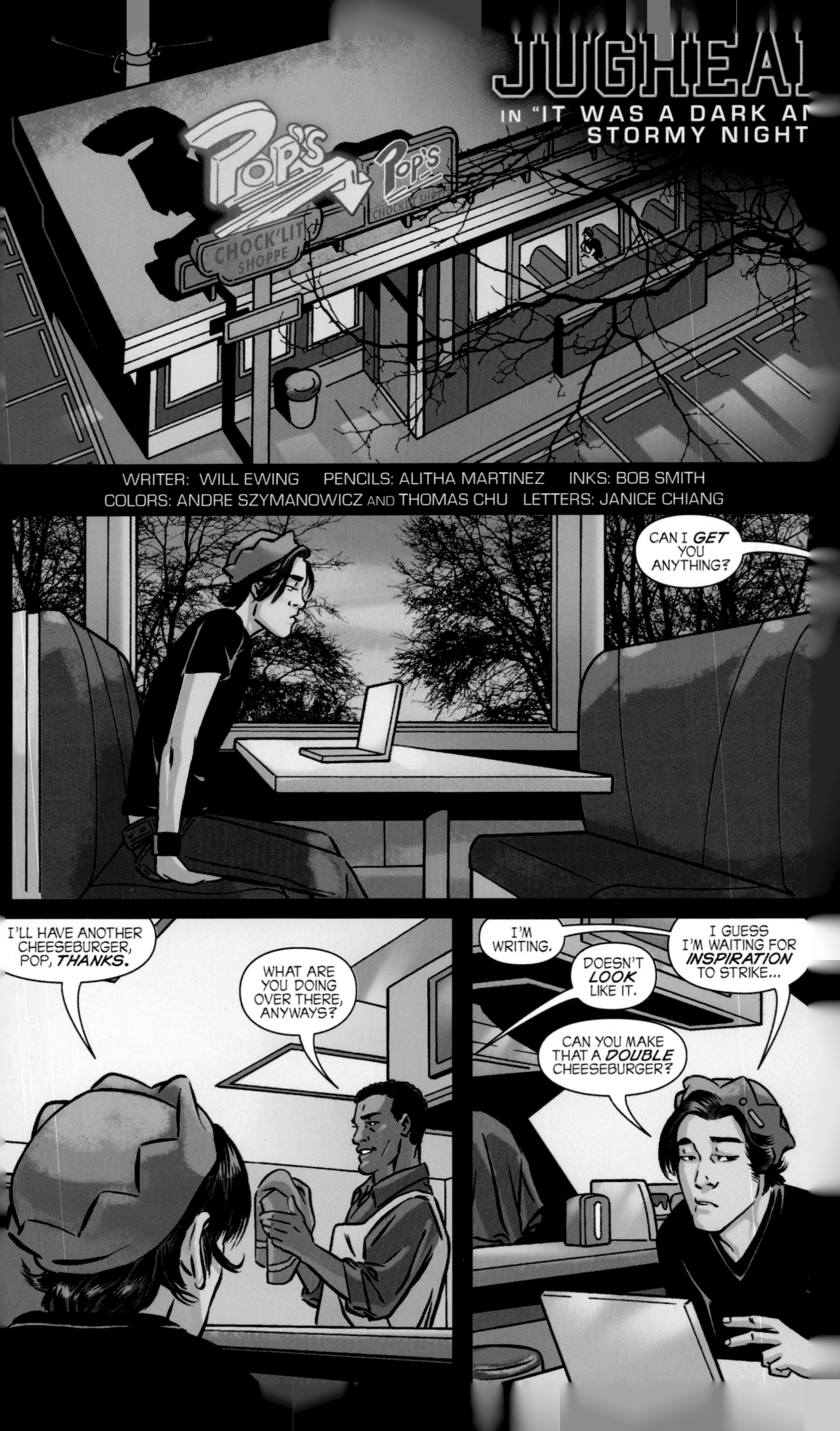

JUGHEAD
IN "IT WAS A DARK AND STORMY NIGHT
POP'S CHOCK'LIT SHOPPE
POP'S CHOCK'LIT SHOPPE
WRITER: WILL EWING PENCILS: ALITHA MARTINEZ INKS: BOB SMITH
COLORS: ANDRE SZYMANOWICZ AND THOMAS CHU LETTERS: JANICE CHIANG
CAN I *GET* YOU ANYTHING?
I'LL HAVE ANOTHER CHEESEBURGER, POP, *THANKS.*
WHAT ARE YOU DOING OVER THERE, ANYWAYS?
I'M WRITING.
DOESN'T *LOOK* LIKE IT.
I GUESS I'M WAITING FOR *INSPIRATION* TO STRIKE...
CAN YOU MAKE THAT A *DOUBLE* CHEESEBURGER?

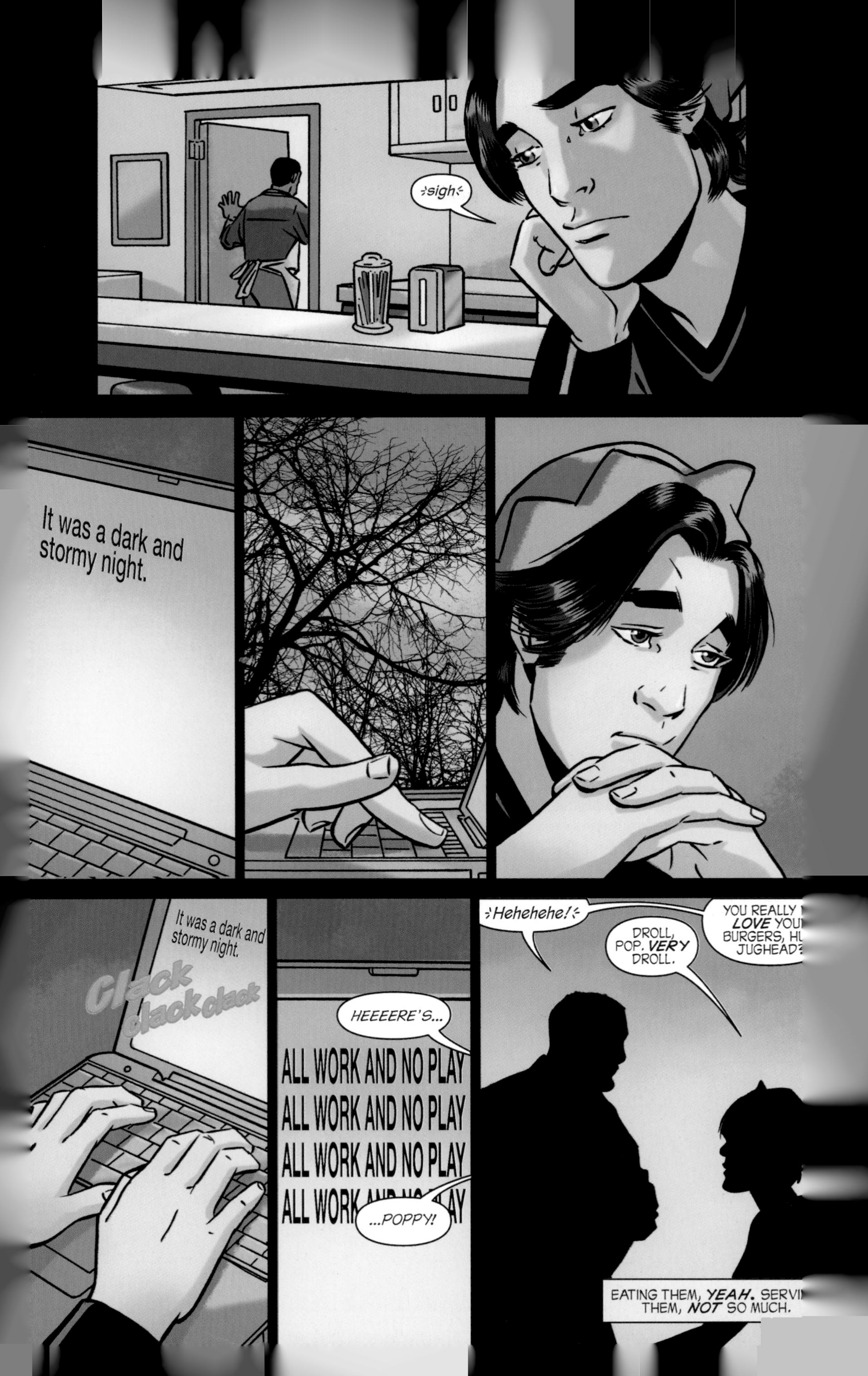

sigh
It was a dark and stormy night.
It was a dark and stormy night.
Clack clack clack
HEEEERE'S...
ALL WORK AND NO PLAY
ALL WORK AND NO PLAY
ALL WORK AND NO PLAY
...POPPY!
Hehehehe!
YOU REALLY LOVE YOUR BURGERS, HUH JUGHEAD?
DROLL, POP. VERY DROLL.
EATING THEM, YEAH. SERVING THEM, NOT SO MUCH.

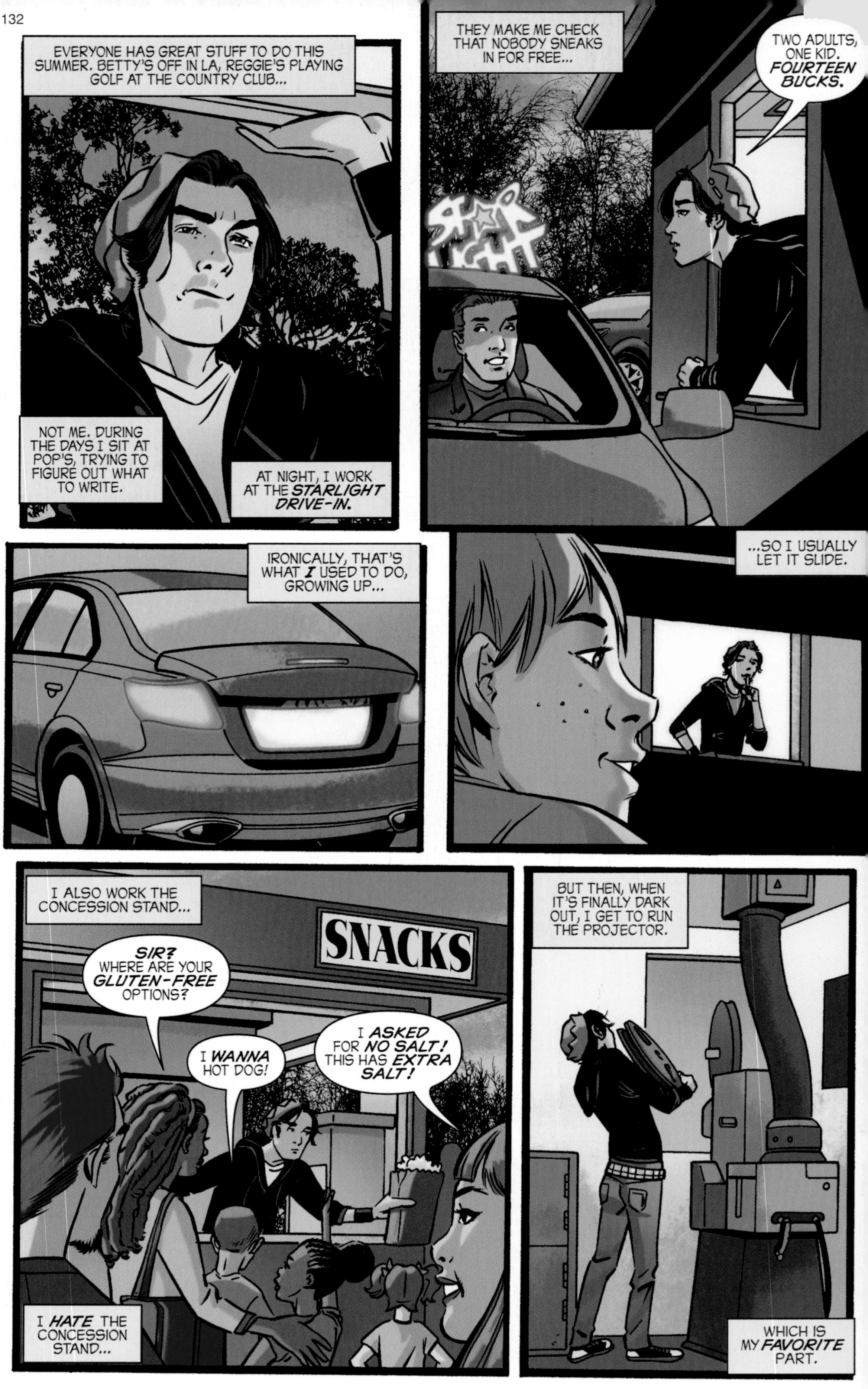
EVERYONE HAS GREAT STUFF TO DO THIS SUMMER. BETTY'S OFF IN LA, REGGIE'S PLAYING GOLF AT THE COUNTRY CLUB...
NOT ME. DURING THE DAYS I SIT AT POP'S, TRYING TO FIGURE OUT WHAT TO WRITE.
AT NIGHT, I WORK AT THE STARLIGHT DRIVE-IN.
THEY MAKE ME CHECK THAT NOBODY SNEAKS IN FOR FREE...
TWO ADULTS, ONE KID. FOURTEEN BUCKS.
IRONICALLY, THAT'S WHAT I USED TO DO, GROWING UP...
...SO I USUALLY LET IT SLIDE.
I ALSO WORK THE CONCESSION STAND...
SNACKS
SIR? WHERE ARE YOUR GLUTEN-FREE OPTIONS?
I WANNA HOT DOG!
I ASKED FOR NO SALT! THIS HAS EXTRA SALT!
I HATE THE CONCESSION STAND...
BUT THEN, WHEN IT'S FINALLY DARK OUT, I GET TO RUN THE PROJECTOR.
WHICH IS MY FAVORITE PART.

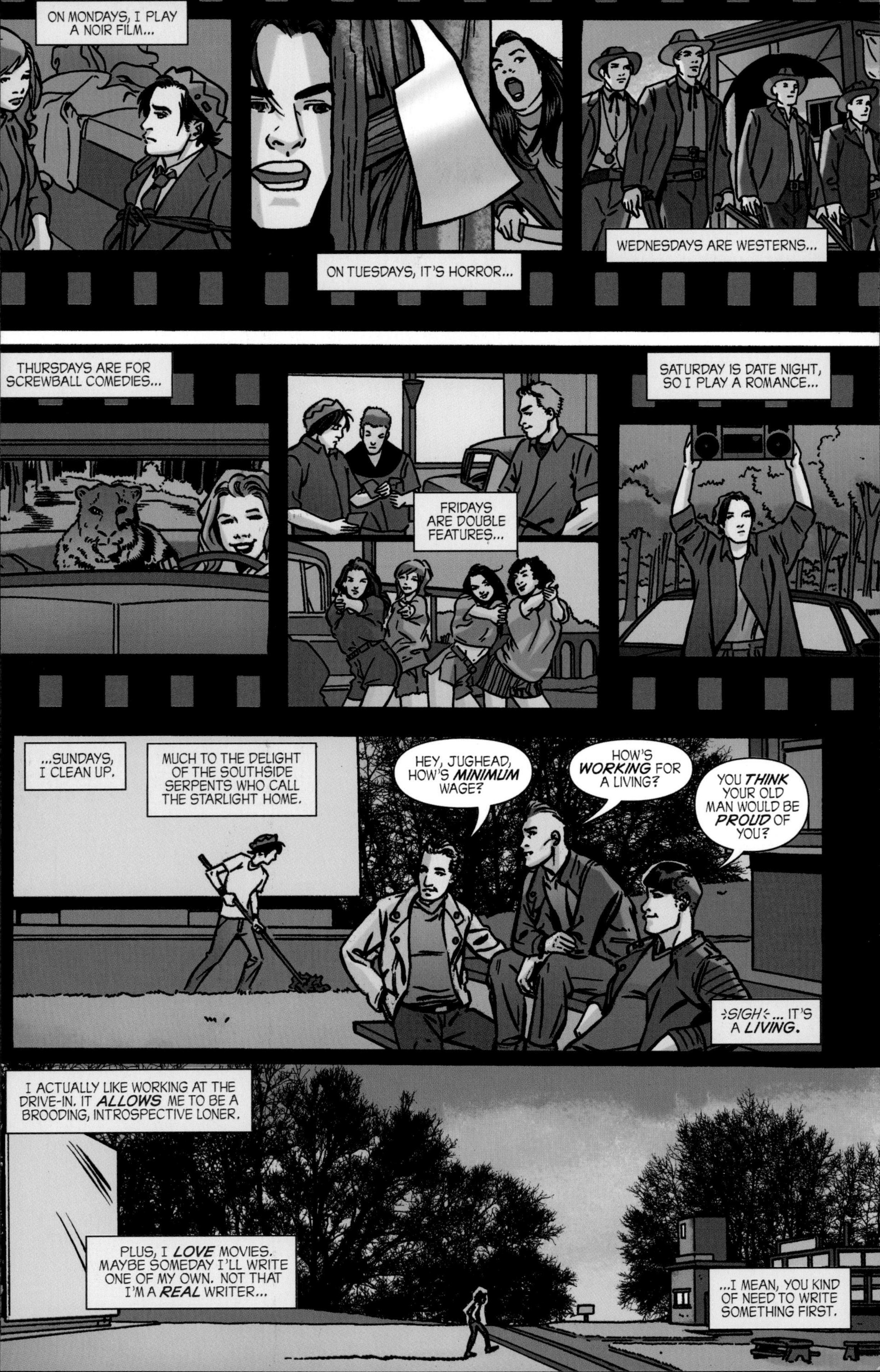
ON MONDAYS, I PLAY A NOIR FILM...
ON TUESDAYS, IT'S HORROR...
WEDNESDAYS ARE WESTERNS...
THURSDAYS ARE FOR SCREWBALL COMEDIES...
FRIDAYS ARE DOUBLE FEATURES...
SATURDAY IS DATE NIGHT, SO I PLAY A ROMANCE...
...SUNDAYS, I CLEAN UP.
MUCH TO THE DELIGHT OF THE SOUTHSIDE SERPENTS WHO CALL THE STARLIGHT HOME.
HEY, JUGHEAD, HOW'S MINIMUM WAGE?
HOW'S WORKING FOR A LIVING?
YOU THINK YOUR OLD MAN WOULD BE PROUD OF YOU?
SIGH... IT'S A LIVING.
I ACTUALLY LIKE WORKING AT THE DRIVE-IN. IT ALLOWS ME TO BE A BROODING, INTROSPECTIVE LONER.
PLUS, I LOVE MOVIES. MAYBE SOMEDAY I'LL WRITE ONE OF MY OWN. NOT THAT I'M A REAL WRITER...
...I MEAN, YOU KIND OF NEED TO WRITE SOMETHING FIRST.

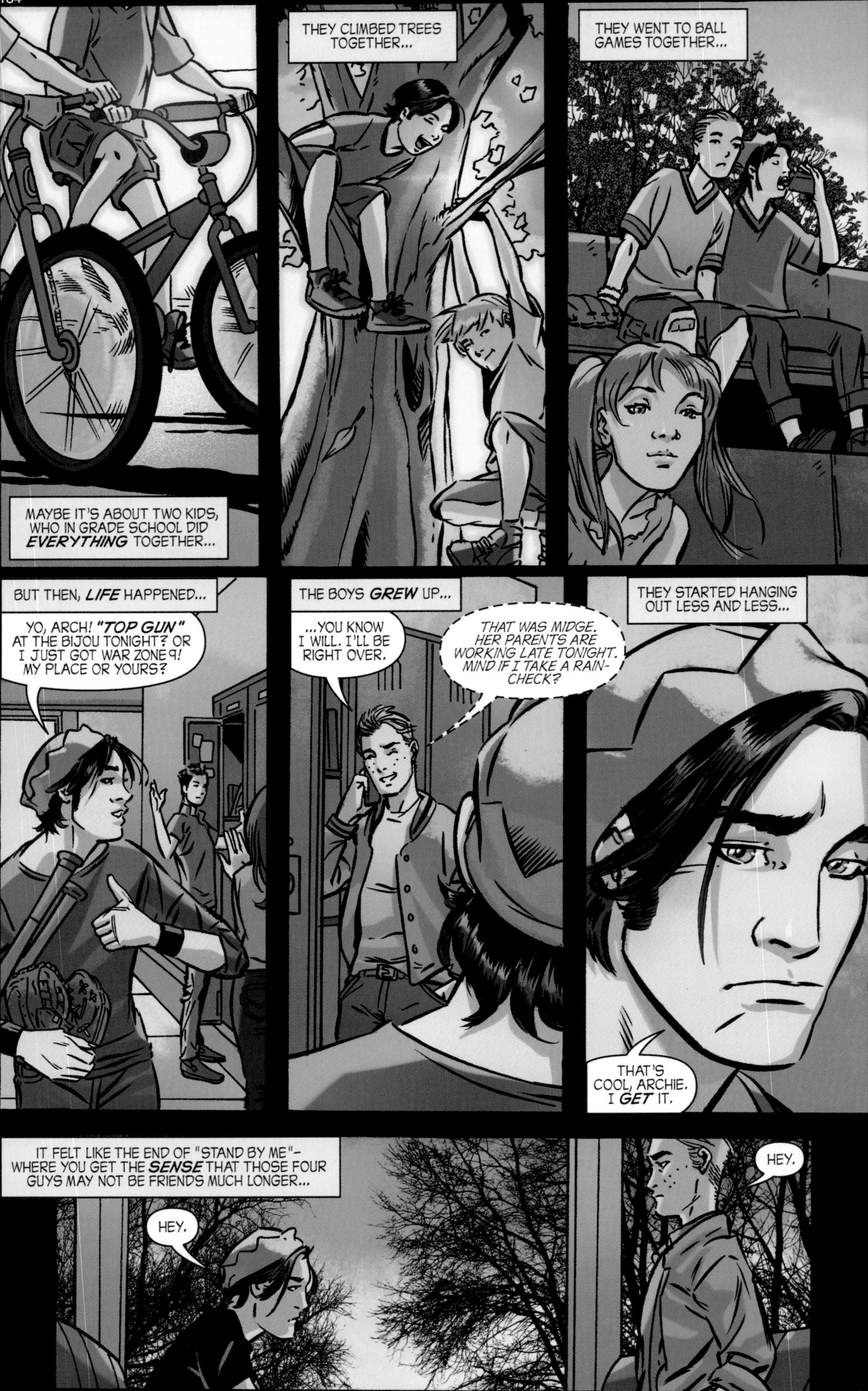
MAYBE IT'S ABOUT TWO KIDS, WHO IN GRADE SCHOOL DID *EVERYTHING* TOGETHER...
THEY CLIMBED TREES TOGETHER...
THEY WENT TO BALL GAMES TOGETHER...
BUT THEN, *LIFE* HAPPENED...
YO, ARCH! *"TOP GUN"* AT THE BIJOU TONIGHT? OR I JUST GOT WAR ZONE 9! MY PLACE OR YOURS?
THE BOYS *GREW* UP...
...YOU KNOW I WILL. I'LL BE RIGHT OVER.
THAT WAS MIDGE. HER PARENTS ARE WORKING LATE TONIGHT. MIND IF I TAKE A RAIN-CHECK?
THEY STARTED HANGING OUT LESS AND LESS...
THAT'S COOL, ARCHIE. I *GET* IT.
IT FELT LIKE THE END OF "STAND BY ME"– WHERE YOU GET THE *SENSE* THAT THOSE FOUR GUYS MAY NOT BE FRIENDS MUCH LONGER...
HEY.
HEY.

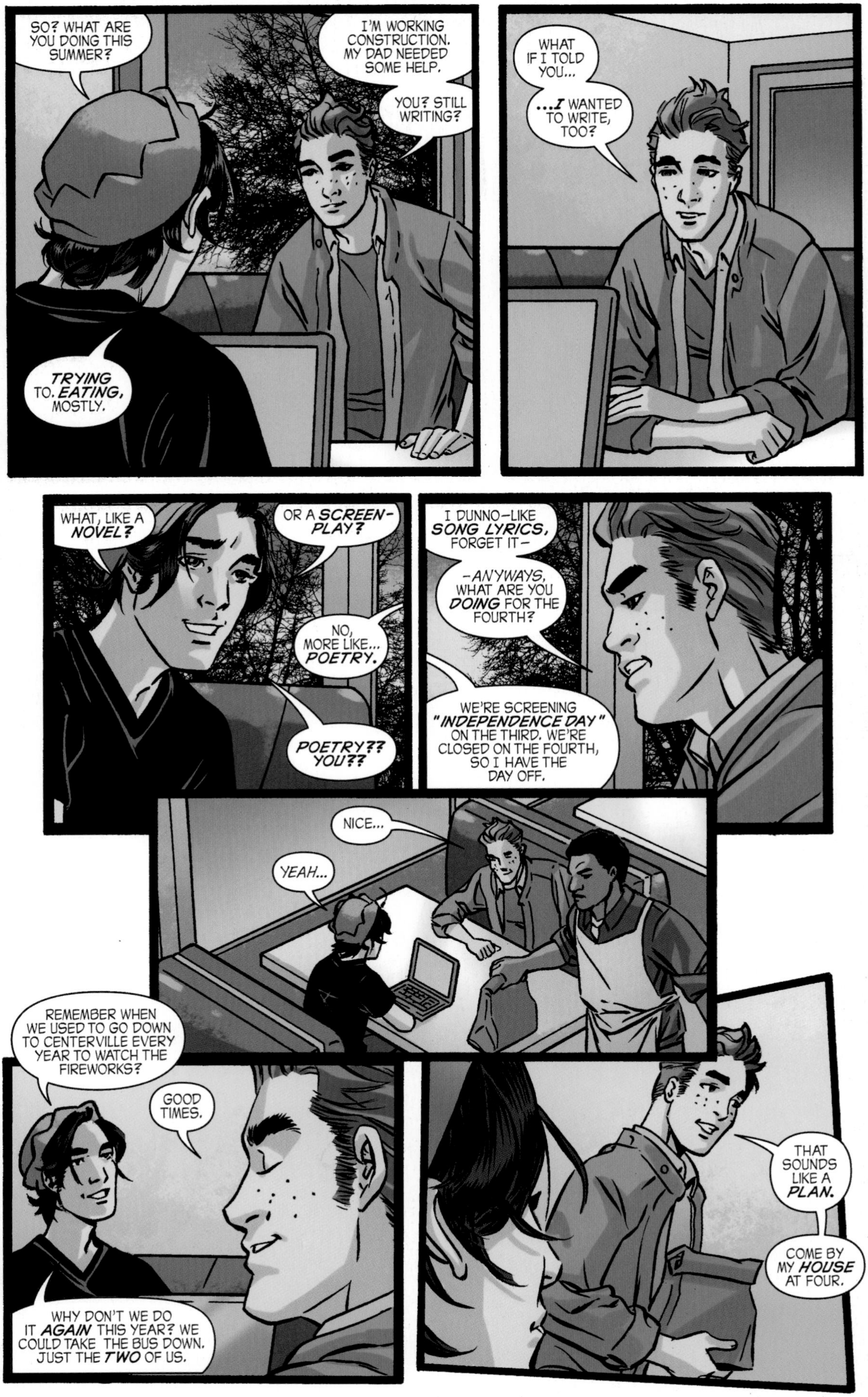
SO? WHAT ARE YOU DOING THIS SUMMER?
I'M WORKING CONSTRUCTION. MY DAD NEEDED SOME HELP.
YOU? STILL WRITING?
TRYING TO. EATING, MOSTLY.
WHAT IF I TOLD YOU...
...I WANTED TO WRITE, TOO?
WHAT, LIKE A NOVEL?
OR A SCREEN-PLAY?
NO, MORE LIKE... POETRY.
POETRY?? YOU??
I DUNNO—LIKE SONG LYRICS, FORGET IT—
—ANYWAYS, WHAT ARE YOU DOING FOR THE FOURTH?
WE'RE SCREENING "INDEPENDENCE DAY" ON THE THIRD. WE'RE CLOSED ON THE FOURTH, SO I HAVE THE DAY OFF.
NICE...
YEAH...
REMEMBER WHEN WE USED TO GO DOWN TO CENTERVILLE EVERY YEAR TO WATCH THE FIREWORKS?
GOOD TIMES.
WHY DON'T WE DO IT AGAIN THIS YEAR? WE COULD TAKE THE BUS DOWN. JUST THE TWO OF US.
THAT SOUNDS LIKE A PLAN.
COME BY MY HOUSE AT FOUR.

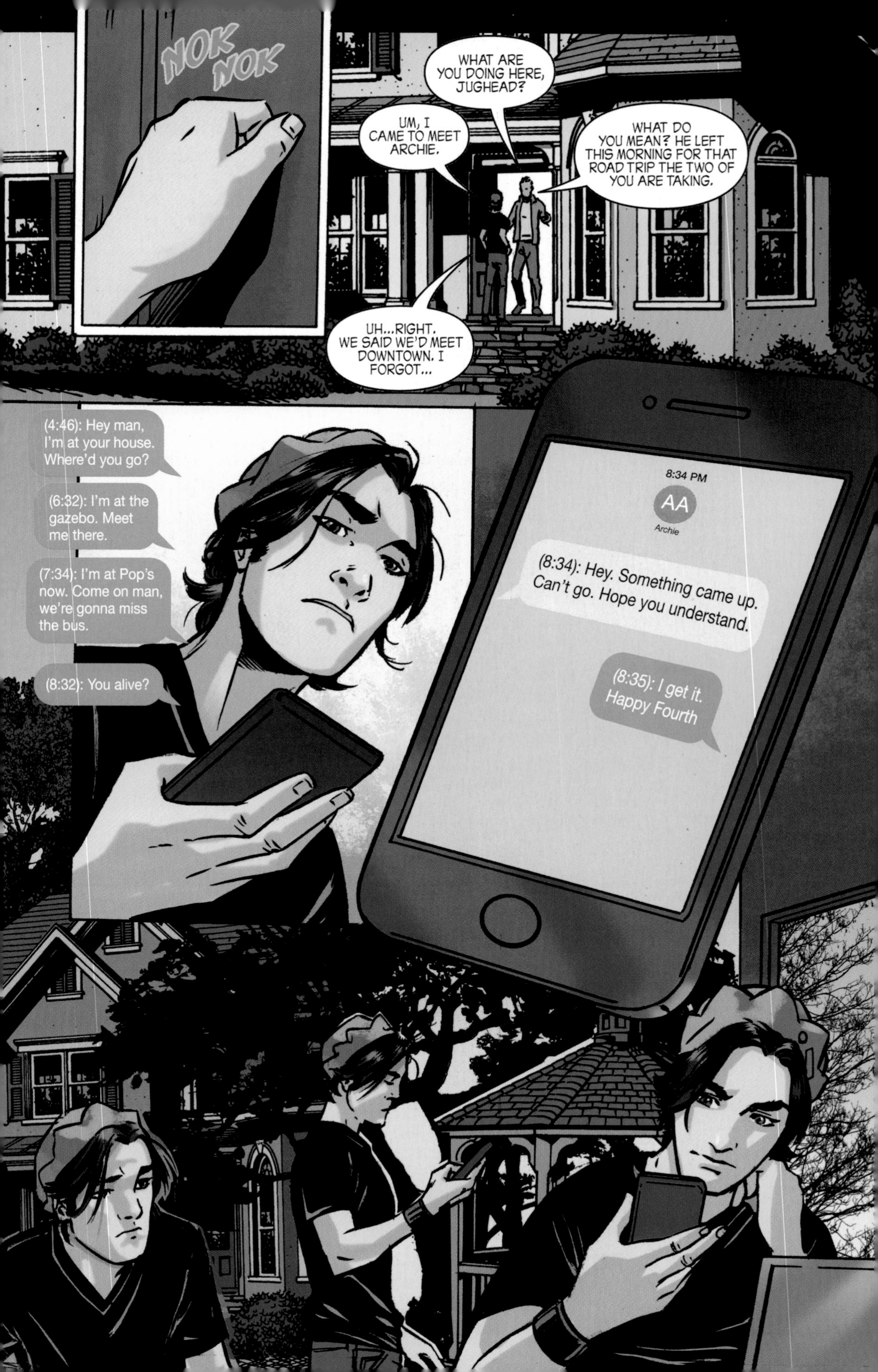
NOK NOK
WHAT ARE YOU DOING HERE, JUGHEAD?
UM, I CAME TO MEET ARCHIE.
WHAT DO YOU MEAN? HE LEFT THIS MORNING FOR THAT ROAD TRIP THE TWO OF YOU ARE TAKING.
UH...RIGHT. WE SAID WE'D MEET DOWNTOWN. I FORGOT...
(4:46): Hey man, I'm at your house. Where'd you go?
(6:32): I'm at the gazebo. Meet me there.
(7:34): I'm at Pop's now. Come on man, we're gonna miss the bus.
(8:32): You alive?
8:34 PM
AA
Archie
(8:34): Hey. Something came up. Can't go. Hope you understand.
(8:35): I get it. Happy Fourth

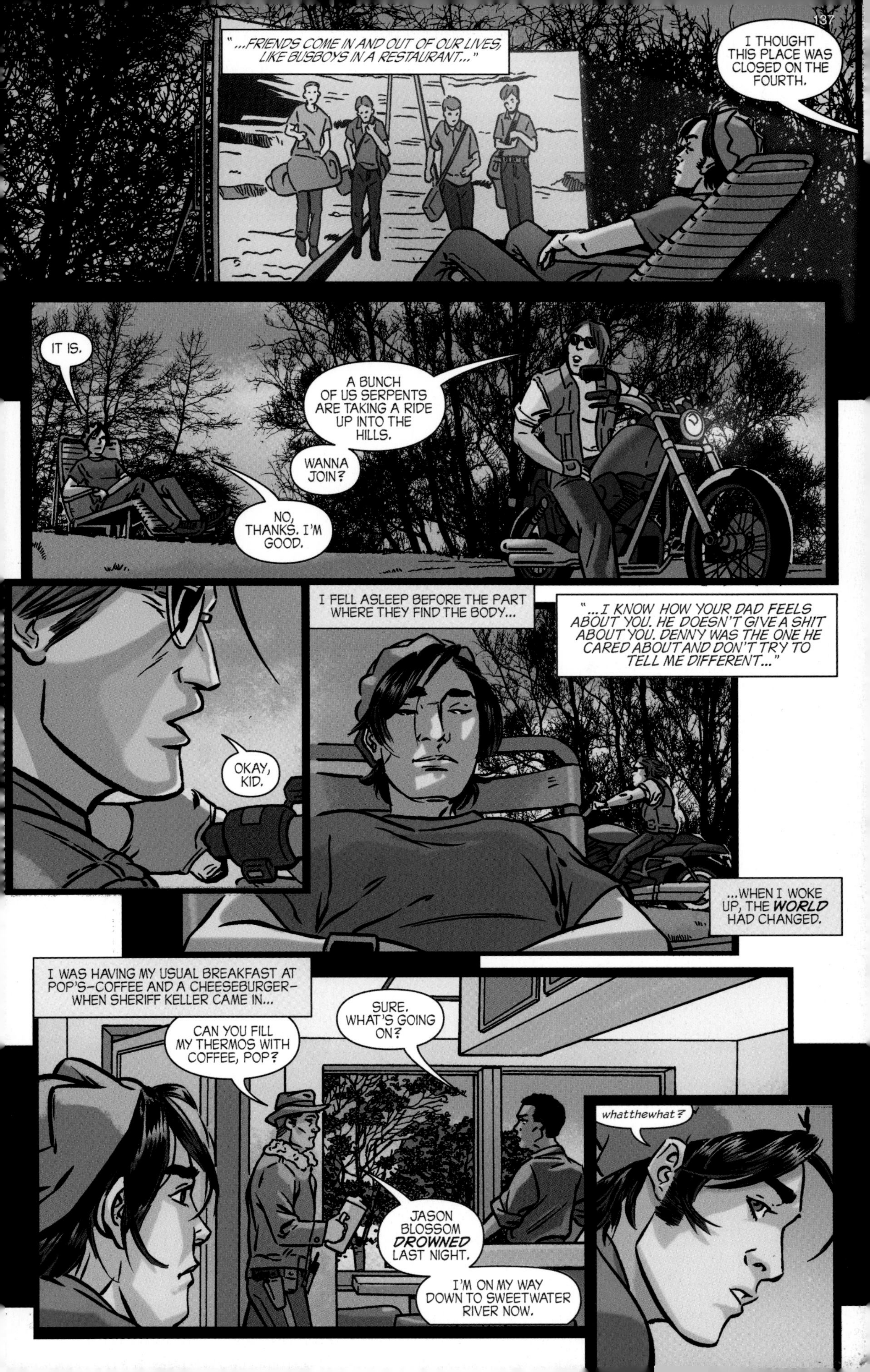
"...FRIENDS COME IN AND OUT OF OUR LIVES, LIKE BUSBOYS IN A RESTAURANT..."
I THOUGHT THIS PLACE WAS CLOSED ON THE FOURTH.
IT IS.
A BUNCH OF US SERPENTS ARE TAKING A RIDE UP INTO THE HILLS.
WANNA JOIN?
NO, THANKS. I'M GOOD.
OKAY, KID.
I FELL ASLEEP BEFORE THE PART WHERE THEY FIND THE BODY...
"...I KNOW HOW YOUR DAD FEELS ABOUT YOU. HE DOESN'T GIVE A SHIT ABOUT YOU. DENNY WAS THE ONE HE CARED ABOUT AND DON'T TRY TO TELL ME DIFFERENT..."
...WHEN I WOKE UP, THE WORLD HAD CHANGED.
I WAS HAVING MY USUAL BREAKFAST AT POP'S—COFFEE AND A CHEESEBURGER—WHEN SHERIFF KELLER CAME IN...
CAN YOU FILL MY THERMOS WITH COFFEE, POP?
SURE. WHAT'S GOING ON?
JASON BLOSSOM DROWNED LAST NIGHT.
I'M ON MY WAY DOWN TO SWEETWATER RIVER NOW.
whatthewhat?

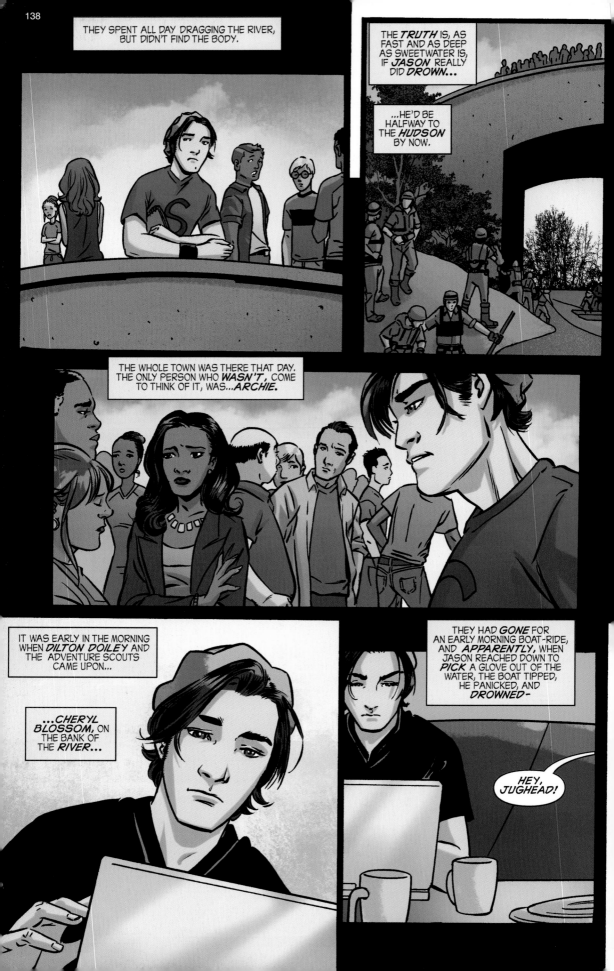

THEY SPENT ALL DAY DRAGGING THE RIVER, BUT DIDN'T FIND THE BODY.

THE *TRUTH* IS, AS FAST AND AS DEEP AS SWEETWATER IS, IF *JASON* REALLY DID *DROWN*...

...HE'D BE HALFWAY TO THE *HUDSON* BY NOW.

THE WHOLE TOWN WAS THERE THAT DAY. THE ONLY PERSON WHO *WASN'T*, COME TO THINK OF IT, WAS...*ARCHIE*.

IT WAS EARLY IN THE MORNING WHEN *DILTON DOILEY* AND THE ADVENTURE SCOUTS CAME UPON...

...*CHERYL BLOSSOM*, ON THE BANK OF THE *RIVER*...

THEY HAD *GONE* FOR AN EARLY MORNING BOAT-RIDE, AND *APPARENTLY*, WHEN JASON REACHED DOWN TO *PICK* A GLOVE OUT OF THE WATER, THE BOAT TIPPED, HE PANICKED, AND *DROWNED*—

HEY, JUGHEAD!

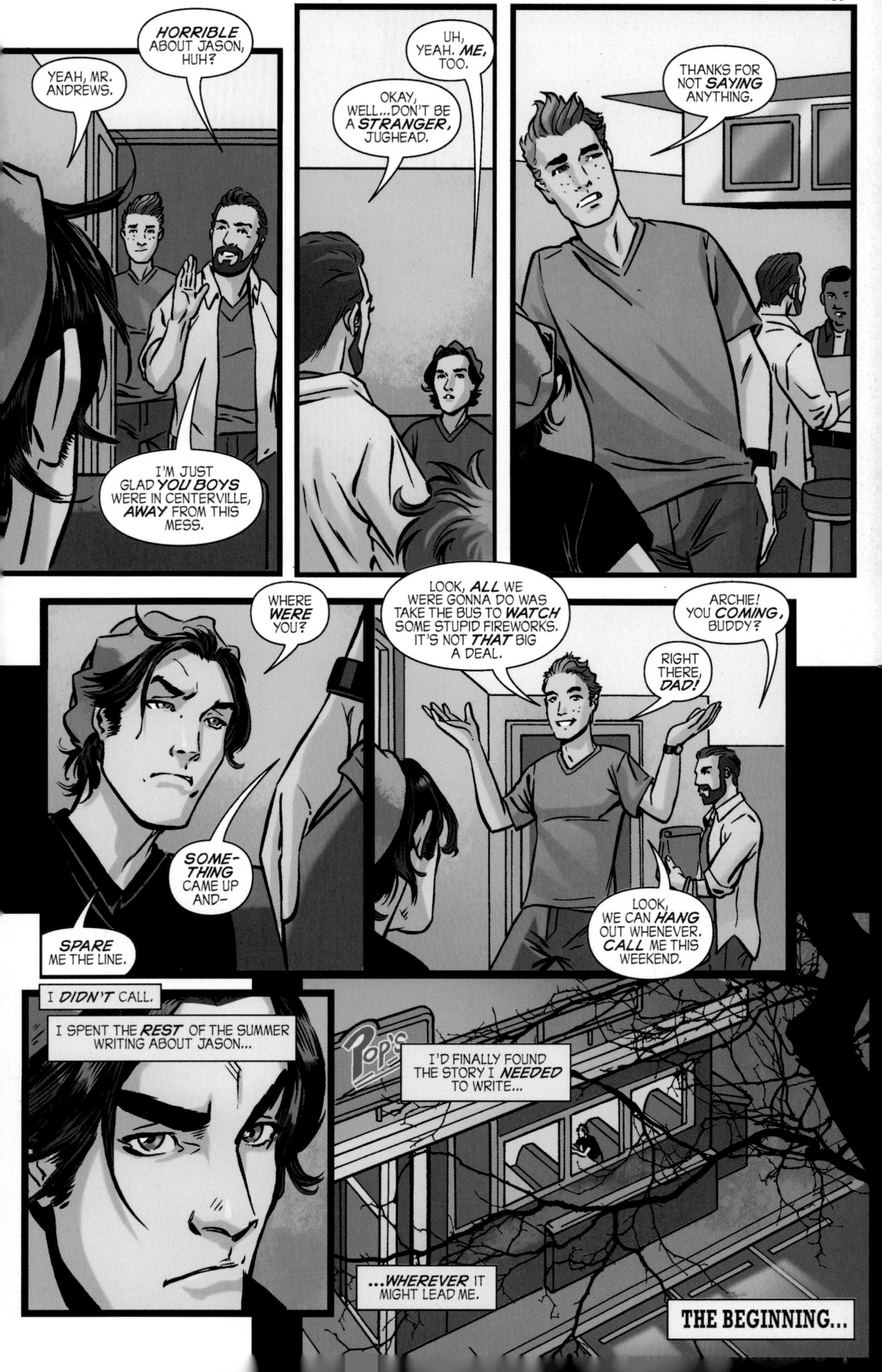
YEAH, MR. ANDREWS.
HORRIBLE ABOUT JASON, HUH?
I'M JUST GLAD YOU BOYS WERE IN CENTERVILLE, AWAY FROM THIS MESS.
UH, YEAH. ME, TOO.
OKAY, WELL...DON'T BE A STRANGER, JUGHEAD.
THANKS FOR NOT SAYING ANYTHING.
WHERE WERE YOU?
SOME-THING CAME UP AND–
SPARE ME THE LINE.
LOOK, ALL WE WERE GONNA DO WAS TAKE THE BUS TO WATCH SOME STUPID FIREWORKS. IT'S NOT THAT BIG A DEAL.
ARCHIE! YOU COMING, BUDDY?
RIGHT THERE, DAD!
LOOK, WE CAN HANG OUT WHENEVER. CALL ME THIS WEEKEND.
I DIDN'T CALL.
I SPENT THE REST OF THE SUMMER WRITING ABOUT JASON...
POP'S
I'D FINALLY FOUND THE STORY I NEEDED TO WRITE...
...WHEREVER IT MIGHT LEAD ME.
THE BEGINNING...

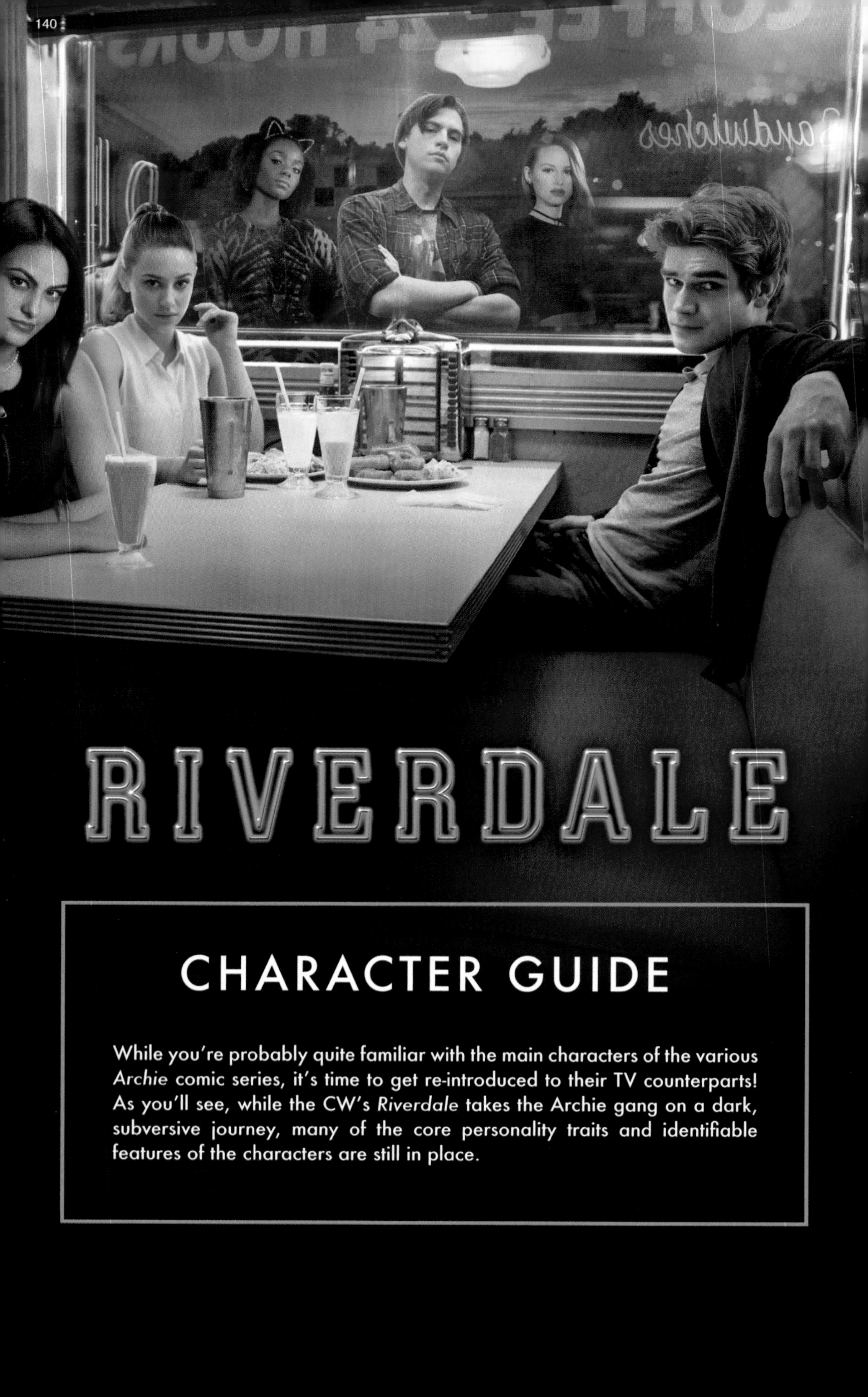

RIVERDALE

CHARACTER GUIDE

While you're probably quite familiar with the main characters of the various *Archie* comic series, it's time to get re-introduced to their TV counterparts! As you'll see, while the CW's *Riverdale* takes the Archie gang on a dark, subversive journey, many of the core personality traits and identifiable features of the characters are still in place.

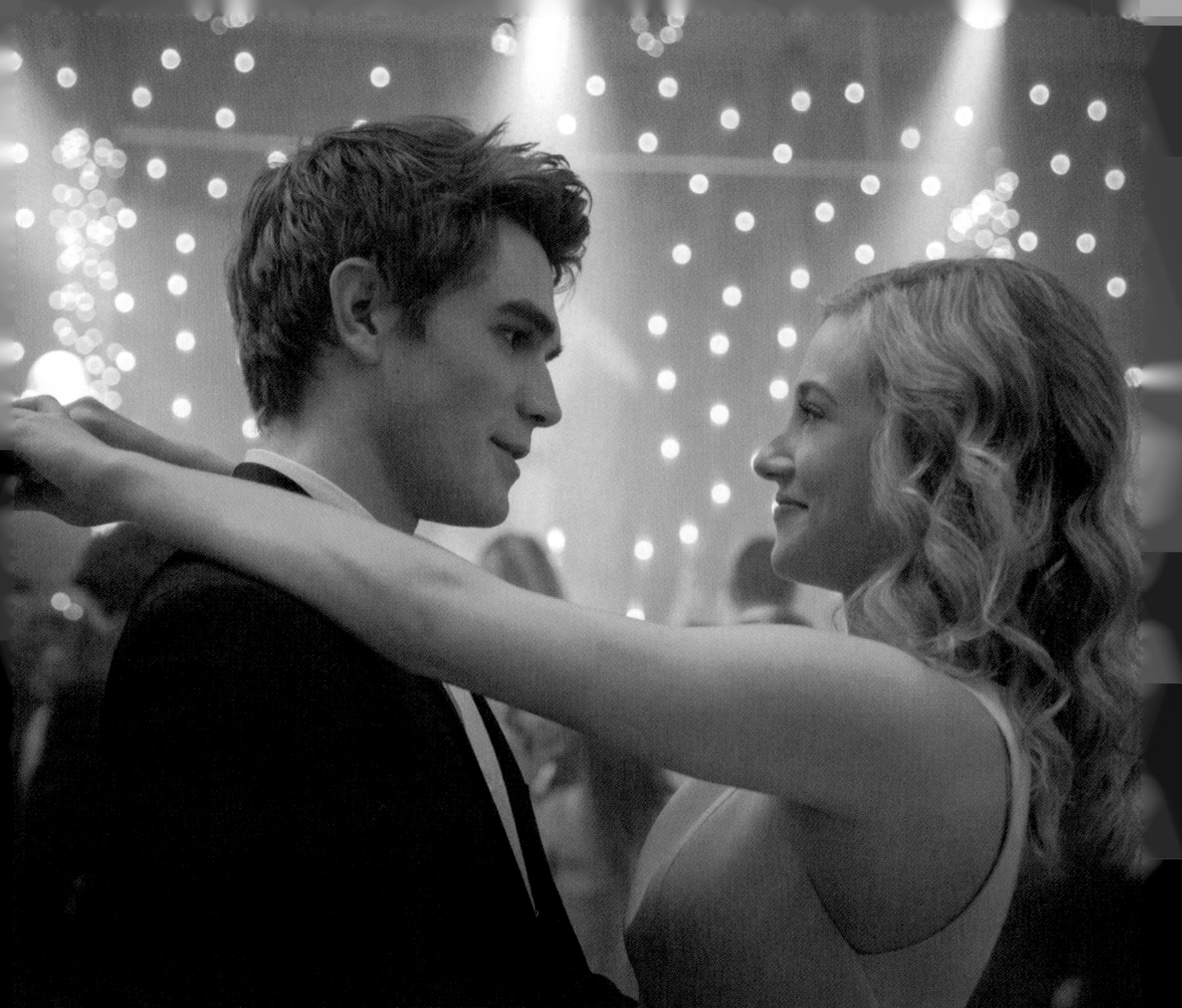

ARCHIE ANDREWS

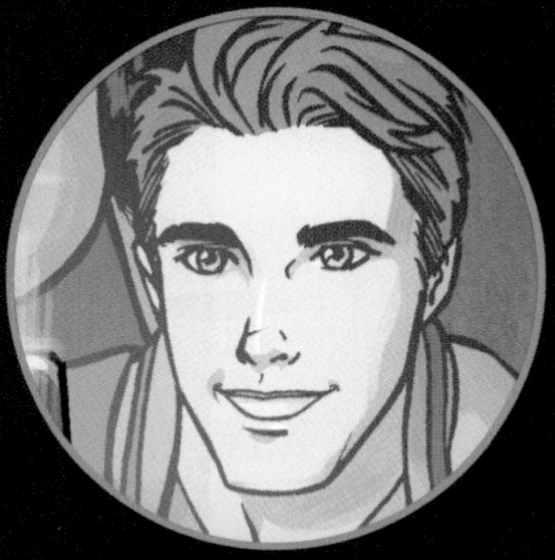

Archie is a small town boy who is well liked in his hometown of Riverdale—though his clumsiness tends to anger various school faculty and adults. He's especially liked by girls, namely Betty Cooper and Veronica Lodge. He is forever caught in a love triangle between the two BFFs.

In *Riverdale,* Archie (played by KJ Apa) is an intense, conflicted teen, juggling the interest of several girls, as well as trying to balance his passion for writing and performing music—against the wishes of his father.

BETTY COOPER

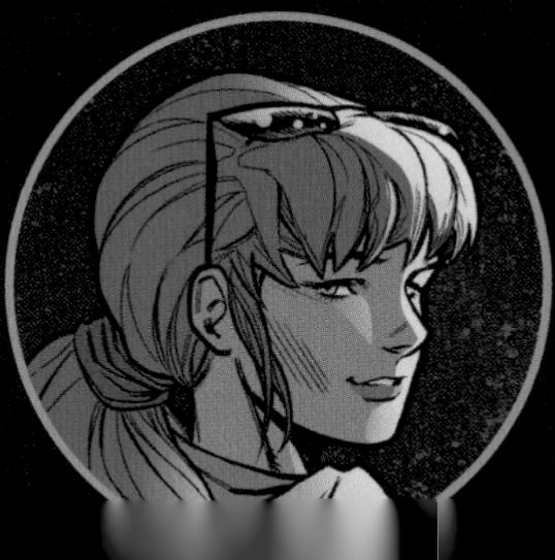

Betty is the quintessential girl-next-door. She enjoys fixing up cars, writing and takes a special interest in the environment and other social issues. Betty is devoted to Archie, but often plays second fiddle to Veronica for his affections.

In *Riverdale,* Betty (played by Lili Reinhart) is a sweet, smart, eager-to-please and wholesome girl with a long time crush on her best friend, Archie. But she is tired of being the perfect daughter, student and sister, so she turns to her new friend, Veronica, for life advice, much to the alarm of her emotionally

VERONICA LODGE

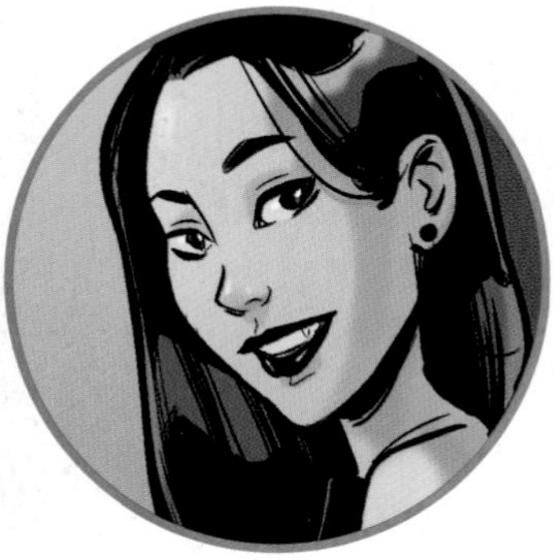

Veronica is gorgeous, sophisticated, sexy, confident and very rich. She is ambitious and would someday like to run her father's company, Lodge Enterprises. Veronica has no problem with boys, except maybe Archie. She is forever trying to win Archie's affection over Betty and uses her looks, brains and money to do so.

In *Riverdale,* Veronica (played by Camila Mendes) is an intelligent, confident high school sophomore. Veronica and her mother return to Riverdale from New York, eager to reinvent themselves after a scandal involving Mr. Lodge.

HERMIONE LODGE

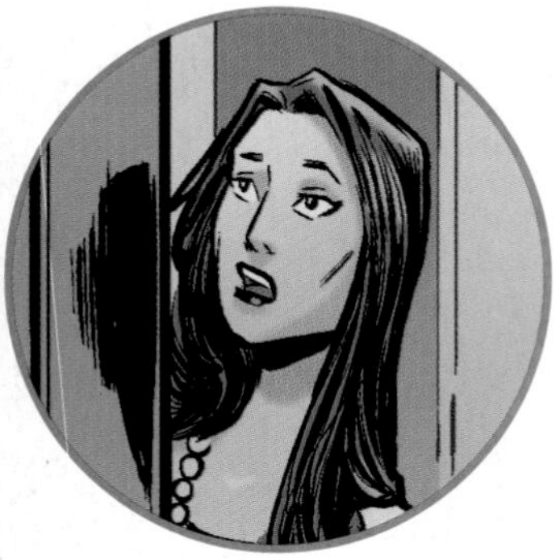

Much like her daughter, Veronica, Mrs. Lodge loves to shop. The two often go on shopping sprees together, sometimes even traveling to other countries to pick up designer clothes. Mrs. Lodge also makes sure to do her part to give back to society as well. If there's a charity bazaar or famous social event, odds are Hermione is one of the organizers.

In *Riverdale,* Hermione (played by Marisol Nichols) returns to Riverdale with Veronica after a scandal involving her husband lands him in jail. Humbled by the experience, Hermione goes back to her roots and accepts a job that's beneath her status, just to make ends meet and provide a healthy family life for her daughter.

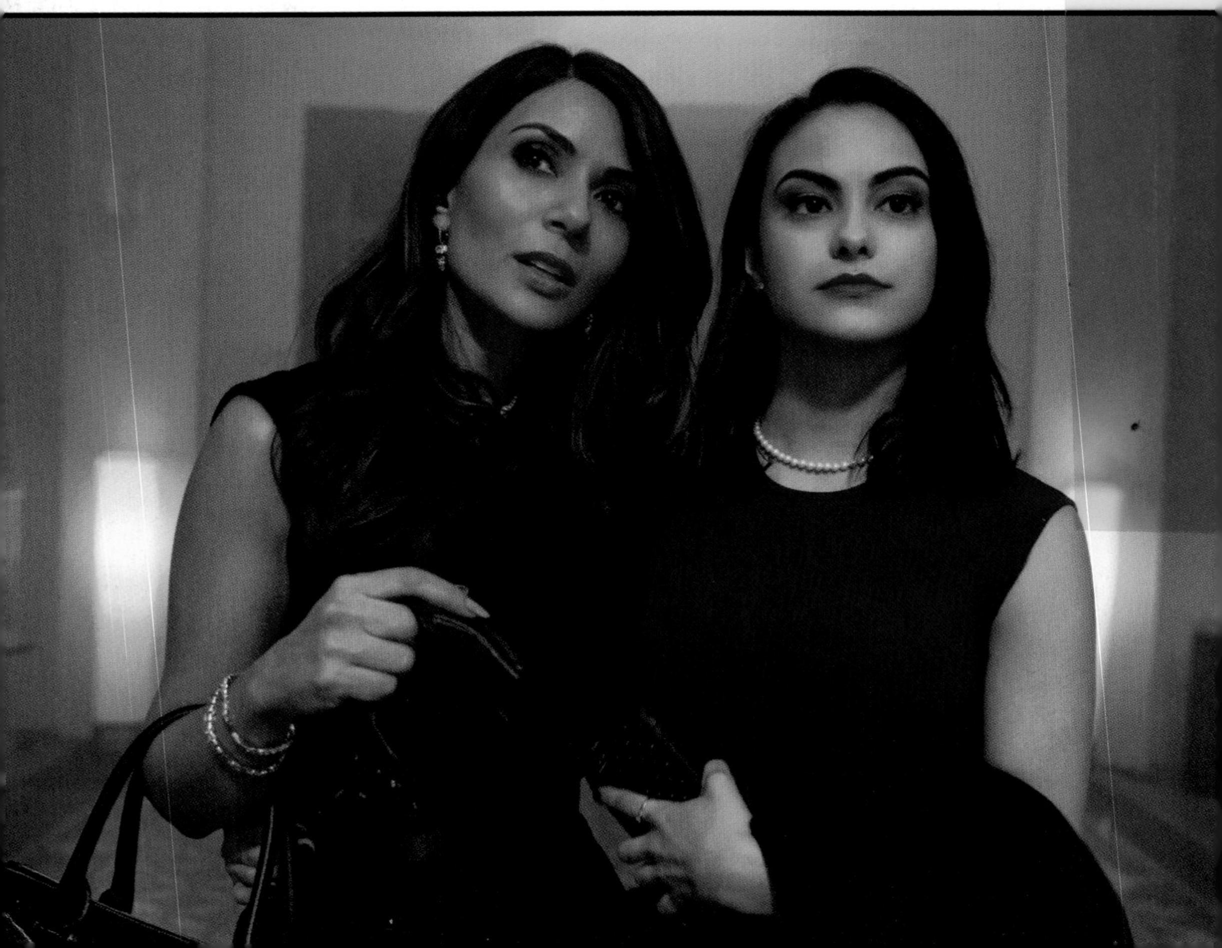

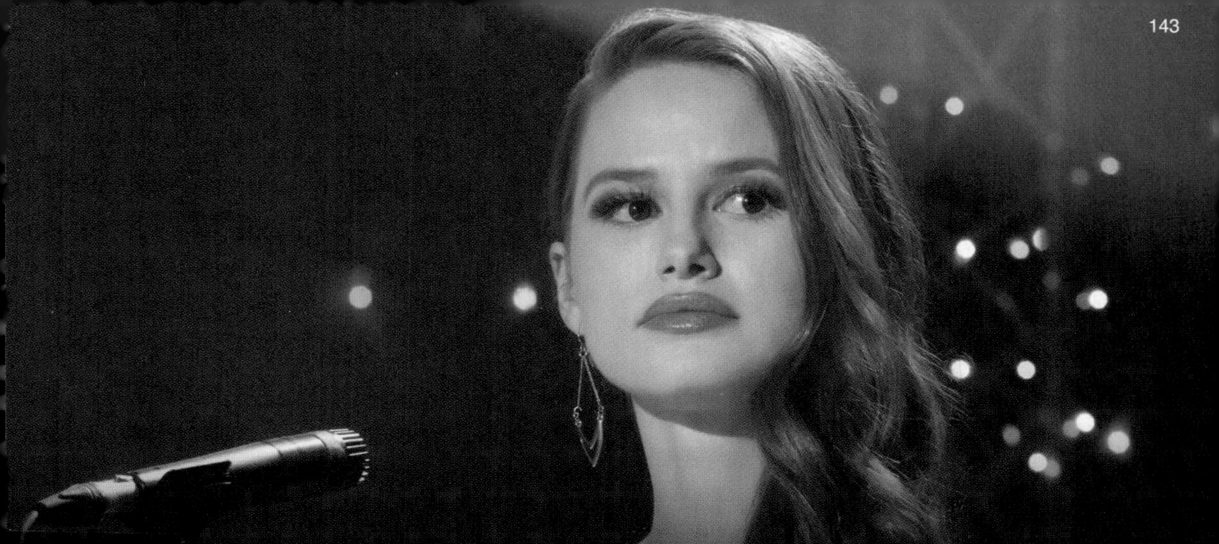

CHERYL BLOSSOM

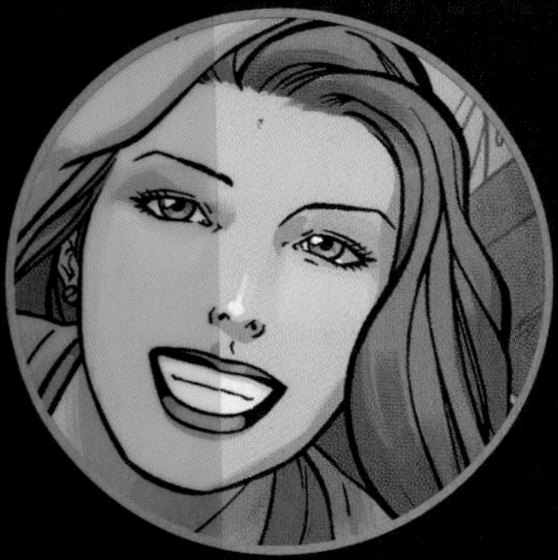

Scheming twins Cheryl and Jason Blossom come from a family that is even richer than the Lodges. Cheryl is snobby and flirtatious, and she is the only girl around who could compete with Veronica when it comes to fashion and beauty. This makes Veronica extremely jealous of her. Cheryl is Betty and Veronica's arch nemesis, especially when it comes to Archie, whom Cheryl dates on and off.

In *Riverdale,* Cheryl (played by Madelaine Petsch) is a rich, entitled, and manipulative girl who recently lost her twin brother in a mysterious accident.

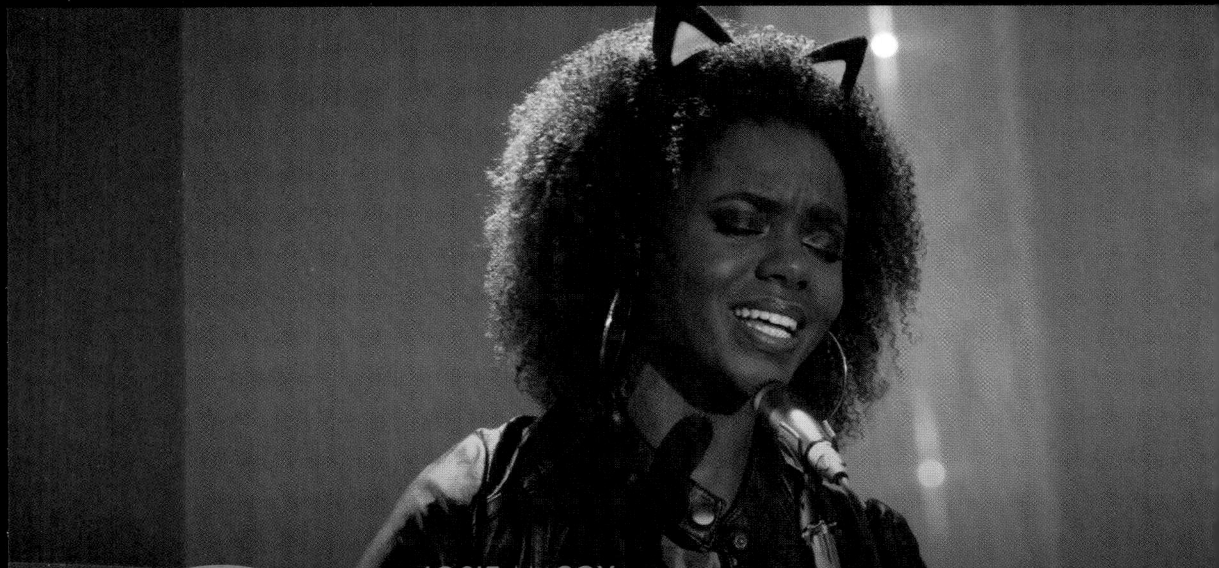

JOSIE McCOY

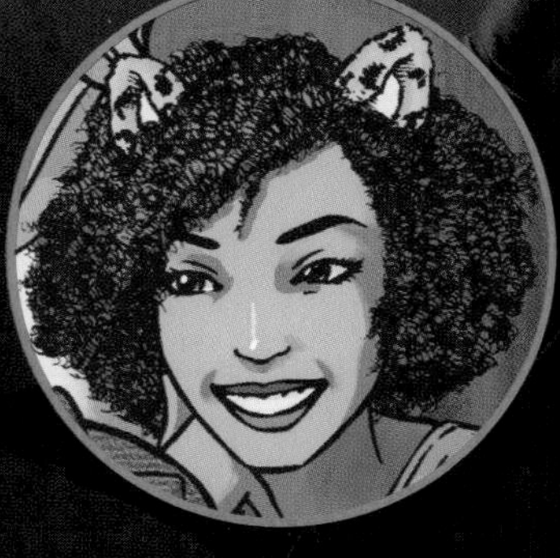

Lead singer and guitarist for "Josie & the Pussycats," Josie is a sweet girl who is actually sort of like a female Archie. She is scatterbrained and goofy, but means well, even though she barely ever knows what she wants! She is the driving force behind her group.

In *Riverdale,* Josie (played by Ashleigh Murray) is a gorgeous, snooty, and ambitious girl who is the lead singer for the popular band Josie and the Pussycats.

JUGHEAD JONES

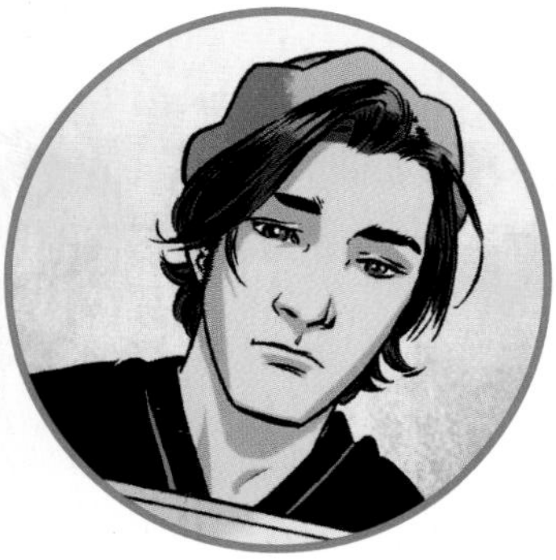

Jughead's favorite activities are eating, sleeping and eating again. Besides his tremendous appetite, Jughead is best known for his grey beanie cap; he rarely goes anywhere without it. He's been known as a "woman-hater," but this is not exactly true; he just avoids complicated romantic situations. Beneath Jughead's exterior lies a sharp-witted and alert person, and he is constantly helping his best pal Archie out of his predicaments.

In *Riverdale,* Jughead (played by Cole Sprouse) is a philosophically-bent heartthrob who was once the best friend of Archie, and who is now dealing with a rift that came between them.

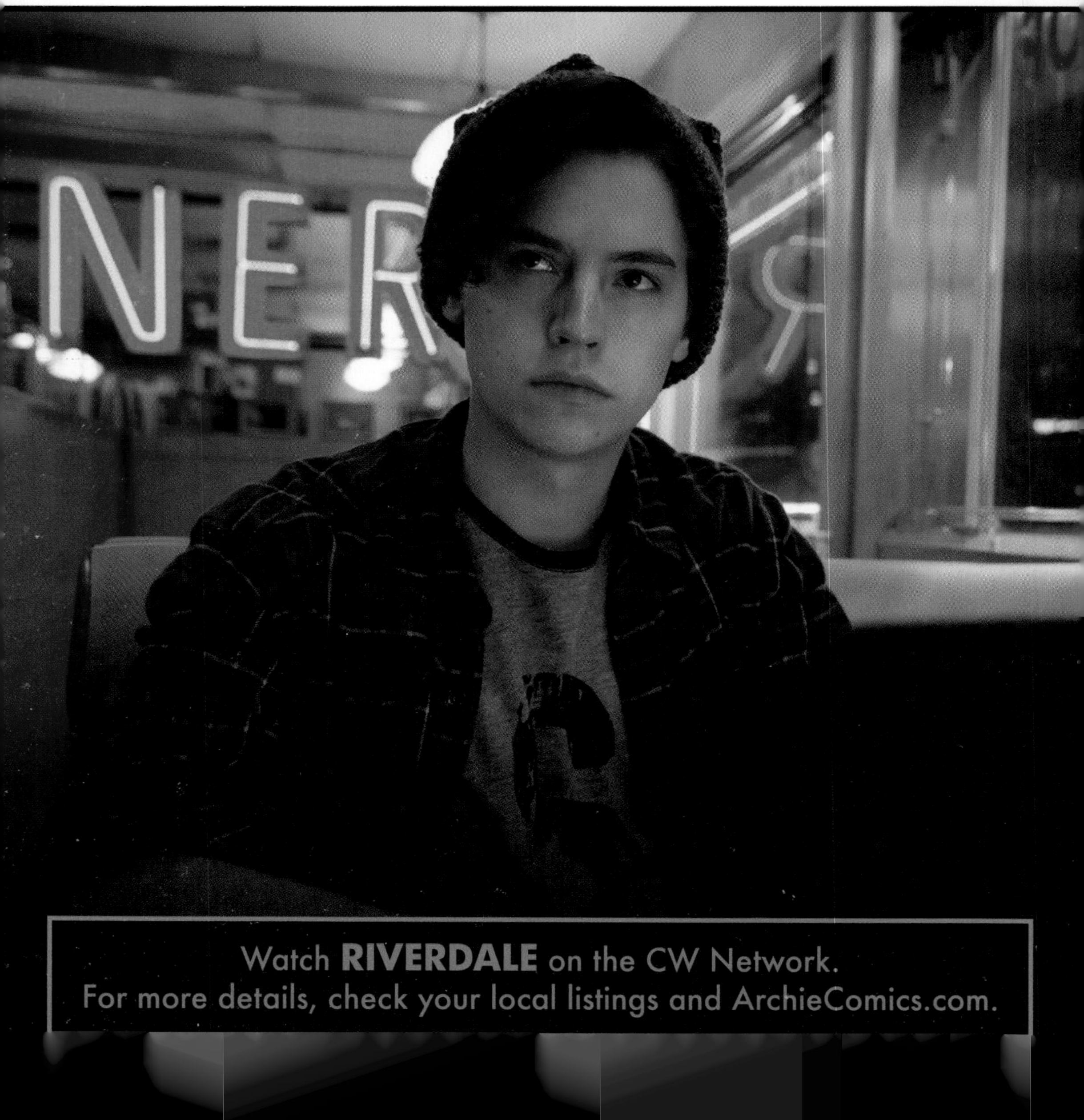
NER
Watch **RIVERDALE** on the CW Network.
For more details, check your local listings and ArchieComics.com.